Glennon Gourmet

from the

GLENNON GUILD

Cardinal Glennon

Published in cooperation with
Reedy Press
PO Box 5131
St. Louis, MO 63139, USA

Library of Congress Control Number: 2011931955

ISBN: 978-1-935806-16-5

Please visit our website at www.reedypress.com.

Design by Jill Halpin

Photo credts:
    Cardinal Glennon: vii, color tabs
    Patti Gabriel: xii
    St. Louis Archdiocese: ix
    St. Louis Review: xi

Printed in China
11 12 13 14 15   5 4 3 2 1

Contents

Acknowledgments

The Cardinal Glennon Guild would like to express our gratitude to everyone who contributed to making this cookbook a reality. Thousands of hours went into the publication of this book, from the submission of recipes, to compiling and editing, recipe testing, design, and creativity.

More than 1,000 recipes were submitted, and due to space limitations we regret that we were not able to include every submission. We attempted to choose a representation of recipes. We apologize for any omissions or mistakes that may have occurred in the publication of this book.

We also would like to extend a special thank you to the restaurants and chefs who submitted recipes.

Cookbook Committee

Guild President:

Constance Reis

Chairs:

Monica Meara
Susan Soucy

Committee:

Laura Baylis
Laurie Caro
Chris Clermont
Ginny Hartman
Sheila Heitz
Kim Lindley
Barbara Lynch
Liz Mantych
Carol Mullinex
Ann Nethington
Joanne Noyes
Gretchen Schulte
Connie Sigmund
Elaine Smith
Linda Tracy
Cathy Wilmott

Support Team

Marian Ahlering
Barbara Ball
Cindy Brooks
Ann Chivetta
Nancy Crippin
Sara Dee
Sarah Dow
Mary Ann Durnien
Mary Foshage

Lori Hartman
Susie Hudspeth
Constance Reis
Kelly Sigmund
Michelle Sullivan
Meg Terry
Carol Watkins
Barb Weiss

Contributors

Joan Aaron
Marian Ahlering
Chef Josh Allen
Chef Nick Angelou
Claire Applewhite
Chef Mohammad Azhar
Barbara Ball
Laura Baylis
Alison Bedell
Maryann Benoist
Lynn Berger
Eleanor Berra
Kelly Bick
Dianne Bishop
Debra Bokulic
Millie Boschert
Chef Ryan Boulware
Bernice Boyette
Carol Brauner
Chef Tim Brennan
Susan Brooker
Cindy Brooks
Chef Ronald Bub
Chef Rachel Buchholz
Jean Buckley
Chef Bethany Budde
Ann Burroughs
Molly Burroughs
Pat Butt
Nancy Cahalin
Jane Cannon
Joan Caro
Laurie Caro
Chef D'Aun Carrell
Lisa Cayse

Becky Chambers
Chris Clermont
Abby Clinton
Tom Coghill
Dottie Connell
Chef Jeffery Conner
Liz Crawford Bockius
Estie Cruz-Curoe
Kelly Dean
Sara Dee
Pam Dennis
Chef Chris Desens
Kim Diederich
Chef Grace Dinsmoor
Barb Doss
Sarah Dow
Kathy Durel
Patty Erker
Barbara Erker-Baumstark
Adriana Fazio
Chef Jim Fiala
Kristine Finlay
Jane Fisher
Cynthia Fitton
Jeanne Flood
Concie Fowler
Margaret Francka
Chef Paul V Frintrup
Sherry Furdek O'Connell
Dorothea Garman
Susan Gausnell
Giuseppi's Restaurant
Chef Sherrill Gonterman
Chris Guyol
Judy Harbaugh

Barbara Harris
Ginny Hartman
Lori Hartman
Cindy Heffernan
Peri Heft
Sheila Heitz
Barbara Hilton
Pam Hobelman
Sue Hodapp
William Hollifield
Susie Hudspeth
Margaret Hvatum
Rosie Intagliata
Donna Jackson
Chef Kris Janik
Mary Jane Johnston
Kathy Judd
Pam Kalkbrenner
Debby Keenan
Chef Eric Kelly
Judy Keran
Helen Klohmann
Debbie Koob
Sydney Koob
Debby Lane
Peggy Lane
Lori Lanham
Jill Lewis
Lewis and Clark Restaurant
Kim Lindley
Nicholas Lindley
Chef Todd Lough
Chef Jon Lowe
Kathleen Luepke
Barbara Lynch
Betty Lou Lynch
Chef Rob Marbs
Mary McGhee
Judy McGraugh
Sue McLean

Brigette McMillin
Monica Meara
Marge Merjavy
Angela Mestres
Gina Meyer
Debi Miller
Pam Miller
Chef David Molina
Susie Montebello
Marlene Moore
Chef Joseph Mueller
Carol Mullenix
Chef Kevin Nashan
The Neelys
Ann Nethington
Dorothy Nix
Anne Noyes
Blake Noyes
Joanne Noyes
Kathy Ohlman
Jan Orlando
Phyllis Otto
Chef Kyle Patterson
Anne Pennell
Kathy Petersen
P.F. Chang's China Bistro
Chef Alexander Pille
Chef Bernard Pilon
Wendy Pleau
Nina Pool
Elizabeth Purcell
Erin Radulski
Donna Reinhardt
Kathy Reuther
Peggy Ritter
Sister Mary Pat Rives
Elizabeth Robb
Lynette Roccia
Janet Ruzycki
Mary Scalzo

Sharon Schardan
Jane Schmidt
Michelle Schneider
Gretchen Schulte
Sara Schulte Dee
Ginny Schwarzmann
Susie Settle
Becky Sewing
Chef Casey Shiller
Valerie Siemer
Connie Sigmund
Kelly Sigmund
Lisa Sigmund
Sharon Sigmund
Elaine Smith
Meara Smith
Susan Soucy
Soulard's Restaurant
Sherri Sprehe
Ginny Stackle
Jim Stanley
Keith Starry
Chef Kevin Storm
Dr. Lisa Suffian
Mary Sullivan
Michelle Sullivan
Augie Swengros
Meg Terry
Dorothy Tracy
Linda Tracy
Chef Lee Tran
Julie Trausch-Azar
Scott Trausch
Diane Uhlenbrock
Chef Mathew Unger

Mary A. Vitale
Connie Vohsen
Judy Wagner
Chef Kirk Warner
Chef Brad Watts
LaVerne Weishaar
Helen Wells Klohmann
Mitzie Westbrook
Linda White
Ellie Williams
Cathryn Wilmott
Francesca Wilmott
Gina Wilmott
Robin Wolf
Paddie Wunderlich
Mary Wyss
Hilary Young
Chef Gregory Ziengnefuss
Chef Amy Zupanci

Preface

Cardinal Glennon Children's Medical Center

SSM Cardinal Glennon Children's Medical Center is a 190-bed, not-for-profit, inpatient and outpatient pediatric medical center. Cardinal Glennon serves children primarily from eastern Missouri and southern Illinois, but it also treats children from throughout the United States and around the world. The hospital is home to a Level 1 pediatric trauma center and a Level 3 neonatal intensive care unit, both the highest available classification. More than sixty pediatric specialties include adolescent medicine, cancer care, cardiology, child development, critical care, emergency medicine, rehabilitation, pulmonology, minimally invasive surgery, fetal surgery, hematology/oncology, sleep disorders, weight management, and others. All of these specialties ensure that we provide the best care and best results to our patients. Cardinal Glennon is a teaching hospital associated with the Saint Louis University Schools of Medicine, Nursing, and nine other medical institutions.

The Vision

The first steps toward construction of a Catholic-sponsored pediatric hospital in the St. Louis region began when Joseph Cardinal Ritter appointed a Board of Governors to raise funds for the building of the hospital to pay tribute to Cardinal John Joseph Glennon, who led the Archdiocese from 1903 to 1946 as Archbishop. The Archbishop's mission was to see a health-care facility open to all children in need of medical care. Peter G. Danis, M.D., one of

Archbishop John J. Glennon on the steps of the New Cathedral.

St. Louis's best-known pediatricians and a Saint Louis University School of Medicine faculty member, had urged Ritter to build a memorial hospital that would meet the needs of young people and enhance educational programs and research in the then-new field of pediatrics. The fundraising campaign began in 1950, with a goal of $5 million to build Cardinal Glennon Memorial Hospital for Children.

The campaign sought donations from all citizens of St. Louis and Missouri, Catholic and non-Catholic alike. Donations ranged from the purchase of a brick for ten cents to huge sums sufficient to establish memorial units such as a whole department or floor. Every member of every union in the AFL Building and Construction Trades Council contributed a day's pay to the campaign to build the hospital that they would help to erect. The original goal of $5 million was reached in early 1950, and the groundbreaking dedication took place in July 1953. The hospital opened its doors on July 5, 1956, with a price tag and donations reaching $6.2 million. Dedication ceremonies were held on April 15, 1956, which was proclaimed "Cardinal Glennon Hospital Sunday." The St. Louis Archdiocese continues to dedicate a "Glennon Sunday" each year to raise awareness and solicit donations for the hospital.

Cardinal Glennon's continued success has led to many improvements since its original construction. In 1965 a $1.5 million addition was added, and from 1976 through 1978 the hospital undertook a $6 million improvement project. In 1985 a $12 million major expansion was announced. The Bob Costas Cancer Center opened in 1998, and in 2003 a new patient care wing and expanded emergency room were opened. A recent $59 million addition includes an expanded sixty-bed neonatal intensive care unit and ten state-of-the-art surgical operating rooms.

A History of Accomplishments and Innovations

From the first days, Cardinal Glennon has pioneered the development of new and improved techniques and facilities to treat children. Renovation and updating has been a characteristic of the hospital since its inception. Over the years, the hospital developed the first neonatal intensive care unit in St. Louis, the first genetic and

An early rendering of the Cardinal Glennon campus.

neurofibromatosis clinics in the state, and the first poison center and pediatric rehabilitation unit in the region. Physicians and surgeons at Glennon were the first to perform open-heart surgery on a child in the city. They also treated the smallest surviving premature baby in St. Louis. A kidney transplant was performed at Glennon on the youngest child in the state to ever undergo this type of surgery.

Cardinal Glennon Children's Medical Center Today

When Cardinal Glennon opened, a commitment was made to offer the finest, most advanced health care available to all children at all times. Each year, the lives of more than 300,000 children are touched at this unique pediatric hospital—children from all backgrounds, all walks of life, and from all religious denominations. The following are examples of the many different ways in which Cardinal Glennon cares for children:

- *Dorothy and Larry Dallas Heart Center:* Key features of the heart center include fetal echocardiology testing, exercise stress-testing, and digital echo technology including cardiac ultrasound with advanced 3D heart

imaging. This state-of-the-art technology, combined with a dedicated cardiology team, ensures the best possible care for patients.

- *Bob Costas Cancer Center:* The center consists of a sixteen-bed inpatient unit, a four-bed bone marrow/stem cell transplant unit, research facilities at the Pediatric Research Institute, and the St. Louis Cord Blood Bank, bringing lifesaving ability of stem cell bone marrow transplants to children. The Day Hospital is a state-of-the-art treatment center allowing many treatments to be delivered on an outpatient basis at convenient hours, permitting children to maintain normal home and school activities.

- *Dan Dierdorf Emergency & Trauma Center:* Glennon's Emergency & Trauma Center is a twenty-four-hour, Level 1, Emergency/Trauma Center with full-time board-certified pediatricians present at all times.

- *Dana Brown Neonatal Intensive Care Unit:* Cardinal Glennon is the only all-private NICU in the St. Louis area, with sixty beds and plenty of room for parents to stay at their baby's bedside. The NICU has advanced life-sustaining and support equipment, electronic monitors, diagnostic equipment, respiratory therapy devices, and special lighting installations required to care for critically ill neonates. A neonatal transport team is available twenty-four hours to assist in transporting these babies via helicopter or ambulance to Glennon.

Since Cardinal John Joseph Glennon's vision became a reality, Cardinal Glennon Children's Medical Center has gained a reputation for excellence and commitment to healing children and finding new ways to help them get well in the future.

The Glennon Guild

A dedicated cadre of women created the Glennon Guild in 1957 to lend financial assistance to the newly established Cardinal Glennon Children's Hospital, now known as Cardinal Glennon Children's Medical Center, and fondly as "Glennon" to those of the Guild who cherish its existence. Under the leadership of Mrs. Howard Benoist Jr., who served as the first Guild Board president from 1957 to 1959, the Guild embarked on fundraising projects. Over the decades these efforts have included numerous designer showhouses, annual fashion show luncheons, Christmas village boutiques, balloon parties in Forest Park, house tours, wine tastings, even an animal fair at a shopping mall, as well as lobby sales of gold jewelry, books, baked goods, Ted Drewes ice cream, hospital "scrubs," and shoes. Notwithstanding the wide array of previous fundraisers, this current endeavor has the distinction of being the FIRST Glennon Guild Cookbook.

The unifying thread for all these events has been the Guild Board's mission "to render service, to promote and advance the welfare of Glennon and its patients by volunteer effort, fund raising, and any other activities." In tandem with this goal is the Guild Board's commitment to keep Glennon in the forefront of the public eye. The Guild Board wants everyone to know and appreciate both the services and needs of this remarkable facility. To that end, the Glennon Guild is comprised of about 600 friends of Glennon, many of whom volunteer or work at Glennon and voluntarily pay annual dues to support Guild activities. The Glennon Guild Board, limited to about seventy members, are active Glennon Guild members who commit to monthly meetings and work year-round planning and organizing the special fundraising projects.

The Guild reflects proudly on its long history and the resulting friendships. It has welcomed illustrious celebrities—baseball great Stan Musial served as fur auctioneer at a Glennon Guild Christmas boutique in the 1980s; artist Mary Englebreit lent her home for a Designer Showhouse; and singer Lou Rawls appeared at a Guild party. Most importantly, the Glennon Guild treasures the gifts we have been given to provide for the needs of the loving and deserving children of Cardinal Glennon Children's Medical Center.

Our love for kids just keeps on growing!

Appetizers & Beverages

Cardinal Glennon Children's Medical Center has a long-standing partnership with Saint Louis University School of Medicine. Our expert doctors serve as faculty at SLU School of Medicine where they're educating the next generation of health-care providers.

Cold Appetizers

Cambodian Summer Rolls

12 Servings

Dipping Sauce:
⅓ cup low-sodium soy sauce
¼ cup water
2 tablespoons sugar
2 tablespoons chopped fresh cilantro
2 tablespoons fresh lime juice
1 teaspoon ginger, peeled and minced
1 teaspoon chili paste with garlic,
  such as sambal oelek
1 garlic clove, minced

Rolls:
6 cups water
36 unpeeled medium shrimp
  (about 1 pound)
4 ounces uncooked rice noodles
12 (8-inch) round sheets rice paper
¼ cup hoisin sauce
3 cups shredded red leaf lettuce
¼ cup thinly sliced fresh basil
¼ cup thinly sliced fresh mint

Prepare dipping sauce by whisking all ingredients together. Set aside.

To prepare rolls, bring 6 cups water to a boil in a large saucepan. Add the shrimp to pan and cook 3 minutes or until done. Remove shrimp, reserving the hot water, and rinse with cold water. Peel shrimp and chill until ready to use. Bring the shrimp water to a boil. Place noodles in a large bowl, cover with boiling water. Let stand for 8 minutes, drain. Add cold water to a large, shallow dish to a depth of 1 inch. Place 1 rice paper sheet in water. Let stand 2 minutes or until soft. Place rice paper sheet on a flat surface.

Spread 1 teaspoon hoisin sauce in the center of sheet; top with 3 shrimp, ¼ cup lettuce, about 2½ tablespoons noodles, 1 teaspoon basil, and 1 teaspoon mint. Fold sides of sheet over filling, roll up jelly-roll fashion, and gently press seam to seal. Place roll, seam side down, on a serving platter; cover to keep from drying. Repeat procedure with remaining rice paper, hoisin sauce, shrimp, shredded lettuce, noodles, basil, and mint.

Serve with dipping sauce.

Pancetta Crisps with Goat Cheese and Pear
6 Servings

12 slices of pancetta
1 large or 2 medium Red Bartlett pears
4 ounces goat cheese, crumbled

honey
pepper

Arrange the pancetta slices in a single layer on an aluminum foil-lined baking pan. Bake at 450°F for 8 to 10 minutes until golden. Transfer to a paper towel lined wire rack. Let stand 10 minutes until crisp. Core pears and cut crosswise into 10 thin rings. Arrange on a serving platter. Top with pancetta and goat cheese. Sprinkle with cracked pepper and drizzle with honey just before serving.

Asparagus and Prosciutto Bundles
Makes 24 Spears

48 thin asparagus spears
2½ ounces goat cheese, room temperature
2 tablespoons chopped fresh basil
1 tablespoon chopped toasted pine nuts
1 tablespoon water
1 teaspoon grated orange peel
2 ounces thinly sliced prosciutto, cut into 24 4×1-inch strips

Cut stalks from asparagus, leaving 2-inch-long tips. Reserve asparagus stalks for another use. Cook asparagus tips in pot of boiling salted water until tender crisp, about 1 minute. Drain. Transfer asparagus to paper towels and drain well. Mix goat cheese, basil, pine nuts, water, and orange peel in bowl to blend. Season with salt and pepper. Spread scant 1 teaspoon filling over each prosciutto strip. Arrange 2 asparagus tips atop filling at short end of prosciutto. Roll up prosciutto, enclosing base of asparagus tips; press to seal. Place on platter.

Note: *Can be made 1 day ahead, cover and chill.*

Crab Salad in Crisp Wontons
Makes 18 Wontons

18 wonton wrappers, thawed
2 teaspoons canola oil

Dressing:	*Salad:*
1 teaspoon lime zest	½ pound lump crabmeat
2 tablespoons fresh lime juice	1 stalk celery, finely diced
¼ teaspoon salt	½ cup finely diced mango
¼ teaspoon black pepper	¼ cup diced red onion
½ teaspoon red pepper flakes	2 tablespoons chopped fresh
2 tablespoons olive oil	cilantro

Spray 2 mini-muffin tins with cooking spray. Brush the wonton wrappers with oil and place each into a section of a mini-muffin tin. Gently press each wrapper into the tin to form a cup shape. Sprinkle with salt and bake at 375°F for 8 to 10 minutes, until browned and crisp. Remove wrappers from the tins and cool.

Meanwhile, whisk together the lime zest, lime juice, salt, pepper, and pepper flakes. Add the oil and whisk until combined. In a medium bowl, toss together the crabmeat, celery, mango, onion, and cilantro. Add dressing and toss to combine. Fill each cup with the crab salad and serve.

Note: *The wonton cups can be made a day in advance and stored in an airtight plastic container until ready to fill.*

Mango-Curry Shrimp Salad in Wonton Cups
Makes 48 Wonton Cups

12 wonton wrappers (from one
  12-ounce package); each
  cut into 4 squares
cooking spray
½ cup mayonnaise
2 tablespoons chopped fresh cilantro
5 teaspoons fresh lime juice

2 teaspoons mango chutney
¾ teaspoon Thai green curry
  paste
12 ounces peeled, cooked,
  medium shrimp, coarsely
  chopped
fresh cilantro leaves

Place wonton squares on work surface; spray with cooking spray. Press each into mini muffin cup, oiled side down. Bake at 325°F until wonton cups are golden brown, about 10 minutes. Cool completely in tins. Remove from tins. Whisk mayonnaise, chopped cilantro, lime juice, chutney, and curry paste in medium bowl to blend. Stir in shrimp. Season to taste with salt and pepper. To assemble: Place wonton cups on serving platter, spoon 1 teaspoon salad into each cup, and garnish with cilantro leaves.

Note: *Wonton cups can be made ahead and stored in an airtight container for up to 3 days. The shrimp salad can also be made ahead and stored, covered, in a refrigerator for 24 hours. Assemble as directed above before serving.*

Smoked Salmon Pâté
Makes 2 Cups

4 ounces smoked salmon, chopped
½ fresh lemon, juiced
1 tablespoon chopped onion
4 ounces cream cheese, softened

2 hard cooked eggs, chopped
2 tablespoons heavy whipping
  cream
salt and black pepper to taste

In food processor, purée the smoked salmon until smooth. Add lemon juice, onion, and cream cheese and process until smooth. Add eggs, whipping cream, salt, and pepper and process for 15 seconds. Scrape into a 2-cup ramekin and refrigerate at least 30 minutes. Spread on your choice of cracker.

Shrimp and Avocado Cocktail Dip
8 Servings

1 pound cooked, peeled, deveined small or medium shrimp, tails removed
12 ounces seafood cocktail sauce
1 avocado, peeled, pitted, and cubed
½ small red onion, chopped
¼ cup chopped fresh cilantro
½ teaspoon hot pepper sauce (optional)
¼ teaspoon ground black pepper
lime wedges

Drain shrimp well, pat dry with paper towels. Cut shrimp if they are larger than bite sized. Combine shrimp, cocktail sauce, avocado, onion, cilantro, hot pepper sauce, and pepper in medium bowl. Chill for 4 to 6 hours before serving. Decorate rim of serving bowl with lime wedges. Serve with tortilla chips.

Gorgonzola Bites
Makes 20 Bites

1 8-ounce sheet frozen puff pastry
4 ounces Gorgonzola or other blue cheese, crumbled fine
pepper, freshly ground

Remove the puff pastry from the package and let it stand at room temperature until pliable (about 30 minutes); unfold it if necessary.

Set the pastry sheet on a work surface and scatter the cheese over the pastry, distributing as evenly as possible. Grind a generous amount of pepper over the entire surface. Drape a piece of plastic wrap over the pastry and gently roll over the wrap with a rolling pin to press the cheese into the pastry (the cheese will not cover the entire surface).

Peel off the plastic wrap and cut the pastry into 1-inch squares or diamonds with a sharp knife; discard odd edges and ends. Transfer the pastry pieces, placing them about ½ inches apart, to ungreased baking sheets. Bake at 350°F until the pastries are puffed and golden, about 25 minutes. Let them cool before serving. If made ahead, store them in an air-tight container for up to 1 day.

Boursin Tray
10 Servings

Dressing:
½ cup olive oil
¼ cup balsamic vinegar
2 tablespoons honey
3 cloves of garlic, finely minced
4 fresh basil leaves, finely chopped
1½ tablespoons grain Dijon mustard
salt and pepper to taste

Sides:
2 5.2-ounce Boursin cheeses
1 avocado
4 plum tomatoes, seeded
14-ounce can artichoke hearts, drained
14-ounce can hearts of palm, drained
12-ounce jar roasted red peppers, drained
4 ounces black olives, drained
Carr's table crackers

Mix olive oil, balsamic vinegar, honey, garlic, basil, mustard, salt, and pepper together in a small bowl and set aside. Set the 2 Boursin cheeses in the middle of a tray. Finely chop the avocado, tomatoes, artichoke hearts, hearts of palm, roasted red peppers, and black olives individually. Put them in mounds surrounding the cheeses; use 2 mounds for each vegetable. Alternate colors for presentation. Pour dressing over the cheeses and vegetables. Serve with Carr's table crackers.

Corn and Black Bean Salsa
10 to 12 Servings

1 11-ounce can shoe peg corn, drained
1 16-ounce can black beans, drained
 and rinsed
1 bunch of green onions, chopped
4 ounces diced feta cheese
fresh cilantro, chopped

Dressing:
6 tablespoons sugar
6 tablespoons raspberry
 wine vinegar
6 tablespoons oil

Gently mix corn, beans, green onions, feta cheese, and cilantro. Combine sugar, raspberry wine vinegar, and oil for dressing. Mix all ingredients together and allow flavors to blend at least several hours in refrigerator. Serve with Scoops tortilla chips or corn chips.

Pesto Cheese Blossom
15 Servings

8 ounces thinly sliced provolone
  cheese
16 ounces cream cheese, room
  temperature
20 pistachios, shelled
2 cloves garlic
½ cup fresh basil leaves

½ cup fresh parsley
½ cup pine nuts
¼ teaspoon salt
¼ teaspoon ground pepper
2 tablespoons olive oil
3 ounces oil-packed sun-dried
  tomatoes

Line a medium bowl with plastic wrap, leaving overhang to cover the top. Reserving 3 slices provolone, line the bottom and sides of the bowl with the remaining provolone, overlapping the slices.

For the cream cheese layer, process the cream cheese, pistachios, and 1 garlic clove in food processor until blended; place in a separate bowl and set aside.

For the pesto layer, process the basil, parsley, pine nuts, and remaining clove of garlic until blended. Dissolve the salt and pepper in the olive oil and mix well. With the food processor running, add the oil in a fine stream. Scrape the mixture into another bowl and set aside.

For the tomato layer, drain the tomatoes, reserving the oil. Purée the tomatoes with a small amount of the reserved oil.

To assemble, spread some of the cream cheese mixture over the cheese slices lining the bowl. Layer the pesto mixture horizontally in the bowl, half of the remaining cream cheese mixture, the sun-dried tomato mixture, and then the remaining cream cheese mixture. Cover with the remaining provolone. Bring the edge of the plastic wrap together over the top and secure with a twist tie. Freeze until firm. Remove the plastic wrap and invert onto a serving platter. Serve with crackers.

White Bean Salsa
6 to 8 Servings

6 slices precooked bacon, chopped
1 15-ounce can navy beans, rinsed and drained
1 large tomato, diced
1 ripe avocado, peeled, seeded, and diced
½ small jalapeno chile, seeded, and finely chopped

½ cup diced red onion
¼ cup loosely packed coarsely chopped fresh cilantro leaves
2 tablespoons lime juice
1 tablespoon extra-virgin olive oil
⅛ teaspoon salt

In medium serving bowl, with silicone spatula, gently stir bacon, navy beans, tomato, avocado, jalapeno, red onion, cilantro, lime juice, olive oil, and salt until well combined. Serve with tortilla chips.

Berry Blue Cheese Spread
16 Servings

½ cup dried blueberries
1 cup boiling water
1 8-ounce package cream cheese, softened
6 ounces blue cheese, crumbled

2 green onions, chopped
1 clove garlic, minced
½ cup chopped pecans
assorted crackers

Place dried blueberries in a small bowl; pour boiling water over berries. Let stand 1 minute, drain, and set aside. In mixing bowl, beat cream cheese and blue cheese until nearly smooth. Stir in drained berries, green onions, and garlic just until combined. Transfer spread to a serving bowl. Cover and refrigerate up to 4 hours before serving. To serve, sprinkle with pecans and serve with crackers.

Layered Greek Dip
12 Servings

14 ounces regular hummus
1 11-ounce jar pitted kalamata olives, drained and chopped

1 pint grape tomatoes, chopped
4 mini cucumbers, chopped
2 ounces feta cheese, crumbled

Spread hummus in bottom of serving dish. Layer olives, tomatoes, and cucumbers, and sprinkle feta cheese over top. Serve with pita chips or Ak-Mak crackers.

Blue Cheese Dip
Makes 2 Cups

4 ounces cream cheese, at room temperature
1 cup sour cream
4 ounces tangy blue cheese, such as Point Reyes

2 tablespoons chopped fresh chives
½ teaspoon freshly ground pepper

In a bowl, using a handheld electric mixer fitted with the beater attachments, beat the cream cheese on medium speed until soft and creamy, about 2 minutes. Reduce the speed to low, add the sour cream, and beat until combined, about 1 minute. Add the blue cheese and beat until the cheese is crumbled and no large lumps remain, about 1 minute. Stir in the chives and pepper.

Transfer the dip to a small serving bowl, cover with plastic wrap, and refrigerate for at least 30 minutes or up to 1 week. Serve with potato chips and crudités.

Curry Vegetable Dip
4 to 6 Servings

1 cup mayonnaise
1 teaspoon curry powder
1 teaspoon garlic salt

1 teaspoon tarragon vinegar
1 teaspoon grated onion
1 teaspoon horseradish

Mix mayonnaise, curry powder, garlic salt, tarragon vinegar, grated onion, and horseradish together. Stir until well mixed and refrigerate several hours for flavors to blend. Serve with vegetables for dipping.

Raspberry Cheese Dip
4 to 6 Servings

2 cups finely shredded
   cheddar cheese
2 cups finely shredded Monterey
   Jack cheese

8 green onions, chopped
1 cup chopped pecans
6 tablespoons mayonnaise
1½ cups raspberry preserves

Line a pie plate with plastic wrap. Combine cheddar cheese, Monterey Jack cheese, onions, pecans, and mayonnaise in mixing bowl. Press ingredients into pie plate. Chill at least 1 hour. Invert on serving tray. Spread raspberry preserves on top. Serve with crackers.

Traditional Hummus
Makes 3 Cups

2 15.5-ounce cans no-salt-added
  chickpeas, rinsed and drained
2 garlic cloves, crushed
½ cup water
¼ cup tahini (sesame seed paste)

3 tablespoons fresh lemon
  juice
2 tablespoons extra-virgin olive
  oil
¾ teaspoon salt
¼ teaspoon black pepper

Place chickpeas and garlic in a food processor; pulse 5 times or until chopped. Add ½ cup water, tahini, lemon juice, olive oil, salt, and pepper; pulse until smooth, scraping down sides as needed. Serve with pita chips or fresh vegetables.

Pretzel Beer Dip
4 to 6 Servings

16 ounces cream cheese, softened
8 ounces Budweiser beer
1 ounce package dry Hidden Valley Ranch mix
2 cups shredded sharp cheddar cheese

Mix cream cheese, beer, Hidden Valley mix, and cheddar cheese together. Serve with pretzels.

Beer Dip
Makes 2 Cups

½ cup mayonnaise
½ cup sour cream
½ teaspoon hickory smoked salt
1 clove garlic, minced
2 tablespoons chopped fresh chives

6 ounces natural cheddar
  cheese, finely grated
4 ounces natural Swiss
  cheese, finely grated
¼ cup beer

Combine mayonnaise, sour cream, smoked salt, garlic, chives, cheddar cheese, Swiss cheese, and beer. Blend well. Refrigerate one hour. Serve with rye crackers.

Warm Appetizers

Roasted Tomato and Ricotta Bruschetta
4 Servings

Josh Allen *opened* Companion Baking Company *in 1993. His vision was to create wholesome and delicious European breads with simple ingredients. In addition to cafes in Clayton and Ladue, Companion Bread is available in many local restaurants and grocers.*

4 medium-size tomatoes	*Ricotta Cheese:*
4 tablespoons herb infused olive oil	½ gallon milk
1 teaspoon fresh thyme	½ cup heavy cream
2 slices Companion Pain Beaucaire	4 tablespoons white vinegar
(cut on bias 1¾-inch thick)	1 tablespoon salt
1 cup homemade ricotta cheese	
(see below), or store bought	
salt and pepper	
shaved Reggiano-Parmigiano	
1 tablespoon toasted pine nuts	
2 tablespoons basil chiffonade	
6 tablespoons extra-virgin olive oil	

Roasted Tomatoes:
Core and cut tomatoes in half; remove seeds. Season with herb infused olive oil, fresh thyme, salt, and pepper. Roast at 250°F for two hours. Remove from oven, let cool, and remove skin over a bowl to reserve juice and oil. Rough chop and put in bowl with juice and oil. Set aside. Makes approximately 1 cup roasted tomatoes.

To Prepare and Serve Bruschetta:
Place 2 slices of bread on a cookie sheet. Divide ricotta cheese in half and place on bread; season with salt and pepper. Divide the tomatoes in half and place on cheese. (The cheese and tomatoes won't all stay on top of the bread, so don't try.) Bake at 350°F for 12 to 15 minutes or until hot all the way through. Remove from the oven. Use a spatula to put bruschetta on to plates. Top with shaved Parmesan, toasted pine nuts, and basil. Drizzle about 3 tablespoons of extra-virgin olive oil over bruschetta.

Ricotta Cheese:
Bring milk and cream to 180°F. Stir in white vinegar and salt. Stir as curds form, about 1 minute. Let set for 1 hour. Strain through a cheese cloth. Tighten cheese cloth every 15 minutes for an hour.

Spicy Shrimp
4 Servings

½ cup olive oil
2 tablespoons Cajun or Creole
  seasoning
2 tablespoons fresh lemon juice
2 tablespoons chopped fresh parsley
1 tablespoon honey

1 tablespoon soy sauce
pinch cayenne pepper
1 pound uncooked large
  shrimp, shelled and deveined
lemon wedges for garnish
French bread slices

Combine the olive oil, Cajun seasoning, lemon juice, parsley, honey, soy sauce, and cayenne pepper in a 9×13 baking dish. Add shrimp and toss to coat. Refrigerate for 1 to 4 hours. Bake at 450°F until the shrimp are cooked, stirring occasionally, about 10 to 15 minutes. Garnish with lemon wedges and serve with French bread.

Individual Baked Crabmeat Appetizer
6 Servings

⅓ cup chopped green pepper
¼ cup chopped green onion
3 tablespoons diced celery
1 2-ounce jar diced pimentos, drained
3 tablespoons unsalted butter, melted
1 tablespoon chopped fresh parsley
1 teaspoon Beau Monde seasoning
½ teaspoon prepared horseradish

½ cup white wine
dash Worcestershire sauce
¼ teaspoon Dijon mustard
¼ teaspoon hot sauce
1 egg, beaten
¼ cup plus 2 tablespoons
  mayonnaise
1½ pounds fresh lump
  crabmeat, drained

In a large skillet, sauté green pepper, green onions, celery, and diced pimentos in butter until tender. Stir in parsley, Beau Monde seasoning, horseradish, white wine, Worcestershire sauce, mustard, and hot sauce. Remove from heat and set aside to cool. Combine egg and mayonnaise and combine with the vegetable sauté. Gently stir in crabmeat. Spoon mixture into 6 individual baking dishes. Bake at 375°F for 12 to 15 minutes until tops are lightly browned.

Prosciutto Wrapped Scallops

Makes 20 Scallops

10 fresh sea scallops
10 thin slices prosciutto,
  halved lengthwise
20 medium fresh basil leaves
salt
black pepper

Roasted Red Pepper Aioli:
½ cup jarred roasted red peppers,
  drained
2 cloves garlic, minced
⅓ cup mayonnaise
2 tablespoons olive oil
⅛ teaspoon salt
pinch of black pepper

Soak 20 6-inch skewers in water for 30 minutes; drain. Preheat broiler. Rinse scallops and pat dry with paper towels. Cut scallops in half, vertically. Lay prosciutto strips on a large cutting board. Top each strip with a basil leaf and scallop half. Starting from a short end, roll up each prosciutto strip around scallop. Thread each appetizer onto a skewer. Sprinkle with salt and pepper.

Place scallop skewers on lightly greased unheated rack of a broiler pan. Broil 4 inches from heat for 6 to 8 minutes until scallops are opaque and prosciutto is crisp, turning once halfway through broiling. Serve with Roasted Red Pepper Aioli.

Roasted Red Pepper Aioli:
In food processor, combine red peppers and garlic and blend until chopped. Add mayonnaise and blend just until combined. Gradually add olive oil through feed tube. Transfer to bowl and season with salt and pepper. Makes about 1 cup. Refrigerate.

Crab Quiche Bake
6 Servings

8 eggs, beaten
2 cups half-and-half
1 large sweet red pepper, chopped
8 ounces chopped crab meat
1 cup soft breadcrumbs
4 ounces shredded Swiss cheese

4 ounces shredded cheddar
  cheese
½ cup chopped green onion
1 teaspoon salt
½ teaspoon pepper

In a bowl, combine eggs, half-and-half, red pepper, crab meat, soft breadcrumbs, Swiss cheese, cheddar cheese, green onion, salt, and pepper. Transfer to a greased 13×9×2 baking dish. Bake uncovered at 350°F for 30 to 35 minutes until knife inserted near center comes out clean. Let stand 10 minutes before serving. Serve with crackers.

J Crab Cakes
16 Servings

¼ cup mayonnaise
¼ cup minced onion
2 eggs, beaten
½ teaspoon Worcestershire sauce
½ teaspoon dry mustard
½ teaspoon salt
¼ teaspoon cayenne pepper

1 pound lump crabmeat
1 cup finely crushed saltine
  crackers, divided
2 tablespoons butter
¼ cup vegetable oil
lemon wedges

Combine mayonnaise, onion, eggs, Worcestershire sauce, mustard, salt, and cayenne pepper. Add crabmeat and ¼ cup crushed crackers. Shape into 1-inch round crab cakes. Coat crab cakes in the remaining crackers crumbs. Refrigerate for 30 minutes before frying. In a large skillet, melt 1 teaspoon butter and 2 tablespoons oil. Cook half of the crab cakes for 2 to 3 minutes per side. Remove from pan and keep warm. Melt the remaining butter and oil in the pan and cook the remaining crab cakes. Serve with lemon wedges.

Crab Cakes
Makes 20 Cakes

2 pounds crab meat
½ cup finely chopped mixed red,
    green, and yellow bell peppers
⅓ cup finely chopped red onions
¼ cup lemon juice
¼ cup chopped chives
2 tablespoons Cajun seasoning

1 tablespoon Old Bay seasoning
1 tablespoon lemon zest
1 tablespoon cayenne pepper
2 eggs
¾ cup mayonnaise
2 cups panko breadcrumbs
olive oil for sautéing

Combine the crab meat, bell peppers, onions, lemon juice, chives, Cajun seasoning, Old Bay seasoning, lemon zest, and cayenne pepper in a bowl. Add the eggs and mayonnaise and mix well. Mix in the breadcrumbs. Shape the mixture into 20 cakes. Sauté in a small amount of oil until golden brown and cooked through.

Dates with Goat Cheese Wrapped in Prosciutto
8 Servings

⅓ cup soft herbed goat cheese
16 Medjool dates, pitted
16 large basil leaves
4 wide, thin slices prosciutto, each cut into 4 long strips
16 toothpicks soaked in water 10 minutes

Spoon 1 teaspoon cheese into each date, wrap with a basil leaf, then a prosciutto strip. Secure with a toothpick. Broil until cheese bubbles, about 3 minutes. Serve warm.

Mini Crab Cakes
Makes 24 Cakes

1 8-ounce package cream
  cheese, softened
¾ cup finely grated Parmesan cheese
1 large egg
¼ cup sour cream
1 teaspoon finely grated orange peel
½ teaspoon finely grated lemon peel

4 teaspoons plus 2 table-
  spoons chopped chives
¼ teaspoon kosher salt
large pinch cayenne pepper
6 ounces lump crabmeat
1 cup panko breadcrumbs
2 ounces melted butter

Beat cream cheese until smooth. Add ¼ cup Parmesan and egg. Beat in sour cream, orange peel, lemon peel, 4 teaspoons chopped chives, salt, and cayenne pepper. Fold in crabmeat. Cover and chill. Can be done one day ahead. Butter 24 mini-muffin tins. Toss panko breadcrumbs, ½ cup Parmesan, and 2 tablespoons chives in a small bowl. Drizzle ¼ cup melted butter over breadcrumb mixture, tossing with fork until moistened.

Press 1 rounded tablespoon panko mixture into each muffin cup, forming crust. Spoon 1 generous tablespoon crab mixture into each cup. Sprinkle rounded teaspoon of panko mixture over each.

Bake at 350°F until golden, about 30 minutes. Cool 5 minutes. Run a knife around the edges of the tins and lift out. Sprinkle with remaining chives and serve.

Note: *Can be made 2 hours ahead. Reheat on baking sheet at 350°F for 6 to 8 minutes.*

Oyster and Artichoke Au Gratin
18 Servings

1¼ quarts fresh oysters, shucked
and liquor (liquid) reserved
2 9-ounce packages frozen
artichoke hearts, halved
2 cups sliced green onions
1 cup unsalted butter
⅔ cup flour
2 tablespoons minced parsley
1 tablespoon minced garlic

2 tablespoons fresh lemon juice
3 tablespoons Worcestershire
sauce
¼ teaspoon Tabasco sauce
2 tablespoons freshly grated
Parmesan cheese
½ cup fresh breadcrumbs
paprika to taste
salt and pepper

In a heavy saucepan, bring oysters and their liquor to a simmer. Cook oysters for 1 minute, or until the edges begin to curl. Drain the oysters, reserving the liquid. In a saucepan, cook the artichoke hearts in 1 cup boiling water with salt to taste for 5 minutes. Drain artichoke hearts, reserving ½ cup of the cooking liquid.

In a large oven-safe stainless steel or enamel saucepan, cook the green onions in butter, stirring over moderate heat for 2 minutes. Stir in flour and cook over low heat for 3 minutes. Add parsley and garlic and cook mixture for 2 minutes. Add reserved liquids and bring to boil, stirring until very thick. Stir in oysters, artichoke hearts, lemon juice, Worcestershire, Tabasco, and salt and pepper to taste. Cook mixture over low heat for 10 minutes. Combine Parmesan cheese with breadcrumbs and sprinkle over dish. Sprinkle with paprika. Bake at 375°F for 20 minutes or until hot and bubbly.

Traditional Pot Stickers
15 Servings

½ pound ground pork
½ medium head cabbage, finely chopped
1 green onion, finely chopped
2 slices fresh ginger root, finely chopped
2 cans water chestnuts, drained and finely chopped
1 teaspoon salt

½ teaspoon white sugar
1 teaspoon sesame oil
1 14-ounce package wonton wrappers
5 tablespoons vegetable oil
¾ cup water
1 tablespoon chili oil
1 tablespoon soy sauce
1 teaspoon rice vinegar

Crumble pork into a large, deep skillet. Cook over medium-high heat until evenly brown. Drain and set aside. In a medium bowl, mix together the pork, cabbage, green onion, ginger, water chestnuts, salt, sugar, and sesame oil. Chill mixture in the refrigerator 6 to 8 hours or overnight. Place a tablespoon of the pork mixture into each of the wonton wrappers. Fold the wrappers, and seal the edges with a moistened fork.

In a large, deep skillet, heat 3 tablespoons vegetable oil over medium-high heat. Place the pot stickers into the oil seam-sides up. Heat 30 seconds to 1 minute. Pour water into the skillet. Gently boil 7 to 8 minutes, until oil and water begins to sizzle; add remaining oil. When the bottoms begin to brown, remove pot stickers from heat.

In a small serving bowl, mix together the chili oil, soy sauce, and vinegar, adjusting proportions to taste. Serve sauce on the side.

Mushroom Turnovers
Makes 30 Turnovers

Pastry:
3 3-ounce packages of cream
cheese, room temperature
½ cup butter, room temperature
1½ cups flour
½ teaspoon salt

Filling:
3 tablespoons butter
1 large onion, finely chopped
8 ounces mushrooms, chopped
¼ teaspoon thyme
½ teaspoon salt
¼ teaspoon pepper
2 tablespoons flour
¼ cup sour cream
1 egg
1 teaspoon milk

Pastry:
Mix cream cheese and butter thoroughly. Add flour and salt; work until smooth. Chill at least 30 minutes. Roll dough to ⅛-inch thickness on lightly floured surface. Cut into 3-inch rounds with a biscuit cutter or glass rim.

Filling:
In skillet heat butter, add onion and brown. Add mushrooms and cook, stirring about 3 minutes. Add thyme, salt, and pepper and sprinkle with the flour. Stir in sour cream and cook gently until thickened.

Place 1 teaspoon filling on each round and fold dough over. Press edges together with a fork. Place on greased cookie sheet, brush tops with egg beaten with 1 teaspoon milk. Bake at 450°F for 10 to 15 minutes until golden.

Honey Apple Brie Bites
Makes 30 Bites

1 teaspoon lemon zest
1 cup chopped toasted walnuts
2 cups finely diced red
  apples (Jonathan)

¼ cup honey
8 ounces Brie with rind
2 packages mini phyllo shells
  (30 shells total)

Combine lemon zest, walnuts, apple, and honey in bowl; mix gently. Cut Brie into 30 ½-inch cubes. Place 1 Brie cube into each phyllo cup. Top Brie with 1 tablespoon of apple mixture. Bake at 400°F for 6 to 8 minutes until Brie is melted.

Cheesy Wonton Appetizer
Makes 48 Wontons

1 12-ounce package wonton wrappers
1 pound bulk pork sausage
1 red bell pepper, finely chopped
2¼ ounce can chopped black
  olives, drained

3½ cups shredded cheddar
  cheese
1 cup ranch-style dressing

Spray a mini muffin pan with cooking spray. Insert wonton wrappers into the muffin pan to form small cups. Bake at 325°F for about 7 minutes or until golden. Allow the baked wrappers to cool. Remove wonton cups from the muffin pan and place on a cookie sheet. Brown the pork sausage, crumble and drain well. In a medium bowl, mix the cooked pork sausage, red bell pepper, black olives, shredded cheddar cheese, and the ranch-style dressing.

Spoon mixture into the baked wonton wrapper cups, filling each slightly more than half full. Bake the filled wonton wrappers at 325°F for 10 minutes until the sausage mixture is bubbly and slightly brown. Watch closely so the wonton wrappers do not burn. Serve warm.

Note: *Wonton cups can be made the day before assembly and stored in an airtight plastic container. The filling can also be made a day ahead and refrigerated until ready to assemble and bake.*

Goat Cheese and Roasted Red Pepper Tart with Basil-Chive Crust

12 Servings

Crust:
1 cup flour
2 tablespoons powdered sugar
4 ounces cold unsalted butter,
   cut into small pieces
2 teaspoons minced fresh basil
1 teaspoon minced fresh chives

Filling:
2 red bell peppers
1 cup fresh goat cheese
½ cup half-and-half
2 tablespoons dry white wine
3 eggs
4 ounces lean prosciutto, chopped
   or sliced into thin pieces

Crust:
Combine flour, sugar, butter, basil, and chives in a food processor and process until the dough forms a large ball. Press dough to about ⅛-inch thickness on the bottom and up the sides of a 9-inch fluted tart pan or pie pan with sides ¾-inch to 1-inch high. Set aside.

Filling:
Roast the peppers over a flame or under the broiler until charred on all sides. Place in a closed paper bag for 15 minutes to steam and then peel off the skin. Cut in half and discard membranes and seeds. Coarsely chop one pepper and cut the other into long thin strips. Purée the goat cheese, half-and-half, wine, and eggs until smooth. Add the prosciutto and chopped pepper, mixing well.

Pour the filling into the crust and decorate the top with the strips of roasted pepper. Bake at 375°F for 45 to 50 minutes just until the mixture has set and the top is slightly browned. Cut into wedges to serve. Can be served warm or at room temperature.

Roasted Tomato Bruschetta
4 to 6 Servings

2 cloves garlic
4 shallots
¼ teaspoon crushed red pepper
  flakes
2 tablespoons chopped fresh basil
2 pounds grape tomatoes
¼ cup olive oil
2 teaspoons balsamic vinegar
salt

black pepper
Ciabatta bread or baguette,
  sliced
additional olive oil
garlic powder
additional fresh basil
freshly grated Parmesan
  cheese

In food processor, pulse garlic, shallots, red pepper flakes, and basil until finely chopped. Mix tomatoes, olive oil, balsamic vinegar, and garlic mixture in bowl until well combined. Spread in a single layer on a baking sheet and roast uncovered at 400°F until tomatoes are very tender and juicy, stirring occasionally, about 30 to 45 minutes. Season with salt and freshly ground pepper to taste.

Slice bread into ½-inch thick slices and place on a baking sheets. Broil one side of bread to lightly toast and then turn over and brush with olive oil and sprinkle with garlic powder. Spoon tomato mixture onto bread slices. Tear a small piece of fresh basil for the top of each toast and grate some fresh Parmesan cheese over the top before heating in a 375°F oven for 5 minutes.

Tomato Bruschetta
12 Servings

8 plum tomatoes, chopped
1 .66-ounce package fresh basil, chopped
2 teaspoons minced garlic
¼ cup balsamic vinegar
¼ cup olive oil

1 10-ounce package Pepperidge Farm Double French Rolls
⅓ cup olive oil
Italian herb seasonings
grated Parmesan cheese

In bowl, combine chopped tomatoes, chopped basil, and minced garlic. In separate bowl, combine vinegar and olive oil and whisk until blended. Pour over tomato mixture and stir well. Slice French roll in ¼-inch slices and place on cookie sheet.

Brush each individual slice with olive oil. Sprinkle with herb seasonings and Parmesan cheese. Broil for 60 to 90 seconds. Watch closely so they do not burn. Place tomato mixture in serving bowl. Place bruschetta on a serving platter. Let guests spoon tomato mixture on bruschetta.

Pesto Appetizers
6 to 8 Servings

2 cups fresh basil leaves
2 cloves garlic, minced
2 tablespoons pine nuts
⅓ cup olive oil

2 tablespoons grated Parmesan cheese
baguette
additional Parmesan cheese

In food processor, process basil, garlic, and nuts until chopped. Slowly add oil unitl emulsified. Add 2 tablespoons Parmesan cheese. Process until combined. Cover and refrigerate. Makes 1 cup. To assemble appetizers, cut a baguette into ½-inch thick slices. Toast lightly. On each toasted bread round, spread 1 tablespoon pesto and top with 1 teaspoon cheese. Broil until bubbly, about 1 minute.

Mississippi Sin
4 to 6 Servings

1 round loaf Hawaiian bread
1½ cups sour cream
2 cups grated sharp cheddar cheese
1 8-ounce package cream cheese,
  softened

⅓ cup chopped green onion
½ cup chopped ham
1 4.5-ounce can green chilies,
  chopped
dash Worcestershire sauce

Remove 1-inch slice from top of bread. Hollow loaf about 1 inch from crust. Save top and insides. Mix sour cream, cheddar, cream cheese, green onion, ham, green chilies, and Worcestershire sauce thoroughly. Place in bread and replace top. Wrap in heavy duty foil. Bake on cookie sheet at least 1 hour at 350°F. Serve with chips, crackers, and/or the toasted cubed bread from the loaf.

California Bread
12 Servings

2 loaves French bread
½ cup butter
4 teaspoons minced garlic
2 tablespoons sesame seeds
1 cup cubed Monterey Jack cheese
1 cup sour cream

½ cup Parmesan cheese
1 14-ounce can artichoke
  hearts, drained and finely
  chopped
1 cup shredded cheddar
  cheese

Cut ¼ top off bread (like a canoe). Scoop out inside of bread leaving a ½-inch border and tear into chunks. Melt butter and sauté garlic and sesame seeds. Add bread chunks and sauté 2 to 3 minutes to absorb butter; remove from heat. Add Monterey Jack cheese, sour cream, Parmesan cheese and stir. Add chopped artichoke hearts. Spoon mixture into crust and sprinkle with cheddar cheese. Bake at 350°F for 30 minutes. Slice into 12 serving pieces.

Goat Cheese Appetizer
4 to 6 Servings

8 ounces goat cheese
4-ounce jar of pesto
1 small tomato, chopped

2 tablespoons pine nuts
1 small loaf of French bread
  sliced

Place goat cheese in glass pie plate. Spoon pesto over goat cheese. Top with tomatoes and pine nuts. Heat in microwave until warm and slightly melted. Serve with sliced French bread.

Jerk Chicken Wings
8 to 10 Servings

8 garlic cloves
4 dried bay leaves
2 jalapeno chilies, chopped
¼ cup red wine vinegar
2 tablespoons fresh thyme leaves

4 teaspoons ground allspice
1 tablespoon coarse salt
2 tablespoons ground pepper
6 pounds chicken wings, cut in
  half at joint

In a food processor, pulse garlic, bay leaves, chilies, vinegar, thyme, allspice, salt, and pepper until coarsely ground. Rinse the chicken and pat dry. In a large shallow dish, toss chicken wings with jerk mixture and refrigerate at least 1 hour or up to 1 day. Arrange chicken on foil-lined rimmed baking sheets and bake at 450°F for 35 to 40 minutes until browned, rotating sheets halfway through.

Hot Corned Beef Tempters
Makes 6 Dozen

2 12-ounce cans corned beef
1 medium onion, finely chopped
1 tablespoon minced parsley
½ cup butter, melted
1 cup flour
1 teaspoon dry mustard

1 teaspoon salt
1 cup milk
1 pound can sauerkraut, drained
2 eggs
¼ cup water
fine dry breadcrumbs

Flake corned beef and mix with onion. Cook with parsley in butter for 5 minutes. Stir in flour, mustard, and salt. Gradually add milk and cook, stirring constantly until thickened. Chop sauerkraut finely and add to meat mixture. Mix thoroughly, then cool. Shape into ½-inch balls. Chill in freezer for 30 minutes. Beat eggs with water. Dip balls into egg mixture and roll in breadcrumbs. Fry in hot vegetable oil for about 2 minutes or until golden. Spread them on cookie sheets, lined with paper towels to drain.

Hot Bacon and Swiss Dip
8 to 10 Servings

1 8-ounce package cream cheese
½ cup mayonnaise
1 cup grated Swiss cheese
2 tablespoons chopped green onions
8 slices bacon, cooked and crumbled
½ cup crushed Ritz crackers

Soften cream cheese in a mixing bowl. Add mayonnaise, Swiss cheese, and green onions; mix well. Transfer to a baking dish. Top with bacon and crackers. Bake at 350°F for 15 to 20 minutes or until bubbly. Serve with Fritos Scoops.

Baked Chicken Cheese Spread
6 to 8 Servings

16 ounces cream cheese, softened
12.5-ounce can chicken
4 teaspoons butter, softened

2 cups shredded mozzarella
cheese
1 cup shredded cheddar
cheese

Mix together cream cheese, canned chicken, butter, and mozzarella cheese. Spread in a 9-inch pie plate. Sprinkle cheddar cheese on top. Bake at 350°F for 10 minutes or until hot.

Enchilada Dip
16 Servings

1 8-ounce package cream cheese, softened
1½ cups Mexican-style shredded cheddar cheese
1 7-ounce can chopped green chilies, not drained
1 teaspoon garlic powder
¼ teaspoon chili powder
½ pound chicken breast, cooked and chopped

Beat cream cheese, 1 cup of the shredded cheese, chilies, garlic powder, and chili powder in small bowl with electric mixer on medium speed until well blended. Stir in chicken. Spread in 9-inch pie plate. Bake at 350°F for 20 to 30 minutes or until dip is lightly browned and heated through. Sprinkle with remaining ½ cup shredded cheese; let stand 10 minutes. Serve as a dip with Wheat Thin crackers.

Buffalo Chicken Wing Dip
6 to 8 Servings

1 8-ounce package cream cheese
½ cup blue cheese salad dressing
¼ cup buffalo wing sauce

1 12.5-ounce can chicken, drained
1 8-ounce package shredded Monterey Jack cheese

In a medium saucepan, melt cream cheese over medium-low heat. Once creamy, add blue cheese, wing sauce, and chicken. Remove from heat. Fold in 4 ounces of Monterey Jack cheese. Pour into square 8×8 oven-safe dish and top with remaining cheese. Bake at 350°F until cheese is melted and bubbly. Serve with celery sticks, crackers, or corn chips.

Hot Buffalo Chicken Wing Dip
12 Servings

4 chicken breasts, boneless, skinless
16 ounces cream cheese
1 cup shredded cheddar cheese

16-ounce bottle ranch dressing
16-ounce bottle buffalo wing hot sauce

Boil chicken breasts until no longer pink and shred into bite-sized pieces. Set aside. Melt cream cheese in microwave; add the cheddar cheese, ranch dressing, and buffalo hot wing sauce. Stir in the shredded chicken. Bake in a 350°F oven for 20 to 30 minutes until bubbly. Serve warm with tortilla chips or crackers.

Note: *For a quick appetizer, you can substitute precooked chicken strips found in the refrigerated section of the grocery store.*

Rosemary Cashews
6 to 8 Servings

1 pound roasted unsalted cashews
2 tablespoons minced fresh rosemary leaves
½ teaspoon cayenne pepper
2 teaspoons light brown sugar
1 tablespoon kosher salt
1 tablespoon unsalted butter, melted

Spread the cashews out on a sheet pan. Toast at 350°F until warm, about 5 minutes. In large bowl combine the rosemary, cayenne pepper, brown sugar, salt, and butter. Thoroughly toss the warm cashews with the spiced butter and serve warm.

Sweet Crispix Mix
10 to 12 Servings

½ cup butter
¼ cup white corn syrup
1 cup brown sugar
1 teaspoon vanilla extract
1 teaspoon baking soda

1 box (12.3 ounces) Crispix cereal
1 bag (8 ounces) mini pretzels
1 can (12 ounces) salted peanuts
1-pound bag M&M's

In a microwave-safe bowl, cook butter, corn syrup, and brown sugar in microwave on high for 2 minutes. Stir. Repeat on high 2 minutes more. Stir in vanilla and baking soda. Pour Crispix, pretzels, and peanuts in large brown paper bag. Pour cooked mixture over and stir with spoon. Microwave in bag 2 minutes on high. Shake and repeat 2 minutes more on high. Shake for 1 minute. Cool mixture on wax paper until cooled. Mix in M&M's.

Beverages

Blueberry-Lime Fizz
1 10-Ounce Serving

Casey Shiller, *CCE, CEPC, is the Coordinator of Baking and Pastry Arts at* St. Louis Community College Forest Park.

½ cup granulated sugar
½ cup water
1 cup fresh or frozen blueberries
1 cinnamon stick

1 bag blackberry flavored
  hot tea
2 limes, zested and juiced
½ cup tonic water

Place sugar, water, blueberries, cinnamon stick, teabag, and lime zest into a small saucepan and bring to a boil. When mixture boils, turn off heat and let the mixture steep for 10 minutes. Strain mixture through fine strainer and cool completely. Fill a glass with ice and pour enough blueberry syrup to cover ¾ of the ice cubes. Add lime juice, and top with a splash of tonic water.

Mexican Margaritas
Makes 4 Drinks

1 6-ounce can limeade
2 ounces triple sec

2 ounces tequila
1 cup ice, plus more as needed

Add limeade, triple sec, and tequila to blender along with 1 cup ice. Blend thoroughly. Add additional ice as needed.

Summer Punch
8 to 10 Servings

12-ounce can frozen limeade
12-ounce can vodka
3 12-ounce bottles Budweiser Select 55 beer

Stir the limeade, vodka, and beer together to mix. Serve very well chilled or with ice.

Pomegranate-Green Tea Cooler
2 12-Ounce Servings

Casey Shiller, *CCE, CEPC, is the Coordinator of Baking and Pastry Arts at St. Louis Community College Forest Park.*

2 cups pomegranate juice
1 cup brewed green tea
¼ teaspoon grated fresh ginger

¼ cup honey
1 small lemon, zested and
 juiced

Freeze pomegranate juice in ice cube trays until solid. In blender, combine green tea, ginger, honey, lemon zest, and lemon juice. Turn blender on medium speed until all ingredients have combined. Turn blender to highest speed and gradually drop in frozen pomegranate juice cubes until mixture is slushy.

Orange Blossom Punch
Makes 50 Drinks

12 ounces frozen lemonade
1 6-ounce can frozen orange juice
9 cups cold water
5 pints pineapple sherbet

1 quart cherry vanilla ice cream
2 quarts ginger ale
orange slices

Combine lemonade, orange juice, and water. Place sherbet and ice cream in punch bowl and break into pieces with spoon. Add the juice mixture and stir. Add ginger ale just before serving. Float orange slice on top of punch.

Note: *This punch is very colorful and makes a large quantity. Perfect for a ladies' luncheon or shower when served in a pretty punch bowl.*

Whiskey Sour Slush
30 Servings

24 ounces frozen orange juice
12 ounces frozen lemonade
1¾ cups sugar

3 cups whiskey
9 cups water
7Up soda for topping off

Mix together orange juice, lemonade, sugar, whiskey, and water. Stir until sugar is dissolved. Keep in a container in the freezer. When serving, spoon out ¾ glass of frozen mixture and then fill the glass with 7Up.

Breads & Brunch

For the children at Cardinal Glennon Children's Medical Center, time can be a precious thing to hold on to. Throughout the hospital, nine ornately designed clocks depict fantastic, child-like worlds of wonder.

Morning Glory Muffins ✓
Makes 30 Muffins

4 cups flour
2½ cups sugar
4 teaspoons baking soda
4 teaspoons cinnamon
1 teaspoon salt
4 cups grated carrots
1½ cups raisins

1½ cups chopped pecans
1 cup chopped dates
3 apples, peeled, cored, and
  grated
6 eggs
2 cups vegetable oil
4 teaspoons vanilla extract

Sift together flour, sugar, baking soda, cinnamon, and salt. Stir in carrots, raisins, pecans, dates, and apples. Beat eggs with oil and vanilla; stir into flour mixture until batter is combined. Spoon into well-greased muffin pans, filling to the top. Bake at 350°F for 35 minutes or until springy to the touch. Cool on wire rack 5 minutes; turn out onto rack and let cool completely.

Applesauce Muffins ✓
Makes 12 Muffins

½ cup butter, softened
½ cup sugar
2 eggs
¾ cup applesauce
1¾ cups flour
1 tablespoon baking powder
½ teaspoon salt

Topping:
¼ cup butter, melted
¼ cup sugar
⅛ teaspoon cinnamon

Cream butter. Gradually add ½ cup sugar, beating until light and fluffy. Add eggs, 1 at a time, beating well after each addition. Stir in applesauce. Combine flour, baking powder, and salt; add to creamed mixture and stir just until moistened. Spoon batter into lightly greased muffin tins, filling ⅔ full. Bake at 425°F for 15 minutes. Remove from pan immediately and dip muffin tops in melted butter. Combine ¼ cup sugar and cinnamon. Sprinkle over top of each muffin.

Bananas Foster Coffee Cake
Makes 6 Muffins

Casey Shiller, *CCE, CEPC, is a St. Louis native and is the Coordinator of Baking and Pastry Arts at* St. Louis Community College at Forest Park. *He was named one of the "Top 10 Rising Star Pastry Chefs of 2000," and has earned several gold and silver medals for his chocolate sculptures and plated dessert displays.*

Coffee Cake Batter:
4 ounces butter, unsalted,
   room temperature
4 ounces granulated sugar
1 egg
5 ounces sour cream
½ teaspoon vanilla extract
5 ounces flour
½ teaspoon baking powder
½ teaspoon baking soda
½ teaspoon salt

Banana Swirl:
4 ounces light brown sugar
1 teaspoon ground cinnamon
1 ounce dark rum
1 ounce banana liqueur
1 tablespoon honey
1 tablespoon vanilla bean
3 ripe bananas

Crumb Topping:
4 ounces quick oats
4 ounces light brown sugar
4 ounces unsalted butter
4 ounces flour
1 teaspoon cinnamon

Coffee Cake Batter:
Cream the butter and sugar until light and fluffy. Mix in egg to incorporate. Add sour cream and vanilla extract, and mix until smooth. Sift the flour, baking powder, baking soda, and salt together, and stir into batter until smooth.

Banana Swirl:
In a 9×13-inch baking pan, pat brown sugar into an even layer. Evenly sprinkle with ground cinnamon, dark rum, banana liqueur, honey, and vanilla bean. Peel the bananas and cut in half lengthwise. Place bananas cut-side-down onto brown sugar. Cover tightly with aluminum foil. Bake at 325°F for 15 minutes. Remove foil, flip bananas over, and baste with the syrup from the baking pan. Replace foil; continue baking for 15 additional minutes. Remove foil, stir bananas; they should be very soft at this point. Return to oven, uncovered, and bake 15 additional minutes.

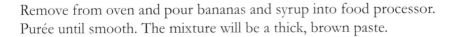

Remove from oven and pour bananas and syrup into food processor. Purée until smooth. The mixture will be a thick, brown paste.

Crumb Topping:
Combine oats, light brown sugar, butter, flour, and cinnamon in mixing bowl. Mix on low speed until butter is reduced to small pea-sized pieces and mixture is crumbly, but will compact when squeezed.

To assemble and bake the coffee cakes:
Portion batter into greased muffin tins. Spoon 2 tablespoons of banana purée onto batter, and swirl in. Place a generous amount of crumb topping on top. Bake at 350 °F until light brown and set, approximately 20 minutes.

Grandma's Banana Nut Bread
Makes 1 Loaf

Chef Joseph Mueller, CEC, is the Executive Chef at the Racquet Club Ladue. Joe earned a degree in Culinary Arts and Hotel/Restaurant Management from St. Louis Community College at Forest Park, and also attended the Culinary Institute of America in both New York and California.

1 cup sugar
½ cup butter, softened
1½ cups mashed ripe bananas
2 whole eggs
2 cups flour

½ teaspoon salt
½ teaspoon baking soda
1½ teaspoons baking powder
1 cup chopped walnuts
1½ tablespoons sour cream
1 teaspoon lemon juice

Cream sugar into butter until well incorporated. Add bananas and eggs, one at a time, while mixing. In a separate bowl, sift flour, salt, baking soda, and baking powder together to combine. Add dry ingredients to banana mixture and stir to incorporate (do not over mix). Fold in walnuts, sour cream, and lemon juice to form a batter. Pour batter into buttered and floured loaf pan. Bake at 325°F approximately 45 minutes. Cool bread on cooling rack at room temperature.

Outrageous Blueberry Muffins
Makes 18 Muffins

2¼ cups flour
1½ cups sugar
¾ cup shortening
¾ cup milk
2 eggs
2½ teaspoons baking powder
1 teaspoon salt
1 teaspoon vanilla extract
½ teaspoon water
1 pint fresh blueberries

Topping:
½ cup flour
½ cup sugar
1 teaspoon cinnamon
¼ cup butter, melted

In a large bowl, mix flour, sugar, shortening, milk, eggs, baking powder, salt, vanilla, and water. Blend on low speed for 2 minutes, scrape sides of bowl, and mix on high speed for 6 minutes. Spoon batter into greased and floured muffin cups, filling each ½ full. Add 6 to 10 blueberries to the batter in each cup. Set aside.

For crumb topping mix ½ cup flour, ½ cup sugar, 1 teaspoon cinnamon, and ¼ cup melted butter. Sprinkle 1 teaspoon of crumb topping and a few blueberries on the top of each muffin cup. Bake at 350°F for about 25 minutes. Remove from oven and cool completely.

Mini Pecan Muffins
Makes 24 Muffins

½ cup butter, melted
2 eggs
1 cup dark brown sugar

½ cup flour
1 teaspoon vanilla extract
1½ cups chopped pecans

Mix all ingredients. Fill greased mini muffin cups ⅔ full. Bake at 350°F for 17 minutes.

Note: *These freeze well.*

Lemon Blueberry Bread
Makes 1 Loaf

Bread:
1 cup sugar
½ cup butter
2 eggs
¾ cup milk
2½ cups flour
2½ teaspoons baking powder
1½ cups fresh or frozen blueberries

Glaze:
¼ cup sugar
3 tablespoons fresh lemon juice

Cream sugar and butter; add eggs and beat well. Add milk and blend well. Fold blueberries into batter. Pour batter into well greased loaf pan or 2 mini-loaf pans. Bake at 350°F for 1 hour and 15 minutes. Gently pierce the top of the loaf with a fork. Spoon glaze over the top of the loaf while it is still hot.

Overnight Pull-Apart Bread ✓
12 Servings

24 ounces frozen dinner roll dough
1 cup brown sugar, packed
1 3.4-ounce package instant
   butterscotch pudding mix

¼ cup white sugar
2 teaspoons ground cinnamon
½ cup chopped walnuts
½ cup butter, melted

The night or several hours before, grease and flour a 9- or 10-inch tube or Bundt pan. Mix brown sugar and pudding mix. Combine white sugar and cinnamon. Place frozen dinner rolls in pan a layer at a time. Sprinkle brown sugar and pudding mixture over first layer of rolls. Sprinkle sugar and cinnamon mixture over the brown sugar and pudding mixture. Spread half the nuts and melted butter over first layer. Repeat with the next layer.

Place pan on counter overnight. Do not cover. Next morning bake at 350°F for 30 minutes. Let stand a few minutes and turn pan over onto serving platter.

English Muffin Bread
Makes 4 Loaves

1 5-pound bag of bread flour
3 packages rapid yeast
3 tablespoons sugar
4 tablespoons salt

1 teaspoon baking soda
5 cups milk
1½ cups water
½ cup cornmeal

Combine 4 cups flour, yeast, sugar, salt, and baking soda. Heat milk and water until warm, 120 to 130°F. Add to dry ingredients. Beat with electric mixer until combined. Stir in the rest of flour. Knead and form into 4 loaves. Put in greased pans sprinkled with cornmeal. Let rise until double. Bake in 400°F oven for 25 minutes.

Note: *This is the best toast in the world, and gives the great smell of bread baking in the oven. Serve with butter and strawberry jam, or use for grilled sandwiches!*

Sour Cream Banana Bread
Makes 1 Loaf

1 cup sugar
½ cup oil
2 eggs
1½ cups mashed ripe bananas
½ cup sour cream

1 teaspoon vanilla extract
1½ cups flour
1 teaspoon baking soda
½ teaspoon salt
chopped pecans (optional)

In large bowl, beat together the sugar and oil. Add eggs, bananas, sour cream, and vanilla; blend well. Add flour, baking soda, and salt. Stir just until dry ingredients are moistened. Pour into greased and floured (bottom only) 9×5 loaf pan. Bake at 350°F for 50 to 60 minutes or until toothpick inserted in center comes out clean. Cool. Remove from pan.

Note: *This recipe will also make 12 muffins.*

Poppy Seed Bread
18 Servings

Bread:
3 cups flour, sifted
1½ teaspoons salt
1½ teaspoons baking powder
3 eggs
1½ cups 2% milk
1⅛ cups vegetable oil
2¼ cups sugar
1½ tablespoons poppy seeds
1½ teaspoons vanilla extract
1½ teaspoons almond extract
1½ teaspoons butter flavoring

Glaze:
½ teaspoon butter flavoring
½ teaspoon vanilla extract
½ teaspoon almond extract
¾ cup sugar
¼ cup orange juice

powdered sugar

Lightly coat two 9-inch loaf pans, 5 mini-loaf pans, or 16 to 18 decorative muffins with non-stick spray. Sift flour, salt and baking powder and set aside. In large bowl of electric mixer, beat eggs, milk, oil, and sugar until very well blended; add the poppy seeds, almond, butter, and vanilla extracts. Mix in the dry ingredients until batter is smooth.

Pour the batter into prepared pans and bake at 350°F until golden brown and toothpick comes out clean. Bake 55-60 minutes for regular loaves; 40 to 50 minutes for mini loaves; 35 to 40 minutes for decorative muffins.

While bread is baking, prepare glaze. Mix together butter flavoring, vanilla extract, almond extract, sugar, and orange juice in a small bowl. After baking, allow bread to rest in pans 5 minutes then turn onto rack to cool. Glaze while bread is warm, allowing glaze to drip down sides. Cool loaves completely. Before serving, sprinkle with powdered sugar.

Note: *Can be frozen once cooled.*

Zucchini Bread
Makes 2 Loaves

2 cups flour
1 teaspoon baking powder
2 teaspoons baking soda
1 teaspoon salt
1 tablespoon cinnamon
3 eggs, beaten

2 cups sugar
1 cup vegetable oil
1 tablespoon vanilla extract
2 cups zucchini, unpeeled,
  grated, and loosely packed
1 cup chopped nuts

In a large bowl, sift flour, baking powder, baking soda, salt, and cinnamon together. Combine eggs, sugar, oil, and vanilla; and stir into dry ingredients. Add grated zucchini and nuts. Pour into 2 greased 9×5×3 loaf pans. Bake at 350°F for 1 hour.

Boston Brown Bread
4 to 6 Servings

1 pound raisins
2 teaspoons baking soda
2 tablespoons butter
3 cups boiling water
2 eggs

1 teaspoon salt
4 cups flour
1 teaspoon cinnamon
2 cups sugar
1 cup pecans

Mince raisins in food processor. Add baking soda and butter. Cover with boiling water and set aside to cool. In another bowl, beat eggs, salt, flour, cinnamon, sugar, and nuts. Add to raisin mixture. Stir well. Grease pans. Bake at 350°F for 1 hour.

Note: *Use either greased, small loaf pans or for the more authentic version, use soup cans (labels off) that have been cleaned well. Place a circle of wax paper in the bottom of each can and fill cans ²/₃ full. Place directly on oven rack and bake as directed.*

Irish Soda Bread
4 to 6 Servings

1¼ cups whole meal or wheat flour
1 teaspoon baking soda
1 teaspoon salt

¾ cup flour
½ pint buttermilk

Mix flour, salt, and soda in bowl. Add almost all the milk and mix to form a loose dough, adding more milk if necessary. Knead lightly on floured board. Turn and flatten to 1½ inch thick. Slash a cross on top; brush with milk. Bake at 400°F for 40 minutes.

Sweet Potato Rolls
Makes 8 to 10 Rolls

1 packet yeast
¼ cup warm water
1 15-ounce can sweet potatoes in
    syrup, drained and mashed
½ cup butter, softened

½ cup sugar
1 teaspoon salt
2½ cups flour
1 teaspoon baking powder

Mix yeast with water according to package. Blend together the sweet potatoes and butter. Stir in the sugar and salt. Add the yeast mixture. Combine the flour and baking powder, and then add to rest of batter. Knead dough on floured surface until dough holds together. Let rise in buttered bowl for 2½ hours.

Roll out dough on floured surface to ½ inch. Cut out rolls with a 2-inch round biscuit cutter. Let each roll rise on a baking sheet for 2 hours. Bake at 400°F for 12 minutes.

Cheddar Cheese and Chive Biscuits
Makes 15 Biscuits

4 cups flour
1 teaspoon salt
2 tablespoons plus ¾ teaspoon
  baking powder
⅓ cup sugar
2 tablespoons dried chives

6 tablespoons grated
  cheddar cheese
¼ cup vegetable oil
⅓ cup margarine, melted
1¼ cups plus 2 tablespoons
  milk

Combine flour, salt, baking powder, sugar, chives, and cheddar cheese; mix thoroughly. Stir in oil and margarine. Add milk and knead just until dough pulls away from side of bowl. Do not over mix. Drop by large spoonfuls onto baking pan. Bake at 400°F about 20 minutes or until golden brown.

Oat Scones
Makes 10 Scones

1¼ cups whole-wheat flour
2 cups flour
¾ cup sugar
¾ teaspoon salt
1 teaspoon baking soda
2½ teaspoons baking powder
2½ cups oats

1 cup roughly chopped
  dried sour cherries
10 ounces chilled unsalted
  butter, cut into ½-inch pieces
⅔ cup buttermilk
1 tablespoon heavy cream
1 tablespoon sanding sugar

Line a 11×17-baking sheet with parchment paper. Combine all dry ingredients, except sanding sugar, with the cherries in a bowl. Add butter and mix on medium-low speed until the mixture resembles coarse meal. Add buttermilk and mix until just combined. Turn out the mixture onto a clean work surface, with hands, quickly pat mixture into a 16×3½-inch rectangle that is 1½ inches high. Score rectangle into 10 triangles. Cover with plastic wrap and transfer to the freezer for at least 2 hours.

Remove dough from freezer, cut into triangles with a sharp knife. Place scones 2 inches apart on the prepared baking sheet. Brush scones with heavy cream and sprinkle with sanding sugar. Bake at 350°F until lightly golden, about 30 minutes.

Apricot Almond Coffee Cake
12 Servings

1 cup butter, softened	2 cups flour
2 cups sugar	1 teaspoon baking powder
2 eggs	¼ teaspoon salt
1 cup sour cream	1 cup sliced almonds
1 teaspoon almond extract	1 10-ounce jar apricot preserves

Cream butter and sugar until fluffy. Beat in eggs; fold in sour cream and almond extract. Sift flour, baking powder and salt; fold into mixture. Place a third of the mixture in a greased and floured Bundt pan. Sprinkle ½ cup almonds and ½ jar preserves over batter. Spoon on remaining batter, add remaining preserves and almonds. Bake at 350°F for approximately 1 hour.

Note: *May vary using vanilla instead of almond extract and a mixture of ½ cup chopped pecans, 3 tablespoons of brown sugar, and 2 teaspoons cinnamon instead of almonds and apricot preserves.*

Perfect Popovers
8 Servings

2 eggs	1 teaspoon salt
1 cup whole milk	dash of cayenne pepper
1 cup flour	2 tablespoons unsalted butter

In a blender or medium bowl, with mixer mix egg, milk, flour, salt, and cayenne pepper until smooth (can refrigerate for 2 days). Grease popover pan cups (sides and bottom) with butter. Additionally, place ½ teaspoon butter in each cup and heat in oven until butter sizzles. Pour batter into cups, ½ to ⅔ full. Bake at 425°F for 25 to 30 minutes or until popovers are puffed and brown. Serve immediately with butter.

Note: *Popover pan is a must! Preheated oven to exactly 425°F is necessary. Do not open oven while they cook.*

Plum Coffee Cake
16 Servings

1 egg
4 tablespoons butter, melted
½ cup sugar
¾ cup milk
2 cups flour, sifted
4 teaspoons baking powder
½ teaspoon salt
Damson plums

Crumb Topping:
1 cup flour
½ cup sugar
4 tablespoons butter

Beat egg; add melted butter, sugar, milk, flour, baking powder, and salt. Mix well. Pour into 2 8- or 9-inch greased baking pans. Place Damson plums cut in half with cut side up over batter. To make crumb topping blend flour, sugar, and butter until pea gravel size and place on top of plums. Bake at 400°F for about 50 minutes.

Note: *Apples, peaches, or cherry pie filling work well in place of the plums.*

Sausage and Hash Brown Muffins
Makes 24 to 30 Muffins

1 pound pork sausage, hot or mild
1 large onion, chopped
2 cups frozen hash browns, thawed
1 cup grated cheddar cheese

3 tablespoons flour
8 eggs, beaten
½ cup milk
1 cup ranch salad dressing

In a large skillet, brown sausage and onion, cooking until sausage is no longer pink. Drain sausage and let it cool. Transfer to a large mixing bowl. Add potatoes and cheese and toss to mix (this part can be done the night before and refrigerated until needed). Stir the flour into the mixture, add eggs, milk, salad dressing, and mix well. Spoon the mixture into greased muffin tins (regular size), filling each cup half way. Bake at 325°F for 15 to 20 minutes until the muffins look golden brown. If using mini-muffin tins, time will be reduced.

Blueberry-Pecan Baked French Toast
8 to 10 Servings

1 loaf French baguette, 24 inches
6 large eggs
3 cups whole milk
1 cup brown sugar, packed
1 teaspoon vanilla extract
½ teaspoon grated nutmeg
2 cups fresh blueberries
½ cup chopped pecans
4 tablespoons butter, melted
powdered sugar for dusting

Blueberry Syrup:
1 cup blueberries
½ cup pure maple syrup
1 tablespoon lemon juice

Cut baguette in 1-inch slices and arrange in single layer in buttered 13×9 baking dish. In large bowl, whisk together eggs, milk, ¾ cup brown sugar, vanilla, and nutmeg. Pour evenly over bread. Chill mixture overnight or at least 8 hours.

Sprinkle 2 cups blueberries, pecans, and then the ¼ cup brown sugar over mixture. Drizzle melted butter over mixture. Bake at 375°F for 25 to 30 minutes until set. Serve with warm syrup and dust with powdered sugar.

Syrup:
Place blueberries and maple syrup in microwave-safe bowl; microwave on high for about 2 minutes. Pour syrup through sieve or small holed colander into a heat-proof bowl, pressing on blueberries to remove skin. Stir in lemon juice.

Overnight Stuffed French Toast with Berry Sauce
12 Servings

1 8-ounce loaf Italian bread
1 8-ounce package strawberry cream cheese
4 eggs
2 cups half-and-half
½ cup brown sugar
1 teaspoon almond extract

Topping:
¼ cup butter
¼ cup brown sugar
½ teaspoon almond extract
powdered sugar
berry sauce

Berry Sauce:
4 cups halved strawberries
¼ cup sugar
¼ cup water
2 teaspoons cornstarch
2 teaspoons grated orange peel

Cut bread diagonally into 30 slices, each ¼-inch thick. Spread about 1 tablespoon cream cheese on ½ of the slices. Top with remaining slices without cream cheese. Place in 9×13 baking dish sprayed with nonstick spray. In large bowl, with hand mixer, beat eggs, half-and-half, ½ cup brown sugar, and 1 teaspoon almond extract. Pour mixture evenly over bread, turning slices as needed to coat completely. Cover and refrigerate overnight.

Topping:
Just before baking, combine butter, ¼ cup brown sugar, and ½ teaspoon almond extract in a 1-cup measuring cup. Microwave on high until butter is melted. Stir until smooth. Drizzle over bread slices. Bake at 375°F for about 30 minutes.

Berry Sauce:
In large saucepan, combine strawberries, sugar, water, cornstarch, and orange peel over medium heat. Bring to boil. Reduce heat and simmer until slightly thickened, about 2 minutes. Drizzle over bread slices. Serve warm!

French Toast Casserole
8 Servings

1 cup brown sugar
1 stick margarine
4 tablespoons white corn syrup
10 to 12 slices white bread
1 cup milk

2 teaspoons cinnamon
1 teaspoon vanilla extract
½ cup sugar
12 eggs

Melt brown sugar, margarine, and corn syrup in a 9×13 baking dish. Cut bread in strips and lay on sugar mixture. Mix together milk, cinnamon, vanilla, sugar, and eggs. Pour over bread and press to soak bread. Bake at 350°F for 45 to 60 minutes. Let set for 10 minutes. Sprinkle with powdered sugar, cut and serve.

Note: *Can also be made with cinnamon bread, French bread, or a combination. May be assembled the night before and refrigerated until ready to bake.*

Whole Grain Strawberry Pancakes
7 Servings

1½ cups whole-wheat flour
3 tablespoons sugar
1 teaspoon baking powder
½ teaspoon baking soda
½ teaspoon salt
3 eggs
⅔ cup fat-free creamy vanilla or
   creamy strawberry yogurt

¾ cup water
3 tablespoons canola oil
1¾ cups sliced fresh
   strawberries
⅔ cup fat-free strawberry
   yogurt

Grease and heat griddle or 12-inch skillet over medium-high heat (375°F). In a large bowl, mix flour, sugar, baking powder, baking soda, and salt. Set aside. In medium bowl, beat eggs, ⅔ cup yogurt, water, and oil with wire whisk until well blended. Pour egg mixture all at once into flour mixture; stir until moistened. For each pancake, pour a little less than ¼ cup batter onto griddle. Cook pancakes 1 to 2 minutes on each side or until golden brown. Place 2 pancakes on each serving plate. Top with ¼ cup sliced strawberries and 1 to 2 tablespoons strawberry yogurt.

Buttermilk Pancakes and Homemade Syrup
4 to 6 Servings

1 well-beaten egg
1¼ cups buttermilk
2 tablespoons oil
1¼ cups flour
1 tablespoon sugar
1 teaspoon baking powder
½ teaspoon baking soda
½ teaspoon salt

Homemade Syrup:
1 cup water
2 cups white sugar
1 teaspoon maple flavoring

Pancakes:
In bowl, beat egg. Add buttermilk and oil and mix together. Separately, mix together flour, sugar, baking powder, baking soda, and salt, and then add to buttermilk mixture. Mix just to moisten; do not over mix. The batter will be lumpy. Fry on lightly greased griddle.

Syrup:
Mix in heavy saucepan, the water, sugar, and maple flavoring. Bring to a boil over medium heat. Cook for 2 minutes, or until thickened, and let cool slightly before serving.

Goat Cheese, Artichoke, and Ham Strata
10 to 12 Servings

2 cups whole milk
2 tablespoons olive oil
1 16-ounce loaf sourdough bread,
   cut into 1-inch cubes
5 eggs
1½ cups half-and-half or light cream
6 cloves garlic, minced
1½ tablespoons herbs de Provence
¾ teaspoon ground black pepper
½ teaspoon grated whole nutmeg
½ teaspoon rubbed sage

½ teaspoon crushed dried
   thyme
2 cups crumbled goat cheese
12 ounces smoked cooked
   ham, chopped
3 6-ounce jars marinated
   artichoke hearts, drained
   and halved lengthwise
5 ounces finely shredded
   Parmesan cheese
1 cup shredded Fontina
   cheese

In a very large bowl, mix milk and olive oil. Add bread cubes; stir to coat. Let stand 10 minutes. In large bowl, whisk eggs, half-and-half, garlic, herbs de Provence, pepper, nutmeg, sage, and thyme. Whisk in goat cheese until combined; set aside.

Spread half of the bread cube mixture in bottom of a greased 13×9 baking dish. Top with half of the ham, artichoke hearts, Parmesan and Fontina cheeses. Repeat layers; drizzle egg mixture over all. Cover and chill 2 to 24 hours. Uncover and bake at 350°F for 1 hour or until set in the center and edges are browned. Let stand 10 minutes before serving.

Brunch Roulade with Red Pepper Cream Sauce
6 Servings

5 eggs, separated
½ teaspoon salt
¼ teaspoon ground white pepper
paprika
1 cup warm milk

Filling:
1 10-ounce package frozen
   chopped spinach
1 cup freshly grated Parmesan cheese
¼ cup chopped roasted red
   peppers (optional)
6 slices bacon, cooked and crumbled

Sauce:
4 tablespoons unsalted butter
1 large red bell pepper, seeded and diced into ¼-inch pieces
¼ cup thinly sliced green onions
¼ cup flour
¼ teaspoon salt
¼ teaspoon white pepper
1¾ cups milk
3 teaspoons fresh lemon juice

Egg Mixture:
Line a jelly-roll pan with parchment or wax paper and spray well with nonstick cooking spray. In a small bowl, combine the egg yolks, salt, and pepper; beat well. Use an electric mixer in a large bowl to beat the egg whites until stiff. Fold the egg yolk mixture into the beaten egg whites. Do not over stir. Use a rubber spatula to spread the egg mixture evenly in the prepared pan. Sprinkle with paprika. Bake at 350°F for 10 minutes or until the top is brown.

Cut around the edge of the baked egg to loosen. Turn the baked egg onto another piece of oversized parchment paper coated with cooking spray (in a pan or tray with a rim), and peel off the first sheet. Pour warm milk over the egg layer, making certain to cover the edges. Let the milk soak in.

Filling:
Cook the spinach according to the package directions. Let cool, then squeeze all of the moisture out of the spinach. Sprinkle the cheese over the egg layer, then distribute the spinach evenly over the cheese.

Distribute the chopped roasted red peppers over the spinach. Finally, top with the crumbled bacon.

Roulade:
Roll the egg, jelly-roll fashion, beginning at one long side, to form a long roll that encloses the filling. Place the roll, seam side down, on a cookie sheet. Bake at 350°F for 15 minutes or until hot. Place on a serving tray; cut into 1½-inch thick slices to serve.

Sauce:
In a small, heavy saucepan, melt the butter and sauté the bell pepper and onions for 2 minutes. Add the flour and sauté over low heat for 3 minutes more. Blend in the salt and white pepper. Gradually whisk in the milk and lemon juice and cook for 1 minute. Place the mixture in a blender and blend on high for 2 minutes or until thoroughly puréed. Spoon over the roulade. Makes about 2 cups.

Note: *This may seem complicated, but it is really very easy. The roulade can be made ahead and refrigerated overnight and brought to room temperature for baking in the morning. The sauce can be made ahead and reheated before serving. The presentation is very pretty!*

Sausage and Egg Casserole
10 to 12 Servings

16 to 20 slices wheat bread
  without crust
1 pound pork sausage,
  browned and drained
1 8-ounce package cheddar
  cheese, shredded

7 eggs
3 cups milk
1 cup crushed cornflakes
2 tablespoons butter

Tear up bread and place half on bottom of greased 9×13 pan. Next, layer sausage, cheddar cheese, and bread. Beat eggs and milk together and pour over the sausage layer. Sprinkle top with crushed cornflakes. Top with chunks of butter. Bake at 350°F for 30 to 45 minutes until firm in middle.

Eggs Benedict √
8 Servings

4 English muffins, split and toasted
16 thin slices Canadian bacon
8 eggs
¼ cup butter
¼ cup flour
1 teaspoon paprika
⅛ teaspoon ground nutmeg

⅛ teaspoon pepper
2 cups milk
2 cups shredded Swiss
  cheese
½ cup dry white wine
½ cup crushed cornflakes
1 tablespoon butter, melted

In a 13×9×2 baking dish, arrange muffins, cut side up. Place 2 bacon slices on each muffin half. Half fill a 10-inch skillet with water; bring just to boiling. Break egg into a dish and carefully slide egg into water. Repeat with 3 more eggs. Simmer, uncovered 3 minutes or until just set. Remove eggs with slotted spoon. Repeat with remaining eggs. Place 1 egg on top of each muffin topped with bacon and set aside.

Sauce:
In a medium saucepan melt ¼ cup butter. Stir in flour, paprika, nutmeg, and pepper. Add all of the milk; cook and stir until thickened and bubbly. Stir in cheese until melted. Add wine. Spoon the sauce over the eggs. Combine cornflakes and 1 tablespoon butter; sprinkle over muffin stacks. If not serving immediately, the dish can be covered and chilled overnight.

When ready to serve, bake uncovered in 375°F oven for 20 to 25 minutes, or until heated through.

Note: *The Eggs Benedict can be made ahead and is a great brunch dish.*

Egg Brunch
12 Servings

4 slices bacon	pepper, to taste
½ pound shredded chipped beef	1 quart 2% milk
½ cup butter, divided	16 eggs
2 4-ounce cans sliced mushrooms, drained	¼ teaspoon salt
½ cup flour	1 cup evaporated milk

Sauté bacon; drain, and dice. Add beef, ¼ cup butter, and 6 ounces of the mushrooms. Sprinkle with flour and pepper. Gradually stir in milk. Cook until thickened. Set aside. Beat eggs, salt, evaporated milk, and ¼ cup melted butter. Scramble in large skillet. Make four layers in casserole dish beginning with egg mixture and ending with meat mixture. Garnish with remaining mushrooms. Cover dish and bake at 275°F for 1 hour.

Note: *Can be made the day before and stored in refrigerator. Baking time will be slightly longer.*

Overnight Brunch Casserole
12 Servings

¼ cup chopped red pepper, sautéed	6 eggs
¼ cup chopped green pepper, sautéed	1¾ cups whole milk
½ cup chopped onions, sautéed	¼ cup flour
1 28-ounce package frozen hashed browned potatoes, diced	1½ teaspoons seasoned salt
8 ounces sharp cheddar cheese crumbles	¼ teaspoon pepper
	6 slices of cooked bacon, crumbled

Mix peppers and onions with the potatoes. Arrange potatoes in a 9×13 baking dish that has been coated with nonstick cooking spray. Top with 1 cup of the cheese. In a medium bowl, beat together the eggs and milk. Whisk in flour and seasonings. Pour the mixture over the potatoes. Cover and refrigerate overnight.

Uncover and bake at 350°F for 30 minutes. Top with remaining cheese. Bake an additional 10 to 15 minutes or until golden brown and set. Crumble bacon and place on top.

Crustless Quiche
8 Servings

4 eggs, beaten
1 pound small-curd cottage cheese
½ pound Swiss cheese, grated
½ pound mild cheddar
  cheese, grated
½ cup milk
½ cup butter, melted

½ cup flour
1 teaspoon baking powder
1 10-ounce package frozen
  spinach thawed and well
  drained
salt to taste

Put all ingredients in large bowl and mix well. Spread into a greased 9×13 pan and bake at 350°F for 1 hour.

Note: *This quiche freezes well before baking. Vary recipe by substituting the spinach with crab meat, shrimp, ham, bacon, sausage, or broccoli.*

Crab Quiche Bake
6 Servings

8 eggs, beaten
2 cups half-and-half
1 large sweet red pepper, chopped
1 8-ounce package imitation crab
  meat, chopped
1 cup soft breadcrumbs

1 cup shredded Swiss cheese
1 cup shredded cheddar cheese
½ cup chopped green onion
1 teaspoon salt
½ teaspoon pepper

In a bowl, combine all ingredients. Transfer to a greased 13×9×2 baking dish. Bake uncovered at 350°F for 30 to 35 minutes until knife inserted near center comes out clean. Let stand 10 minutes before serving.

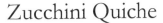

Zucchini Quiche
6 Servings

2 tablespoons butter
2 cups trimmed and coarsely
    chopped zucchini
½ cup chopped onion
¾ teaspoon salt, divided
½ teaspoon oregano
¼ teaspoon basil
¾ cup shredded Swiss or cheddar cheese

1 9-inch pie shell
1½ cups half and half
1½ teaspoons cornstarch
3 eggs
pinch nutmeg
dash liquid hot pepper sauce

Melt butter in a large skillet over medium heat. Add zucchini, onion, ½ teaspoon salt, oregano, and basil. Cook and stir until zucchini is tender, about 5 minutes. Increase heat and continue to cook until moisture is completely evaporated, stirring occasionally. Remove from heat. Toss with cheese and immediately distribute evenly on bottom of pie shell. In bowl, mix half-and-half with cornstarch. Whisk in eggs, nutmeg, hot pepper sauce, and remaining salt. Pour into pie shell. Bake at 400°F until set and lightly browned on top, about 40 minutes. Cool 10 minutes before serving.

Note: *If using a frozen shell, use a 9-inch deep-dish shell or a 10 inch regular shell. Also, this is good made with milk rather than half-and-half if you want to cut calories.*

Cheese Grits
4 to 6 Servings

1 cup stone-ground grits
1 teaspoon salt
4½ cups boiling water
¾ cup grated sharp white Vermont
    cheddar cheese

¼ cup freshly grated
    Parmesan cheese
3 tablespoons butter
freshly ground black pepper
Tabasco

Whisk the grits and salt into the boiling water; reduce to simmer, and cook for 35 to 40 minutes, stirring frequently. When the grits are tender, turn off the heat and stir in the cheeses and butter until melted and combined. Season to taste with pepper and Tabasco.

Quiche Lorraine
6 Servings

1 9-inch pastry shell, unbaked
12 bacon slices, crisply fried
  and crumbled
1 cup shredded natural Swiss cheese
⅓ cup finely chopped onion

4 eggs
2 cups half-and-half
¾ teaspoon salt
¼ teaspoon pepper
⅛ teaspoon cayenne pepper

Sprinkle bacon, cheese, and onions on bottom of pastry. Beat eggs slightly with a wire whisk, add half-and-half, salt and both peppers, and whisk together. Pour egg mixture into pastry. Bake at 425°F for 15 minutes. Reduce heat to 300°F and bake 30 minutes until knife comes out clean when inserted half way between center and edge. Let stand before serving.

Note: *To prevent crust from browning too much use aluminum foil strips to cover crust during baking. Try substituting other ingredients for the bacon and onion, or use a different cheese.*

Cheese Grits Casserole with Jalapeno Peppers
4 to 6 Servings

4 cups hot grits, cooked in milk
1 pound grated white cheddar
  cheese
½ cup butter
½ teaspoon ground mace
1 teaspoon salt

¼ teaspoon cayenne pepper
2 to 3 garlic cloves, finely
  chopped
¼ cup finely chopped
  jalapeno peppers (optional)
6 eggs

Combine the hot grits, cheddar cheese, butter, mace, salt, cayenne pepper, garlic, and jalapeno peppers, and stir well. Beat eggs well and add them into the grits mixture. Pour into a buttered 2-quart casserole or 9×12-inch baking dish. Bake at 350 °F until set and lightly browned, 30 to 45 minutes.

Baked Oatmeal
6 to 8 Servings

3 cups oatmeal
¾ cup brown sugar
½ cup margarine

2 eggs
2 cups milk
2 teaspoons baking powder
1 teaspoon salt

Mix all ingredients together. Pour in a 13×9 buttered pan. Bake at 375°F for 25 minutes.

Note: *Serve with dried fruits, nuts, or honey. Pour into small ramekins for baking and serving individually.*

Granola
6 Servings

3 cups old-fashioned rolled oats
1 cup slivered almonds
1 cup cashews
¾ cup shredded sweet coconut
¼ cup plus 2 tablespoons
    dark brown sugar

¼ cup plus 2 tablespoons
    maple syrup
¼ cup vegetable oil
¾ teaspoon salt
1 cup raisins or dried
    cranberries

In a large bowl, combine the oats, nuts, coconut, and brown sugar. In a separate bowl, combine maple syrup, oil, and salt. Combine both mixtures and pour onto 2 sheet pans. Bake at 250°F for 1 hour and 15 minutes, stirring every 15 minutes to achieve an even color. Remove from oven and transfer into a large bowl. Add raisins or cranberries and mix until evenly distributed. Serve with vanilla yogurt for breakfast.

Baked Fruit √
12 Servings

1 15-ounce can peaches	½ cup brown sugar
1 15-ounce can pineapple chunks	2 teaspoons curry powder
1 15-ounce can pears	(optional)
1 15-ounce can apricots	¾ stick butter or margarine
½ cup maraschino cherries	½ cup chopped pecans

Drain fruit well and place in a shallow baking dish. Mix brown sugar and curry powder. Sprinkle over fruit, dot with butter. Add nuts. Bake at 350°F for 30 to 40 minutes.

Note: *Almond extract, vanilla, or nutmeg may be substituted for the curry powder.*

Summer Berries with Yogurt Cream
4 Servings

1 pint strawberries, hulled and cut in half	1 teaspoon balsamic vinegar
2 cups mixed berries such as blue-	2 tablespoons heavy cream
berries, raspberries, or blackberries	⅓ cup nonfat vanilla yogurt
1 tablespoon orange juice	½ teaspoon vanilla extract
1 tablespoon sugar	

Toss fruit with orange juice, sugar, and vinegar. Allow to stand for 15 minutes. Toss again. Combine yogurt and vanilla. Whisk cream until slightly thickened. Fold into yogurt mixture. Serve berries in stemmed glasses and dollop with yogurt mixture.

Soups, Salads, & Sandwiches

The St. Louis Cord Blood Bank, a program of Cardinal Glennon Children's Medical Center, is the second largest cord blood bank in the nation. It is a non-controversial source for adult stem cells and distributes donated cord blood all over the world, sustaining millions of lives every year.

Soups

Harvest Rice and Wild Mushroom Soup
10 to 12 Servings

Culinary Institute of America graduate Sherrill Gonterman *started* LaChef Catering *30 years ago with her mother.* LaChef *specializes in healthy, creative cuisine for residential and corporate clients.*

1 large onion, diced
1 pound carrots, diced
5 stalks celery, diced
½ cup butter
1 teaspoon thyme
1 teaspoon marjoram

1 bay leaf
3 quarts chicken stock
1 pound roasted turkey, diced
8 ounces wild rice
1 pound shiitake mushrooms
½ cup sherry
½ cup chopped parsley

Sauté onions, carrots, and celery in butter for 10 minutes. Add thyme, marjoram, bay leaf and cook for 2 minutes. Add stock, turkey, and rice. Simmer for 1 hour. Add mushrooms and sherry to soup and cook for 15 minutes. Stir in parsley, salt, and pepper to taste. Remove bay leaf before serving.

Note: *Serve soup in a hallowed pumpkin in the fall.*

Lentil Soup
4 Servings

Edwardsville native Amy Zupanci *is the chef and owner of* Fond Restaurant *and* Township Grocer *in Edwardsville, Illinois. Zupanci is gaining a reputation for sustainable, beautifully presented cuisine in the heart of the Midwest. Fond has received many accolades, including the distinction of best new restaurant of 2009.*

¼ cup olive oil
1 large onion, minced
4 cloves garlic, minced
1 cup diced carrot
1 cup diced celery
2 cups green lentils
½ teaspoon cayenne
½ teaspoon cumin

1 tablespoon Turkish oregano
8 cups water
1 large can tomatoes, diced
3 cups chopped kale
2 cans garbanzo beans, drained and rinsed
1 tablespoon sherry vinegar
salt and pepper to taste

In a large heavy pot, warm oil. Add onions and garlic; sweat for about 5 minutes. Add carrots and celery and coat with oil and aromatics. Add lentils and spices, stirring to coat the lentils with all the vegetables, cayenne, cumin, and oregano. Cover with water. Add tomatoes. Bring to a bubble and simmer for about 45 minutes. Add kale and garbanzo beans. Season with salt and pepper. Continue cooking 20 minutes or until lentils are tender. Finish with vinegar and salt and pepper if needed.

Mushroom Bisque
4 Servings

Bernard Pilon, CEC, was a chef in Montreal and Maryland before arriving in St. Louis in 1995. He has been the Executive Chef at Norwood Hills Country Club since 2000, and won the Chef of the Year Award in 2007. His family includes his wife Stephanie, his daughter Olivia, and his son Brian.

8 ounces mixed mushrooms, chopped
1 small onion, diced
2 tablespoons olive oil
2 tablespoons butter
2 cups chicken stock
2 cups cream containing 45% fat

¼ cup Madeira wine
salt and pepper to taste
2 ounces mushrooms for garnish
2 ounces smoked salmon for garnish

Sauté mushrooms and onion in olive oil and butter. Add stock and cream. Cook and reduce until creamy. Purée in food processor. Add Madeira wine, salt and pepper. Garnish with mushrooms and salmon.

White Chicken Chili
8 Servings

Paul V Frintrup, CCC, is a St. Louis native who began his career as a cook at Two Nice Guys and The Seventh Inn. Paul is the Executive Chef at the Country Club of St. Albans. He currently resides in Webster Groves with his wife and son.

¼ cup olive oil
9 ounces diced onion
4 ounces diced celery
2 ounces minced fresh
  serrano peppers
4½ ounces whole butter
4½ ounces flour
½ gallon chicken broth
14 ounces navy beans (drained weight)

14 ounces garbanzo beans
  (drained weight)
1½ teaspoons cumin
2 teaspoons dry basil
2½ cups heavy cream
1 pound 4-ounce baked
  chicken, diced

In stockpot, heat oil and sweat onions, celery, and peppers. Add butter, melt, and add flour to form roux. Cook this mixture for 5 to 7 minutes stirring frequently. Add broth and bring to a light boil. Once thickened, add beans, spices, and cream. Simmer 10 to 15 minutes. Add chicken and just warm through. Season with salt and pepper to your liking.

Poached Lemon Sole in Rich Coconut Ginger Soup
4 Servings

Mohammad Azhar *is the Executive Chef at the* Ritz Carlton St. Louis. *He was raised in Northern India, where he was exposed to a wide array of cooking that fused unique Indian cuisine with modern influences to create the flavorful repertoire that Azhar is now known for. He learned the food ethics and cuisines of the regions where he has worked, and pays homage to them in every menu he creates.*

Soup:
2 thinly sliced shallots
4 thinly sliced garlic cloves
2 thinly sliced ounces ginger
1 ounce thinly sliced lemongrass, divided
2 ounces butter
1 pint chicken stock, lightly reduced
12 ounces coconut milk
2 Kaffir lime leaves
4 sprigs coriander, rinsed and roughly chopped

Fish and Presentation:
4 Sole fillets (each cut in 3 pieces)
1.5 pint Coconut Ginger Soup
1 mango, cut into ¼-inch dice
1 avocado, cut into ¼-inch dice
5 cilantro sprigs
1 tablespoon olive oil

To Prepare the Soup in Advance:
Sweat the shallots, garlic, ginger, and ½ of the lemongrass in butter and season very lightly. Cook until the shallots are transparent. Add chicken stock and cook for 10 to 15 minutes. Add coconut milk and cook 5 minutes more. Add remaining lemongrass, Kaffir lime leaves and coriander and cook 2 to 3 minutes. Remove from heat and let steep for 10 to 15 minutes. Strain through a chinoise (or fine mesh strainer) and season.

To Serve:
Season lemon sole and sear on a hot pan with little olive oil. Place soup in saucepan and begin to heat. Arrange diced avocado and mango in bottom of soup plate and set aside. Place seared sole in the middle of the plate by stacking all three pieces. Squeeze lime onto plate and pour the soup to barely cover avocado and mango. Garnish plate with cilantro sprigs.

Wild Mushroom Bisque

6 Servings

Paul V Frintrup, *CCC, is a St. Louis native who began his career as a cook at Two Nice Guys and The Seventh Inn. Paul is the Executive Chef at the* Country Club of St. Albans. *He currently resides in Webster Groves with his wife and son.*

8 ounces button mushrooms	5 ounces diced white onion
8 ounces shiitake mushrooms	3 fluid ounces white wine
4 ounces portabella mushrooms	1 quart chicken stock
3 ounces whole butter	8 fluid ounces heavy cream
3 ounces flour	4 ounces shredded smoked Gouda

Wash, pat dry, and rough chop button mushrooms. Remove stems of shiitake and portabella. With a spoon, scrape the gills underneath the portabella. Rough chop all mushrooms, dice onions, and set aside. In a separate pan, melt butter and stir in flour to form a roux. Cook this until a nutty aroma fills the kitchen. In a heated stockpot, sweat onions add mushrooms and cook until all liquid evaporates. Deglaze with white wine and reduce liquid by half. Add stock and bring to a boil. Once thickened, reduce heat and stir in cream and shredded cheese. Let this simmer for approximately 10 to 15 minutes. In a blender, pulse until soup is completely macerated. Season the soup with salt and pepper to suit your own personal needs.

Note: *Garnish: Fresh chopped parsley or Parmesan Crisp.*

Smoked Gouda, Peppered Bacon, and Mushroom Soup

4 Servings

Chris Desens *is currently the program director for the* Culinary Institute at Hickey College. *He has thirty years of varied industry experience including national and international culinary competitions. He is a certified culinary judge through the American Culinary Federation, a Certified Executive Chef, and a member of the American Academy of Chefs.*

1 strip peppered bacon, julienned
1 strip peppered bacon, diced
3 tablespoons butter
¼ cup diced yellow onions
¼ cup diced celery
2 cups mushrooms, cremini, shiitake, and domestic, sliced
½ teaspoon minced garlic
¼ cup flour

⅛ cup Madeira wine
⅛ cup sherry
2 cups chicken stock
1 cup heavy cream
1 cup smoked gouda cheese, grated
⅛ teaspoon fresh thyme
1 bay leaf
salt and pepper to taste

Croutons:
bread, crust removed, diced
butter, clarified
fresh thyme

Shiitake Bacon:
¼ cup shiitake mushrooms, stems removed, thinly sliced
1 teaspoon mushroom soy
1 teaspoon olive oil
black pepper, to taste

Heat julienned bacon in pot and cook until crisp; remove, drain, and reserve as garnish. Add diced bacon and cook until nearly crisp. Add butter, onions, celery, and mushrooms and cook until mushrooms release their liquid. Add garlic and continue to cook briefly. Add flour and stir to make a roux. Add Madeira wine and sherry and stir well, then add chicken stock.In a separate pot, heat cream and cheese together until cheese melts. Purée in blender and fold into thickened soup base. Add herbs, bay leaf, and season to taste. Cook until flour taste disappears. Remove bay leaf before serving.

Croutons:
Heat butter in skillet and add bread cubes and thyme. Toast over medium heat until golden brown and crisp. Reserve for soup.

Shiitake Bacon:
Combine mushrooms with soy and olive oil; lay out on rack and bake in oven until crisp. Add pepper to taste. The mushrooms will resemble diced bacon. Reserve for soup.

To Serve: Ladle soup into bowls and garnish with croutons, crisp bacon, and shiitake bacon.

Note: *This soup works well for any occasion. It offers a nice variation on a classic favorite.*

Wisconsin Beer Cheese Soup
6 Servings

Paul V Frintrup, *CCC, is a St. Louis native who began his career as a cook at Two Nice Guys and The Seventh Inn. Paul is the Executive Chef at the* Country Club of St. Albans. *He currently resides in Webster Groves with his wife and son.*

¼ pound bacon
½ pound white onion, small dice
4 ounces chopped celery
2 ounces chopped red pepper
2 ounces chopped yellow pepper
3 ounces whole butter

4 ounces flour
3 cups chicken stock
2 cups heavy cream
1 12-ounce bottle light beer
(we use Busch)
1 tablespoon granulated sugar
2 cups shredded sharp
cheddar cheese

In hot stockpot, render bacon until crispy. Add onions, celery, and peppers; cook until tender. Melt butter in pot, then add flour to form a blonde roux. Whisk in chicken stock and bring to a gentle simmer, stirring frequently. Simmer for 10 to 15 minutes and then pour in cream and beer. Gently bring back to a simmer and sprinkle in sugar and cheese while stirring so that it melts evenly. With an immersion blender or upright blender, purée in batches until a smooth consistency is reached. To finish, season with salt and pepper to taste.

Beet Soup with Horseradish Crème Fraîche, Apples, and Watercress
4 Servings

8 cups water, divided
2 tablespoons plus 1 teaspoon sherry vinegar, divided
1 tablespoon plus ½ teaspoon salt, divided
1 tablespoon sugar
1 pound small red beets, trimmed
¼ olive oil
½ cup chopped shallots
⅛ teaspoon ground ginger

2 cups vegetable broth
1 tablespoon vinegar
½ cup crème fraîche
1 tablespoon prepared horseradish, drained
1 teaspoon lemon juice
2 apples
1 tablespoon grape-seed oil (or olive oil)
salt and pepper to taste
watercress sprigs and extra olive oil for garnish

In a medium saucepan, combine 6 cups water, 1 tablespoon vinegar, 1 tablespoon salt, and sugar. Reserve 2 tablespoons of liquid. Add beets to saucepan; bring to a boil. Reduce heat and simmer for 45 minutes or until beets are tender. Let cool to room temperature, then peel and dice.

In saucepan, heat olive oil over medium-low heat. Add shallots, remaining ½ teaspoon salt, and ginger. Sweat until softened, about 8 to10 minutes. Do not brown. Add beets, broth, 2 cups water, and 1 tablespoon vinegar to saucepan. Bring to a boil. Reduce heat and simmer for 10 minutes.

Meanwhile, in a small bowl, combine crème fraîche, horseradish, remaining vinegar, and lemon juice. Season with salt and pepper. Refrigerate until ready to use. With a melon baller, scoop out about 12 balls from the apples, leaving the peel intact. Toss apple balls with reserved liquid. Set aside.

Working in batches, purée soup and grape-seed oil in a blender until smooth. Season with salt and pepper and ladle into individual bowls. Garnish with apple balls, a drizzle of crème fraîche mixture, and watercress. Drizzle with olive oil.

Butternut Squash Soup
6 Servings

1 tablespoon butter
1 tablespoon olive oil
1 medium onion
3 medium Granny Smith apples,
    cored, peeled, and chopped
3 cups peeled and diced
    butternut squash

1½ cups apple cider
3½ cups chicken broth
pinch of nutmeg
coarse salt and pepper
shaved Parmesan

In a large pot, heat butter and oil over medium heat. Add onion, cook, stirring frequently, until soft. Stir in apples and butternut squash, cook for 3 to 5 minutes until softened. Add apple cider and chicken broth and simmer for 20 to 30 minutes or until vegetables are very soft. Purée in batches in food processor. Add additional chicken stock if soup is too thick. Season with nutmeg, salt and pepper. Serve hot with shaved Parmesan cheese on top.

Note: *You can find already peeled and cut butternut squash at Trader Joe's. As a time saver, you may use 3 packages of frozen squash purée (in frozen vegetable section) instead of the fresh butternut squash. Add this when you add the liquids to the pot so that it can defrost in the soup. You will still need to purée the soup.*

Creamy Pumpkin Soup
5 Servings

¼ cup butter or margarine
1 small onion, chopped
1 clove garlic, minced
2 teaspoons packed brown sugar
1 14½-ounce can chicken broth
½ cup water

½ teaspoon salt (optional)
¼ teaspoon ground black pepper
1 15-ounce can pumpkin
1 12-ounce evaporated milk
  (can use skim)
⅛ teaspoon ground cinnamon

Melt butter in a large saucepan over medium heat. Add onion, garlic, and sugar; cook 1 to 2 minutes or until onions are soft. Add broth, water, salt and pepper; bring to boil, stirring occasionally. Reduce heat to low; cook, stirring occasionally for 15 more minutes. Stir in pumpkin, evaporated milk, and cinnamon. Cook, stirring occasionally, for 5 minutes. Remove from heat. If a smoother consistency is desired, transfer to a food processor or blender and process until smooth. Return to saucepan and serve warm.

Baked Potato Soup
8 Servings

4 medium potatoes
6 tablespoons butter or margarine
¼ cup chopped onion
⅓ cup flour
1 teaspoon salt
1 teaspoon ground black pepper
3 cups half-and-half

2 cups chicken broth
1 cup sour cream
1½ cups shredded cheddar
  cheese
¼ cup chopped green onions
½ cup bacon, cooked and
  crumbled

Bake the potatoes at 400°F for 60 minutes or until fork tender. After cooling, do not peel; dice into 1-inch pieces. Melt butter in a Dutch oven or large saucepan. Add onion and sauté until tender. Add flour, salt, and pepper. Add half-and-half and chicken broth. Cook over medium heat until boiling and it starts to thicken. Stir in diced potatoes and sour cream. To serve, ladle into bowls and top with cheddar cheese, green onions, and bacon.

French Onion Soup
4 Servings

1 pound, 6 ounces peeled onions
3 ounces butter or margarine
1 tablespoon Spanish paprika
1 teaspoon freshly ground or cafe
  ground pepper
2 bay leaves
1½ cups flour

1½ quarts beef bouillon (from
  cubes or canned)
1½ teaspoons salt
French bread for topping
6 ounces grated Swiss cheese
  (Emmentaler or Gruyere
  preferred)

Cut onions in half and slice with the grain about ⅛-inch thick. Melt butter and add sliced onions. Sauté slowly for 20 minutes, stirring frequently. Add paprika, pepper, bay leaves, and flour. Mix well, keeping flame low. Stir while cooking for 5 minutes.

Gradually add hot bouillon while stirring, preferably with a wooden spoon. Simmer soup, covered, for at least 30 minutes. If a rich brown color is desired, add caramel coloring. Taste soup and season with salt. Remove bay leaf.

Heat soup and fill oven-proof casserole or individual oven-proof crocks with 8 ounces soup. Top with thin slices of French bread and cover each serving with 1½ ounces grated Gruyere cheese. Place under broiler and melt cheese until golden brown.

Kansas City Steak Soup
4 Servings

8 tablespoons butter
½ cup flour
40 ounces canned beef broth
¼ cup medium-dice carrots
¼ cup medium-dice onions
¼ cup medium-dice celery
½ cup diced canned tomatoes
1 tablespoon browning sauce
   (Kitchen Bouquet)

¾ teaspoon Lawry's salt
¼ teaspoon black pepper
5 ounces frozen mixed
   vegetables
½ pound ground chuck, chili
   grind, browned and drained

Place the butter in a soup pot; melt without browning. Add flour and stir to form a smooth paste. Cook the mixture (roux) over medium heat, without browning, for 3 minutes, stirring constantly. Add broth to the roux and stir until smooth and lightly thickened. Bring to a full boil. Add the carrots, onions, celery, tomatoes, Kitchen Bouquet, Lawry's salt, and pepper; return to a boil. Reduce heat and simmer until vegetables are just barely tender (20 to 30 minutes).

Add the frozen vegetables and the browned ground chuck. Simmer an additional 15 minutes. Be sure to simmer long enough that the flavors become well blended.

Leek and Salmon Chowder
6 to 8 Servings

12-ounce salmon fillet
3 cups bottled clam juice
1 tablespoon butter, softened
1 tablespoon flour
4 bacon slices, chopped
2 medium leeks, thinly sliced, soaked in water for about 10 minutes

1 large white-skinned potato, peeled, cut into ½-inch pieces
2½ cups milk
½ cup whipping cream
2 tablespoons chopped fresh chives
salt and pepper

In medium skillet, simmer salmon in clam juice covered, for 10 minutes. Transfer salmon to plate. Reserve clam juice. Flake salmon into small pieces. Mix butter and flour in a small bowl. Cook bacon in heavy saucepan over medium-low heat until crispy. Transfer bacon to paper towels to drain.

Add leeks to drippings in saucepan and sauté 3 minutes. Add potato and reserved clam juice and bring to a boil. Reduce heat. Cover and simmer until potato is tender, about 10 minutes. Add milk, bring to a boil, and whisk in flour mixture. Stir in cream, chives, salmon, and bacon. Season with salt and pepper to taste.

Note: *Serve chowder with crusty bread and a salad for a great meal!*

Cajun Jambalaya
4 Servings

12 medium shrimp, peeled, deveined,
  and chopped
4 ounces diced chicken
1 tablespoon Creole seasoning,
  recipe follows
2 tablespoons olive oil
¼ cup chopped onion
¼ cup chopped green bell pepper
¼ cup chopped celery
2 tablespoons chopped garlic
½ cup chopped tomatoes
3 bay leaves
1 teaspoon Worcestershire sauce
1 teaspoon hot sauce
¾ cup rice
3 cups chicken stock
5 ounces andouille sausage, sliced
salt and pepper

Creole Seasoning:
2½ tablespoons paprika
2 tablespoons salt
2 tablespoons garlic powder
1 tablespoon black pepper
1 tablespoon onion powder
1 tablespoon cayenne pepper
1 tablespoon dried oregano
1 tablespoon dried thyme

In a bowl, combine shrimp, chicken, and Creole seasoning and work in seasoning well. In a large saucepan, heat oil over high heat with onion, pepper, and celery for 3 minutes. Add garlic, tomatoes, bay leaves, Worcestershire, and hot sauce. Stir in rice and slowly add broth. Reduce heat to medium and cook until rice absorbs liquid and becomes tender, stirring occasionally, about 15 minutes. When rice is just tender add shrimp and chicken mixture and sausage. Cook until meat is done, about 10 minutes more. Season to taste with salt, pepper, and Creole seasoning. Remove bay leaves before serving.

Creole Seasoning:
Combine all ingredients thoroughly.

Jambalaya
6 to 8 Servings

1 pound smoked sausage, sliced
and quartered
¼ cup olive oil
1 cup chopped onion
1 cup chopped red pepper
1 cup chopped celery
1 box of Zatarain's Jambalaya mix

1 pound cooked and shredded
chicken, preferably cooked
and smoked on grill
32 ounces of chicken stock
30 shrimp, peeled, deveined,
and cooked

In a large stockpot, sauté smoked sausage until all of the fat has rendered, about 20 minutes. Remove the sausage and set aside.

Add the olive oil to the fat rendered from the sausage. Add the onion, pepper, and celery. Sauté until tender. Add the sausage back to the stockpot. Add the rice and seasoning mix from the Zatarain's box and stir will until all of the seasoning is broken down. Add the pulled chicken to the pot. Add the chicken stock to the pot and bring to a boil. After it boils, reduce the heat to a simmer and cover. Allow rice to cook about 30 to 45 minutes. Do not stir while rice is cooking. Add the shrimp on top of rice after 20 minutes of cooking time.

Crescent City Gumbo
8 Servings

3 tablespoons canola oil, divided
½ pound skinless, boneless chicken thighs, cut into bite-sized pieces
1 pound low-fat smoked sausage (such as Healthy Choice) or turkey kielbasa, cut into ½-inch-thick rounds
2 cups chopped onion
1 cup chopped green bell pepper
½ cup chopped celery
1 tablespoon minced fresh garlic
1 teaspoon chopped fresh thyme
½ teaspoon ground red pepper
⅓ cup flour
5 cups fat-free, low-sodium chicken broth
1 14.5-ounce can no salt-added diced tomatoes, not drained
3 cups fresh okra, cut into 1 inch slices
2 bay leaves
¼ cup chopped fresh flat-leaf parsley
1 pound medium shrimp, peeled and deveined
2⅔ cups hot cooked long-grain rice

Coat a large Dutch oven with cooking spray and heat over medium-high heat. Add 1 teaspoon oil, chicken, and sausage; sauté for 3 minutes or until browned. Remove from pan (leave drippings in pan). Add onion, bell pepper, and celery to pan; sauté 4 minutes. Add garlic, thyme, and red pepper; sauté for 4 minutes or until onion is tender and garlic is fragrant. Remove from pan.

Add remaining oil to pan. Add flour to pan, stirring constantly with a whisk. Cook 10 minutes or until roux is light brown, stirring constantly with a whisk. Gradually add broth, stirring constantly with a whisk. Add chicken and sausage, onion mixture, tomatoes, okra, and bay leaves; bring to a boil. Cover, reduce heat, and simmer 45 minutes, stirring occasionally. Stir in parsley and shrimp; cook 5 minutes or until shrimp are done. Discard bay leaves. Serve over rice.

Seafood Gumbo
12 Servings

4 tablespoons vegetable oil, divided
3 medium onions, chopped
2 pounds okra, sliced
2 teaspoons red wine vinegar
3 cloves garlic, minced
1 green pepper, chopped
6 celery stalks, chopped
½ cup minced fresh parsley
14.5 ounces diced tomatoes
8 ounces tomato sauce
2 quarts hot water
2 bay leaves
1 teaspoon thyme

¼ teaspoon rosemary
3 tablespoons chicken bouillon
1 6-ounce can tomato paste
¼ cup Worcestershire sauce
salt and pepper
3 pounds medium shrimp,
  shelled
1 pound lump (or claw) crabmeat
2 tablespoons Old Bay
  seasoning
hot sauce to taste (be gentle
  with shakes)
rice

Heat 2 tablespoons of oil in a large pot over medium-low heat. Add onions, okra, and vinegar and cook until okra is no longer stringy, stirring occasionally, about 30 minutes.

In a large soup pot (approximately 10-quart) heat remaining 2 tablespoons vegetable oil. Sauté garlic, green pepper, and celery until soft. Add parsley and cook for 5 minutes. Add onion and okra mixture to the large soup pot. Cook 5 minutes. Add diced tomatoes, tomato sauce. Simmer 5 minutes. Gradually add hot water, bay leaves, thyme, rosemary, chicken bouillon, tomato paste, and Worcestershire sauce. Simmer 45 minutes. Salt and pepper to taste. At this point, if soup seems too thick, add more hot water.

Add shrimp and crabmeat. Bring to a boil; add Old Bay seasoning and simmer just until shrimp turn pink. Salt and pepper to taste. Add a few shakes of hot sauce. Cool completely; refrigerate overnight. This allows the flavors to blend together and enhances the soup. When you are ready to eat the gumbo, return the soup to a low simmer to heat. Adjust your seasonings to taste. Be careful not to boil the soup because you don't want the shrimp to get tough. Discard bay leaves. Serve with rice. To serve, spoon a few tablespoons of rice into large soup bowls. Ladle gumbo over rice.

Note: *Great served with a green salad and hot French bread.*

Easy Creole Gumbo
6 to 8 Servings

1 green pepper, finely chopped
½ cup chopped onion
½ cup sliced celery
1 clove garlic, minced
2 tablespoons butter
1 6-ounce can tomato paste
1½ cups water

1 teaspoon salt
½ teaspoon thyme
1 teaspoon gumbo file powder
⅛ teaspoon pepper
3 cups cooked shrimp
1 large can or 2 small cans of
  oysters

Cook green pepper, onion, celery, and garlic in butter until tender. Add tomato paste, water, salt, thyme, gumbo file powder, and pepper. Simmer for 15 minutes stirring easily. Add seafood and heat thoroughly for 15 minutes.

Note: *Good served over rice.*

White Chili
4 to 6 Servings

1 medium onion, chopped
1 teaspoon olive oil
3 cloves garlic, minced
3 cans chicken broth
2 cups cooked chopped chicken
3 cans great northern beans
1 can chopped green chilies

1 can chopped tomatoes
1 teaspoon cumin
1 teaspoon oregano
1 teaspoon nutmeg
1 teaspoon cayenne pepper
1 8-ounce bag shredded
  Monterey Jack cheese

In small skillet, sauté onion in olive oil until translucent. Add garlic for 1 minute; remove from heat. In saucepan, combine chicken broth, chicken, beans, chilies, tomatoes, cumin, oregano, nutmeg, and cayenne pepper. Add onion and garlic to broth mixture. Simmer for 2 to 3 hours. Top each individual serving with grated cheese.

Vegetarian Chili
8 Servings

1 16-ounce can diced tomatoes, in juice
1 16-ounce can pinto beans
1 16-ounce can kidney beans
1 16-ounce can black beans
½ cup chopped onions
½ cup chopped green pepper
½ cup chopped celery
½ teaspoon Tabasco sauce

1 tablespoon chili powder
1 tablespoon cumin
1 teaspoon black pepper
2 teaspoons garlic salt
2 teaspoons oregano
2 teaspoons parsley
1 teaspoon coriander

Place tomatoes, beans, onions, green pepper, celery, Tabasco sauce, chili powder, cumin, pepper, garlic salt, oregano, parsley, and coriander in a large pot and simmer 1 to 2 hours.

Note: *This is also delicious served in tortillas, with lettuce, cheese, and tomatoes.*

Chili
6 Servings

2 tablespoons vegetable oil
1½ pounds ground beef
½ teaspoon salt
1 10-ounce can condensed onion soup
1 tablespoon chili powder
2 teaspoons cumin

½ teaspoon pepper
2 teaspoons cocoa powder
1 21-ounce can kidney beans, not drained
1 6-ounce can tomato paste
1 8-ounce can tomato sauce
1 cup cola soda (not diet)

In large skillet, heat oil; add crumbled beef and salt. Pack firmly in pan and cover. Cook over low heat 20 minutes. Remove from heat and drain. Meanwhile, put soup in blender and blend for 1 minute. Add to beef and mash until it looks like rice. Add chili powder, cumin, pepper, and cocoa. Cover and simmer 5 minutes. Add beans, tomato paste, tomato sauce, and cola. Simmer on low for 1 hour.

Note: *Can be heated in crock pot on low for 6 hours or high for 2 hours.*

Vegetarian Chili
4 to 6 Servings

1 tablespoon vegetable oil
1 cup chopped onions
1 cup chopped carrots
3 cloves garlic
1 cup chopped green bell pepper
1 cup chopped red bell pepper
¾ cup chopped celery
1 tablespoon chipotle chili powder
   (if you don't have, use regular chili
   powder but use more BBQ sauce)
1½ cups chopped fresh mushrooms

1 28-ounce can of whole
   tomatoes not drained,
   chopped
1 19-ounce can southwestern
   style kidney beans not drained
1 11-ounce can of sweet corn,
   not drained
1 tablespoon cumin
1½ teaspoons dried oregano
1½ teaspoons dried basil
3 to 5 squirts of BBQ sauce to
   taste

Heat oil in a large saucepan over medium heat. Sauté onions, carrots, and garlic until tender. Stir in green pepper, red pepper, celery, and chili powder. Cook until veggies are tender (about 6 minutes). Stir in mushrooms and cook 4 minutes. Stir in tomatoes, kidney beans, and corn. Season with cumin, oregano, basil, and BBQ sauce. Season to taste. Bring to a boil; reduce heat to medium. Cover and simmer for 20 minutes, stirring occasionally.

Note: *BBQ sauce and/or chipotle chili powder gives it a rich, sweet flavor.*

Tuscan Bean Soup
6 to 8 Servings

1 leek, halved lengthwise
  and thinly sliced
1 onion, finely chopped
1 carrot, finely chopped
1 celery stalk, finely chopped
2 cloves garlic, minced
3 tablespoons olive oil
1 ham bone, trimmed of excess meat
3 Roma tomatoes, skinned,
  seeded and diced
¼-½ head savoy cabbage, shredded
2 cups cannellini beans, soaked
  overnight in lightly salted water

1 long sprig rosemary (leaves
  only), finely chopped
3 sprigs thyme
2 bay leaves
4 quarts water
chicken bouillon paste, to taste
salt and pepper, to taste
3 medium Yukon Gold
  potatoes, boiled to mashing
  consistency
12 ounces orzo pasta, boiled,
  until not quite al dente

Over medium heat, sauté the leek, onion, carrot, celery, and garlic in olive oil until onion has started to turn color, but not browned. Add ham bone, tomatoes, cabbage and beans, and stir well. Add rosemary, thyme, and bay leaves, and stir well. Add water, chicken bouillon paste, salt and pepper. Simmer, covered until beans begin to soften.

Purée some of the beans, all of the potatoes, and add back to soup. Add cooked orzo to soup. Discard bay leaf. Heat thoroughly and serve.

Bean and Pasta Soup
12 Servings

½ cup pasta, cooked and drained
2 celery ribs, diced
2 cups diced mini carrots
½ large onion, diced
1 teaspoon diced garlic
1 tablespoon oil
4 cups fat-free chicken broth
3 16-ounce cans diced tomatoes
1 teaspoon dried basil
¼ teaspoon dried, crushed rosemary

⅛ teaspoon pepper
1 teaspoon oregano
1 8-ounce can green beans, drained
1 16-ounce can northern beans, drained and rinsed
1 16-ounce can kidney beans, drained and rinsed
1 small zucchini, diced

Cook pasta. Meanwhile, in a large non-stick skillet, sauté the celery, carrots, onion, and garlic in oil for 5 minutes. In large pot, pour in broth, tomatoes, basil, rosemary, pepper, and oregano. Add sautéed vegetables. Then add green, northern, and kidney beans. Bring to a boil. Add pasta and zucchini. Reduce heat, cover, and simmer for 10 minutes, or until carrots are soft. Can be frozen.

Black Bean Soup
4 to 6 Servings

2 15.5-ounce cans of black beans, not drained
2 cups chicken stock or broth
1 medium yellow onion

1½ teaspoons cumin
salt and pepper
sour cream

In a pot or large saucepan, heat black beans (with can liquid) and chicken broth. While beans and broth are heating, caramelize onions in a sauté pan. Once onions are caramelized, add to black bean and broth mixture. Add cumin and salt and pepper to taste. Simmer for 15 minutes. Remove from heat and purée until desired consistency. Serve with a dollop of sour cream.

Chickpea and Vegetable Stew
6 Servings

1 tablespoon canola oil	½ teaspoon salt
2 cups cubed zucchini	¼ teaspoon ground cinnamon
1 cup chopped onion	¼ teaspoon ground black pepper
½ cup chopped carrot	1 15½-ounce can chickpeas,
1 tablespoon minced garlic	drained
1 cup fat-free, low-sodium	1 14½-ounce can stewed
chicken broth	tomatoes, not drained
2 tablespoons raisins	1½ cups water
1¼ teaspoons ground ginger	1 cup uncooked couscous
1¼ teaspoons ground cumin	
¾ teaspoon ground coriander	

Heat oil in large nonstick skillet over medium-high heat. Add zucchini, onion, carrot, and garlic. Sauté 5 minutes. Stir in broth and raisins, ginger, cumin, coriander, salt, cinnamon, pepper, chickpeas, and tomatoes; bring to boil. Cover, reduce heat, and simmer 8 minutes, stirring occasionally.

While the chickpea mixture simmers, prepare the couscous. Bring water to boil in a medium saucepan; gradually stir in couscous. Remove from heat; cover and let stand 5 minutes; fluff with fork. Serve 1 cup stew over ½ cup couscous.

Spicy Vegetable Soup
6 to 8 Servings

1 pound ground beef
1 cup chopped onion
2 cloves pressed garlic
1 30-ounce jar chunky garden style
  spaghetti sauce with mushrooms
  and peppers
2 10½-ounce cans beef broth
2 cups water
1 cup sliced celery

1 teaspoon sugar
1 teaspoon salt
½ teaspoon freshly
  ground pepper
1 10-ounce can diced
  tomatoes with green chiles
1 16-ounce package frozen
  mixed vegetables

Cook ground beef, onion, and garlic in a large Dutch oven over medium heat until meat is browned, stirring to crumble. Drain and return meat to Dutch oven. Add spaghetti sauce, beef broth, water, celery, sugar, salt, and pepper. Bring to a boil; cover, reduce heat and simmer 20 minutes, stirring occasionally. Stir in tomatoes and mixed vegetables; return to a boil. Cover and simmer 10 to 12 minutes or until vegetables are tender.

30-Minute Minestrone Soup
6 Servings

4 cups water
2 cups mini carrots
1 16-ounce can northern beans
1 16-ounce can diced tomatoes
1 cup chopped onions
2 teaspoons beef bouillon granules
1 teaspoon garlic powder
½ teaspoon basil

½ teaspoon oregano
¼ teaspoon pepper
1 8-ounce package frozen
  green beans
1 small zucchini, diced
½ cup small or short pasta,
  uncooked
¼ cup grated Parmesan cheese

In large saucepan, combine water, carrots, northern beans, tomatoes, onion, beef bouillon granules, garlic powder, basil, oregano, and pepper. Over high heat, bring to a boil. Add the frozen green beans, zucchini, and uncooked pasta, return to boil. Reduce heat. Simmer, covered, for 10 minutes or until pasta is done. Spoon into bowls. Sprinkle with Parmesan cheese.

After Thanksgiving Turkey Soup
10 Servings

1 turkey carcass
4 quarts water
6 small potatoes, diced
4 large carrots, diced
2 stalks celery, diced
1 large onion, chopped
1½ cups shredded cabbage
1 7.5-ounce can diced
  tomatoes, drained
½ cup barley, uncooked

1 tablespoon Worcestershire
  sauce
1½ teaspoons salt
1 teaspoon parsley flakes
1 teaspoon basil
1 bay leaf
½ teaspoon pepper
½ teaspoon paprika
¼ teaspoon poultry seasoning

Place turkey carcass in stockpot with water and bring to boil. Reduce heat and simmer for 2 hours. Take out carcass, leaving water in pot, and remove all meat from the bones. Add meat back to pot and add potatoes, carrots, celery, onion, cabbage, tomatoes, barley, Worcestershire sauce, salt, parsley, basil, bay leaf, pepper, paprika, and poultry seasoning. Simmer another hour. Remove bay leaf and serve.

Albondigas Soup with Mini-Bacon Meatballs
4 Servings

Albondigas Soup:
1 cup diced onion
2 tablespoons olive oil
4 cloves garlic, minced
2 teaspoons chili powder
2 cups low-sodium beef broth
2 cups water
2 (6 inch) corn tortillas, chopped
1 cup halved grape tomatoes, divided
1½ cups fresh or frozen corn kernels
2 cups sliced button mushrooms (8 ounces)
1 recipe Mini-Bacon Meatballs
salt and black pepper
fresh lime juice
2 tablespoons torn fresh cilantro
sour cream

Mini-Bacon Meatballs:
(28 meatballs)
2 strips bacon, diced
¼ cup diced onion
1 clove minced garlic
½ pound ground sirloin
¼ cup dry breadcrumbs
2 tablespoons minced fresh
  parsley
½ teaspoon paprika
½ teaspoon kosher salt
½ teaspoon black pepper
1 egg, beaten

Sauté onion in oil in a large pot over medium heat until softened, about 5 minutes. Add garlic and chili powder; cook 1 minute. Add broth, water, tortillas, and ½ cup tomatoes. Simmer soup 5 minutes. Purée soup in a blender and return to the pot. Skim off any tomato skins and add remaining tomatoes, corn, mushrooms, and meatballs. Simmer soup over medium-low heat for 5 minutes. Season with salt, pepper, and lime juice before serving. Ladle soup into bowls and garnish each serving with cilantro and sour cream.

Mini-Bacon Meatballs:
Coat a broiler pan with nonstick spray. Cook bacon in a skillet over medium-high heat until starting to crisp, about 4 minutes; remove and set aside on a paper-towel-lined plate. Pour off all but 1 tablespoon drippings from skillet. Sauté onion in same skillet in the 1 tablespoon drippings over medium until softened, about 3 minutes. Add garlic to skillet; cook 1 minute. Combine sirloin, cooked bacon, onion mixture, breadcrumbs, parsley, paprika, salt, and pepper in a large bowl. Stir in beaten egg. Form mixture into 1-inch meatballs and place on prepared broiler pan. Bake meatballs at 400°F until fully cooked, about 10 minutes.

Taco Soup
8 to 10 Servings

2 pounds 90% lean hamburger
1 cup chopped yellow onion
1 clove garlic, crushed
1 package taco seasoning mix
1 package dry ranch salad
 dressing mix
2 cans whole kernel corn,
 not drained
2 cans pinto beans, not drained

2 cans Mexican style stewed
 tomatoes (cut up tomatoes
 with kitchen scissors; or use
 one large can of crushed
 tomatoes and 1 to 2 cans of
 original-style Rotel)
1 4-ounce can of mild
 chopped green chilies
sharp cheddar cheese,
 shredded, for garnish
corn chips for garnish

Brown hamburger with the chopped yellow onion and crushed garlic.
Just before you finish browning the meat, add taco seasoning mix and dry
ranch salad dressing mix. Combine well.Put browned hamburger into a
big soup pot and add corn, pinto beans, stewed tomatoes (or crushed tomatoes and Rotel), and chilies. Simmer on low for 2 hours in a crock pot
or on the stove top; 2 hours allows for better flavor, but it can be served
earlier in a pinch. Garnish with shredded, sharp cheddar cheese and corn
chips.

Cold Dill Shrimp Soup
4 Servings

1 cup thinly sliced celery
6 radishes, thinly sliced
4 to 5 green onions, chopped
⅛ teaspoon powdered mustard
1 quart buttermilk, divided

1 pound shrimp, cooked,
 peeled, deveined, and
 chopped
fresh dill to taste
salt and pepper to taste

Chop celery, radishes, and onions in food processor; set aside. Mix
powdered mustard with ½ cup of the buttermilk. Add shrimp, dill, salt,
pepper, in a large bowl. Add remaining buttermilk and the chopped vegetables to the mixture. Combine and chill for 4 to 6 hours before serving.

Tortilla Soup
4 Servings

1 quart chicken broth, canned	1 serrano or jalapeno pepper,
3 to 4 chicken breasts, skinned	seeded and chopped
and boned	1 cup Monterey Jack cheese
1 medium tomato, finely chopped	1 cup vegetable oil
1 avocado, cubed	1 small package corn tortillas
1 bunch cilantro, chopped	

In a pan, bring the broth to a boil then poach the chicken breasts, uncovered in the broth for 30 minutes over medium heat. Remove the chicken and slice it before putting it back into the broth. On the side, mix the tomato, avocado, cilantro, pepper, and cheese.

In a skillet, heat the oil. Roll up the corn tortillas into small flutes. Cut the rolled up tortillas crosswise into long, thin strips. Fry the tortilla strips in the oil for 3 to 4 minutes until they are crisp. Remove them and drain on paper towels. Place equal amounts of fried tortilla strips into bowls. Spoon equal amounts of mixed vegetables and cheese over the chips. Ladle the broth and chicken on top. Serve immediately.

Salads

Mixed Field Greens
with Strawberry-Merlot Vinaigrette
6 Servings

Chef Ryan Boulware *has been leading the culinary direction at* Dierdorf and Hart's American Bistro and Steakhouse *for more than seven years. Their recent renovations and Chef Boulware's fresh and creative menu offerings have brought exciting changes to a St. Louis classic.*

½ cup goat cheese
1 pound bag of mixed field greens
1 cup strawberry-merlot
   vinaigrette dressing
½ cup sliced toasted almonds
1 tablespoon balsamic reduction
sliced strawberries for garnish

Strawberry Merlot Vinaigrette:
½ pint fresh strawberries (reserve
   ¼ for garnish)
½ cup sugar
¼ cup red wine vinegar
¼ cup strawberry liqueur
½ cup Merlot wine
¼ cup honey
1 teaspoon vanilla extract
1 cup canola oil
salt and freshly cracked black
   pepper to taste

Cut the goat cheese into small pieces and reserve. Wash the greens well and dry thoroughly. In a large bowl toss the chilled greens with vinaigrette to coat the leaves. Plate onto well-chilled dish and top with nuts, cheese, and balsamic reduction drizzled atop for presentation. Garnish with sliced strawberries.

Strawberry Merlot Vinaigrette:
Mix strawberries, sugar, vinegar, strawberry liqueur, wine, honey, and vanilla extract in a food processor or blender. Slowly drizzle while whisking in the oil to incorporate. Chill and reserve.

Mexican Salad with Chicken
4 Servings

This recipe was provided by Lewis and Clark Restaurant, *St. Charles, Missouri.*

vegetable oil, for deep frying
4 10-inch flour tortillas

Chicken:
1 ounce canned diced mild green
   chiles (about 2½ teaspoons)
1 cup bottled chili sauce
¾ teaspoon chili powder
2 tablespoons plus 2 teaspoons
   Lawry's taco seasoning
¼ teaspoon ground red (cayenne)
   pepper
½ cup water
1½ pounds cooked white meat
   chicken, diced

1 pound iceberg lettuce,
   shredded
2 cups refried beans, warmed
6 ounces Monterrey Jack
   cheese, shredded
6 ounces shredded cheddar
   cheese
8 ounces diced tomatoes
8 to 10 black olives, sliced
8 ounces sour cream
8 ounces guacamole
2 cups salsa
corn tortilla chips

To Fry the Tortilla Bowls:
Heat oil in a small pan or deep fryer to 350°F. Wrap the tortillas in a damp paper towel and heat for a few seconds in the microwave until pliable. One at a time, place the tortillas in a wire tortilla form and deep-fry, or gently press into the hot oil with a strainer, potato masher, or other broad, flat utensil. The center of the bowl should be 5 to 6 inches across. Fry about 20 seconds or until tortilla is puffed and crisp. Drain well, upside down or on paper towels. If the bottoms of tortillas are not flat arrange each on a shallow bed of shredded lettuce to hold the bowl upright.

To Prepare the Chicken:
Stir together chiles, chili sauce, chili powder, taco seasoning, cayenne, and water in a small saucepan. Add chicken and toss well. Cook over medium heat until heated through, 7 to 10 minutes. (Makes about 4½ cups.) In fried tortilla bowls, layer lettuce, then beans, dividing evenly; top with chicken. Toss cheeses together to mix well and divide among tortilla bowls. Sprinkle on tomatoes and olives. Top with a scoop of sour cream and another of guacamole. Serve with salsa (for dressing) and tortilla chips on the side.

Shrimp and Avocado Salad
4 Servings

The Crossing *is an upscale French-American restaurant located in Clayton, Missouri. The setting is intimate and the eclectic menu features anything from game to pasta to seafood.* Jim Fiala, *is the chef and owner of* The Crossing, *and his top priority is quality control; he believes that every meal should be a great meal.*

2 pounds jumbo shrimp, peeled and deveined	½ cup diced red onion
3 avocados, peeled and sliced	1 cup ground cherries, halved, plus extra for garnish
1 Zavory pepper or other mild pepper, minced	salt and pepper to taste
¼ cup chopped cilantro	olive oil to taste
	½ to 2 cups micro greens

Cook the shrimp very slowly in simmering water until tender. Cool on a sheet pan. Meanwhile, thoroughly mix the avocados, pepper, cilantro, red onion, ground cherries, and salt in a bowl. Place equal portions of avocado mixture onto four plates. Season the shrimp with olive oil, salt, and pepper and place equal amounts atop the avocado mixture on each plate.

In a separate bowl, season the micro greens with olive oil and salt; place equal portions on top of the shrimp. Garnish with a few whole or halved ground cherries.

Grilled Salmon Niçoise
8 Servings

4 pounds fresh salmon filets
olive oil
kosher salt
freshly ground black pepper
¾ pound haricots verts, stems
 removed and blanched
2 pounds small cooked Yukon
 gold potatoes, thickly sliced
2 pounds ripe tomatoes, cut
 into wedges (6 small tomatoes)
8 hard-cooked eggs, peeled and
 cut in half
½ pound kalamata black olives, pitted
1 bunch watercress or arugula
1 can anchovies, drained (optional)

Vinaigrette:
3 tablespoons champagne
 vinegar
½ teaspoon Dijon mustard
½ teaspoon kosher salt
¼ teaspoon freshly ground
 black pepper
10 tablespoons good-quality
 olive oil

To grill salmon, get a charcoal or stove-top cast-iron grill very hot. Brush the fish with olive oil and sprinkle with salt and pepper. Grill each side for only 5 minutes until the center is barely raw. Remove to a plate and cover tightly with aluminum foil. Set aside for 15 minutes. Arrange the salmon, haricots verts, potatoes, tomatoes, eggs, olives, watercress, and anchovies, if used, on a large flat platter. Cover with plastic wrap and refrigerate.

Vinaigrette:
Combine the vinegar, mustard, salt, and pepper. Slowly whisk in the olive oil to make an emulsion. To serve, unwrap platter and drizzle some of the vinaigrette over the fish and vegetables, and serve the rest in a pitcher on the side.

Note: *This is a beautifully presented salad with lots of color and texture.*

Roasted Beet Salad with Blue Cheese
4 Servings

3 medium yellow beets (about
  1 pound), stems trimmed off
3 medium red beets (about
  1 pound), stems trimmed off
2 tablespoons extra-virgin olive oil
salt and freshly ground black pepper
4 cups baby leaf spinach
¼ pound whole piece blue cheese (frozen)
toasted almonds

Dressing:
3 cups tangerine juice
  or orange juice
1 tablespoon lemon juice
pinch salt and pepper
¾ cup extra-virgin olive oil

Place the beets in a baking pan, drizzle with the oil, and season with salt and pepper. Cover with foil. Bake at 350°F for about 1 hour, or until tender when pierced with a knife. Cool. When cool enough to handle, peel the beets and thinly slice them into rounds. Arrange on a serving platter and drizzle with the dressing.

In a large bowl, toss the spinach with the remaining dressing and place spinach on top of beets in the center of the platter. Remove the wedge of blue cheese from the freezer. Using a micro-plane grater, grate the desired amount over the salad. Garnish with toasted almonds.

Dressing:
In a 1-quart non-reactive saucepan, over medium-high heat, reduce the tangerine juice to about ¾ cup. Add the lemon juice. Remove from the heat and strain with a fine sieve. Return to the saucepan; add salt and pepper. Over medium heat, reduce to about ¼ cup until the mixture bubbles and has a syrup-like consistency. Remove from the heat and strain again. Let cool to room temperature. Add the olive oil. Set aside. (Can be stored in refrigerator for up to 1½ weeks.)

Pear Salad
6 Servings

mixed greens
1 red pepper, sliced
4 ripe pears, cubed or sliced
1 container grape tomatoes
6 slices bacon, cooked and
   crumbled
½ bag toasted almonds, original
   flavor
1 4-ounce container crumbled
   blue cheese

Dressing:
¾ teaspoon coarse black pepper
½ cup olive oil
2 tablespoons honey
1 tablespoon sugar
1 tablespoon red wine vinegar
1 tablespoon balsamic vinegar
1 tablespoon water
1 tablespoon Dijon mustard
1 tablespoon chopped red,
   yellow or white onion

Arrange greens on salad plates. Top with red peppers, pears, tomatoes, bacon, almonds, and blue cheese. Drizzle dressing on top. Serve chilled.

Dressing:
Mix pepper, olive oil, honey, sugar, red wine vinegar, balsamic vinegar, water, Dijon mustard, and onion together and set aside.

Field Greens, Crumbled Blue Cheese, and Spicy Pecans
8 Servings

⅔ cup sugar
1 teaspoon dry mustard
1 teaspoon salt
⅔ cup distilled white vinegar
3 tablespoons apple cider vinegar
4½ teaspoons onion juice
2 tablespoons Worcestershire sauce
1 cup vegetable oil
4 to 5 cups mixed field greens
2 green onions, chopped
4 ounces blue cheese, crumbled (1 cup)
1 Granny Smith apple, cored, seeded, and chopped
¼ cup coarsely chopped spicy pecans

Spicy Pecans:
2 large egg whites
1½ teaspoons salt
¾ cup sugar
2 teaspoons Worcestershire sauce
2 tablespoons Hungarian paprika
1½ teaspoons cayenne pepper
4½ cups pecan halves
6 tablespoons unsalted butter, melted and cooled

Combine sugar, dry mustard, salt, white vinegar, and apple cider vinegar. Stir until sugar is dissolved. Whisk in onion juice and Worcestershire. Add oil slowly, whisking continuously until blended. Toss greens, green onions, blue cheese, apple, and pecans in a salad bowl. Add vinaigrette, tossing to coat.

Spicy Pecans:
Beat egg whites with salt until foamy. Add sugar, Worcestershire, paprika, and cayenne. Fold in pecans and melted butter. Spread pecans evenly on a baking sheet. Bake at 325°F for 30 to 40 minutes, stirring every 10 minutes. Remove from oven and cool. Store pecans in an airtight container. Yields 4½ cups (enough for more than one salad).

Strawberry Fields
8 Servings

1 cup strawberries, hulled and halved
2 tablespoons raspberry vinegar
2 tablespoons brown sugar, firmly packed
¼ cup olive oil
¼ teaspoon sesame oil
½ teaspoon fresh lemon juice
coarse salt

freshly ground pepper
4 cups mixed field greens
1 cup strawberries, hulled and halved
1 medium jicama, peeled and julienned
¼ cup chopped toasted pistachios

Strawberry Dressing:
Process 1 cup strawberries, vinegar, brown sugar, olive oil, sesame oil, and lemon juice in food processor or blender until smooth. Season with salt and pepper. Set aside.

Combine greens, strawberries, and jicama in a salad bowl. Just before serving, toss dressing with salad and sprinkle with pistachios.

Caesar Salad
4 Servings

3 tablespoons olive oil
1 tablespoon red wine vinegar
1 tablespoon Miracle Whip
1 teaspoon Grey Poupon mustard
1 teaspoon Worcestershire sauce

1 teaspoon fresh lemon juice
½ cup Parmesan cheese
4 cloves garlic, crushed
romaine lettuce

Combine olive oil, red wine vinegar, Miracle Whip, Grey Poupon, Worcestershire, lemon juice, Parmesan cheese, and garlic. Mix thoroughly and toss with romaine lettuce just before serving.

Strawberry Spinach Salad
10 to 12 Servings

3 10-ounce packages fresh spinach
1 pound strawberries, sliced (4 cups)
1 pound seedless grapes, halved (2 cups)
1 sweet onion, thinly sliced
½ pound fresh bean sprouts or alfalfa sprouts

1½ cups prepared white wine vinaigrette
¼ cup sugar
2 teaspoons Worcestershire sauce
⅔ cup slivered almonds
⅓ cup sugar

Rinse spinach, if needed; drain and pat dry. Remove and discard any tough stems. Break into bite-size pieces; place in large salad bowl. Add strawberries, grapes, onion, and sprouts. In small jar with tight fitting lid, shake together white wine vinaigrette, sugar, and Worcestershire. Pour over salad; toss to coat. Top with almonds. Serve immediately.

Almonds:
In small heavy skillet, combine ⅔ cup slivered almonds with ⅓ cup sugar. Cook over medium-high heat, stirring constantly, until sugar melts and almonds are lightly toasted, about 5 minutes. Spread on parchment paper to cool. Break apart if needed. Store in airtight container.

Asian Chicken Salad
2 to 4 Servings

Chicken Salad:
salt
ground pepper
1 3-pound chicken
1 stalk celery, finely diced
1 carrot, finely diced
1 medium onion, finely diced
1 clove garlic, minced
1 bay leaf
fresh or dried thyme
¼ cup unsalted butter, melted
1 tablespoon sesame seeds
2 small heads or 1 medium head
   Napa cabbage
1 cup romaine lettuce cut into ¼-
   inch strips
10 snow peas, cut into ¼-inch strips

Chinese Mustard Vinaigrette:
2 teaspoons dry Chinese or
   English mustard
¼ cup rice wine vinegar
1 teaspoon soy sauce
2 tablespoons light sesame oil
2 to 3 tablespoons peanut oil
salt
freshly ground black pepper

Chicken Salad:

Salt and pepper chicken inside and out. Combine celery, carrot, onion, garlic, bay leaf, and thyme to taste. Use mixture to stuff cavity of
chicken. Place chicken on a rack in a roasting pan; baste with some of the
butter. Roast at 425°F for 1½ hours or until done, basting every 15 to 20
minutes with the butter and the drippings. When chicken is done, juices
will run clear and breast should measure 160°F with an instant-read thermometer. While chicken is roasting, spread sesame seeds in a sauté pan;
toast over medium heat until lightly browned. Watch carefully to avoid
burning. When browned, remove quickly from hot pan. Set aside.

Select 4 to 8 nice-looking leaves from Napa cabbage and reserve them.
Roll remaining cabbage leaves into tubes; slice into ¼-inch strips. Set
aside. When chicken is done, let rest until cool enough to handle. Remove
and discard stuffing. Using your fingers, shred meat from the breasts and
thighs of the chicken, making each piece roughly the same size. (Save
remaining meat and carcass for chicken stock.)

Combine chicken, sliced cabbage, romaine, and snow peas in a bowl; toss with enough vinaigrette to coat. Arrange reserved cabbage leaves around the edge of a large serving plate. Mound salad in the center, sprinkle with sesame seeds and serve.

Vinaigrette:
Place mustard, vinegar, soy sauce, and sesame oil in blender; process until smooth. Transfer to bowl; slowly whisk in peanut oil. Add salt and pepper to taste. Set aside.

Asian Tossed Salad
8 Servings

1 cup sliced almonds
6 tablespoons sugar
iceberg and green leaf lettuce (any
  two or more kinds is fine)
3 stalks celery
1 bunch green onions
1 large can mandarin oranges,
  drained

Dressing:
½ cup vegetable oil
4 tablespoons sugar
4 tablespoons vinegar
2 tablespoons snipped parsley
  or flakes
1 teaspoon salt
pinch of black pepper
pinch of red pepper sauce

In a skillet, cook almonds and 6 tablespoons sugar over low heat, slow, continuously stirring, until browned. Pour onto parchment paper to cool then break apart as needed. Tear up lettuces. Add chopped celery, chopped green onions, mandarin oranges, and caramelized almonds when ready to serve.

Dressing:
Stir oil, sugar, vinegar, parsley, salt, pepper, and red pepper sauce together. Pour over salad before serving. Dressing may be prepared in advance, but do not store in refrigerator.

Shredded Chicken Salad
4 Servings

4 boneless, skinless chicken breasts
2 tablespoons balsamic vinegar
2 tablespoons soy sauce
2 tablespoons canola oil
2 teaspoons sugar
½ teaspoon salt
1 clove garlic, minced

1 tablespoon water
mixture of iceberg and romaine
   lettuces (about ½ head of
   each), torn
½ cantaloupe, cubed
cracked black pepper

Poach the chicken breasts in salted water about 20 minutes or until tender; cool. Shred the chicken with 2 forks.

In a large bowl, combine vinegar, soy sauce, canola oil, sugar, salt, garlic clove, and 1 tablespoon water; stir to dissolve sugar. Add chicken and toss to coat. Allow to marinate for ½ hour (or longer) in refrigerator.

Put torn lettuces on a large platter or in a large bowl. Arrange cantaloupe on top of the lettuce; top with chicken. Sprinkle with cracked pepper. Optional additions to this salad are: sliced strawberries, blueberries, green onions, celery.

Note: *For an easy summer salad, you can poach the chicken early in the day, shred it, and store it in the fridge until ready to toss and serve.*

BLT Overnight Salad
8 to 10 Servings

2 cups grape or cherry tomatoes, halved
9 cups chopped iceberg lettuce
8 slices bacon, diced and cooked crisp
4 ounces shredded mozzarella
   cheese (1 cup)

1 8-ounce container light
   sour cream
¾ cup light mayonnaise
1 tablespoon milk
1 0.4-ounce package dry
   ranch dressing mix

In large serving bowl, layer tomatoes, lettuce, bacon, and cheese. In medium bowl, combine sour cream, mayonnaise, milk, and ranch dressing mix. Spread enough dressing over top of salad to completely cover cheese; refrigerate remaining dressing for other uses. Chill for several hours or overnight. Just before serving, toss until mixed well.

Three Cheese Salad
6 to 8 Servings

¼ cup shredded Asiago cheese
1 cup shredded Swiss cheese
½ cup shredded Parmesan cheese
romaine lettuce
cherry tomatoes, halved
1 cup seasoned croutons
chopped bacon
sliced almonds, toasted

Dressing:
2 tablespoons lemon juice
¾ cup vegetable oil
crushed garlic
1 teaspoon salt
½ teaspoon pepper

Combine three cheeses. Combine with lettuce, tomatoes, croutons, bacon, and almonds. Mix dressing and toss salad.

Asparagus Salad
6 Servings

1½ pounds fresh asparagus spears
1 egg
1 egg yolk
1 tablespoon plus 1½ teaspoon
  lemon juice, divided
¼ teaspoon garlic salt
½ cup plus 2 tablespoons olive oil

¼ cup loosely packed fresh
  basil leaves
3 fresh mint leaves
½ teaspoon grated lemon rind
3 large ripe tomatoes

Prepare asparagus by removing tough ends and scraping scales off ends. Blanche in boiling water for 3 minutes until crisp. Plunge into bowl of ice water. Drain. Using food processor or blender, mix egg, egg yolk, 1 tablespoon lemon juice, and garlic salt. Process for 20 seconds or until smooth. Add oil in steady stream while processing until dressing is thickened and well mixed. Add basil, mint, and lemon rind. Continue processing until herbs are finely chopped. Add remaining 1½ teaspoons lemon juice. Process until blended. Cut each tomato into 8 wedges. Arrange asparagus in a fan shape on salad plate. Place 4 tomato wedges at base of asparagus. Place a dollop of mayonnaise dressing at base of tomatoes.

Balsamic Pea Salad
24 Servings

3 16-ounce packages frozen green peas
1½ cups chopped almonds
1½ cups chopped green onions
1½ cups feta cheese, crumbled

2¼ cups low-fat mayonnaise
¼ cup plus 2 tablespoons
  white balsamic vinegar
black pepper to taste

Place peas (one package at a time is better) in a colander and run warm water over them until thawed. Drain; blot dry with a towel and place in large bowl. Toast the almonds at 350°F for 3 to 5 minutes (check frequently; when you begin to smell them toasting, pull them out). Stir in onions, feta cheese, and mayonnaise. Mix in balsamic vinegar, and season with cracked black pepper. Add the peas and almonds. Cover and refrigerate.

Note: *This is a great make-ahead recipe for a potluck or family gathering. You can substitute cheddar cheese and pecans or cashews to suit your family's tastes.*

Broccoli Salad
4 to 6 Servings

3 to 6 cups broccoli, cut into very
    small florets
⅓ cup white raisins
¼ cup chopped red onion
8 slices bacon, cooked and crumbled
¼ cup sunflower seeds

2 to 4 ounces crumbled
    Gorgonzola cheese
½ cup mayonnaise
2 tablespoons sugar
2 tablespoons lime juice
1 to 2 teaspoons vinegar

Mix broccoli, raisins, onion, bacon, sunflower seeds, and cheese in bowl.
Set aside. Whisk together mayonnaise, sugar, lime juice, and vinegar.
Combine with broccoli mixture just before serving.

Summer Tomato Salad
4 Servings

1 pound fresh tomatoes
1 cup seedless red grapes (½ pound)
1 medium cucumber
½ small red onion

½ cup crumbled feta cheese
¼ cup balsamic vinaigrette
¼ cup sliced (not slivered)
    almonds

Wash and core the tomatoes, but do not peel them. Chop the tomatoes
into ½-inch pieces and place in a 2-quart serving bowl. Slice the grapes in
half (quarter any large ones). Add to the bowl. Dice the cucumber; add
to the bowl. Peel and finely dice the onion; add to the bowl. Add the feta
and vinaigrette; toss to mix. Sprinkle with almonds and serve.

Stacked Tomato Salad with Tapenade and Basil Dressing
8 Servings

2 cups kalamata olives, pitted
(about 10 ounces)
4 cloves garlic
4 anchovy fillets
2 tablespoons pine nuts
½ cup olive oil
salt and pepper
¼ cup white wine vinegar
2 tablespoons honey
1 tablespoon Dijon mustard

¾ cup olive oil
12 large, fresh basil leaves,
thinly sliced
8 to 10 large tomatoes, cut
crosswise into ½-inch
slices (preferably heirloom
tomatoes of assorted colors)
2 8-ounce balls fresh water-
packed mozzarella, drained
and cut into ⅓-inch slices

Tapenade:
Blend olives, garlic, anchovies, and nuts in food processor until almost smooth. With machine running, add ½ cup olive oil; process until blended. Season with salt and pepper.

Dressing:
Whisk vinegar, honey, and mustard in a bowl. Gradually whisk in ¾ cup olive oil and stir in basil. Season with salt and pepper.

Place 1 tomato slice on each of 8 plates. Spread each with generous tablespoon tapenade and top with a slice of mozzarella. Repeat layering. Top each stack with a third tomato slice. Chop remaining tomato slices, placing in bowl, and toss with 2 tablespoons dressing. Spoon some dressing over each stack and spoon chopped tomatoes alongside.

Note: *Tapenade can be made 2 days ahead of serving and be kept in refrigerator. Dressing can be made 8 hours ahead of serving and stand at room temperature.*

Greek Cucumber Salad
6 Servings

1 shallot, minced
¼ cup red wine vinegar
¼ cup extra-virgin olive oil
1 teaspoon Cavender's All Purpose
  Greek seasoning
¼ teaspoon kosher salt

8 lemon cucumbers or 3
  English cucumbers, peeled,
  seeded, and sliced
3 sprigs fresh oregano,
  stems removed
½ cup crumbled feta cheese
  (about 2 ounces)
¼ cup pine nuts, toasted

Coarsely ground black pepper to taste. Combine shallot and vinegar in a small bowl. Let stand about 10 minutes. Add olive oil, Greek seasoning and salt, whisking well. Pour vinaigrette over cucumbers and toss well. Sprinkle with oregano, cheese, and pine nuts. Season with black pepper.

Black-Eyed Pea Salad
8 Servings

5 cups cooked and drained
  black-eyed peas
4 slices bacon, cooked until crisp and
  crumbled, fat reserved separately
½ cup plus 2 tablespoons red
  wine vinegar
½ cup olive oil
½ cup finely chopped red onion
  (½ medium onion)
½ cup chopped red bell pepper
3 tablespoons finely chopped
  green onions

2 tablespoons finely chopped
  jalapenos
2 tablespoons finely chopped
  fresh parsley leaves
1½ teaspoons minced garlic
1½ teaspoons Cajun or Creole
  seasoning
¾ teaspoon salt
½ teaspoon freshly ground
  black pepper

Combine the peas, crumbled bacon, 3 tablespoons of the reserved bacon fat, vinegar, olive oil, red onion, bell pepper, green onions, jalapenos, parsley, garlic, and seasonings in a large bowl. Toss well to combine. Cover and refrigerate for at least 4 hours or overnight (preferable), stirring occasionally. Allow salad to come to room temperature for 30 minutes before serving and toss well just before serving.

Zucchini, Garbanzo, and Edamame Salad
4 to 6 Servings

½ cup frozen edamame, blanched
½ cup rinsed garbanzo beans
1 zucchini, quartered and
 chopped lengthwise (¼ inch thick)
½ small onion, thinly sliced
1 tablespoon fresh basil or
 ½ teaspoon dried

4½ teaspoons fresh lemon juice
2 to 3 tablespoons olive oil
⅛ teaspoon red pepper
¾ teaspoon coarse red pepper
 flakes (can be found where
 pizza is sold)
salt and pepper

Combine edamame, garbanzo beans, chopped zucchini, onion, and basil in a bowl. Whisk together lemon juice, olive oil, red pepper, course red pepper flakes, salt and pepper. Add to vegetables and mix well.

Note: *Delicious for a summer salad or anytime you want something a little different!*

Corn and Blueberry Salad
8 to 10 Servings

6 ears fresh sweet corn
1 cup fresh blueberries
1 small cucumber, sliced
¼ cup finely chopped red onion
¼ cup chopped fresh cilantro
1 jalapeno pepper, seeded and
 finely chopped

2 tablespoons fresh lime juice
2 tablespoons olive oil
1 tablespoon honey
½ teaspoon ground cumin
½ teaspoon salt

Cook corn and allow to cool (see note). Cut kernels from cobs. In serving bowl, combine corn, blueberries, cucumber, red onion, cilantro, and jalapeno. For dressing, in screw-top jar, combine lime juice, oil, honey, cumin, and salt. Cover and shake well to combine. Add to salad and toss. Cover and refrigerate overnight (up to 24 hours).

Note: *Great way to cook fresh corn: Remove most of the outer (dark) layers of husk. Cut off both ends of the ear. Microwave at high power 2 minutes per ear. Let cool; corn silk will easily come off when you peel remaining husk.*

Watermelon Salad
2 to 4 Servings

Dressing:
½ cup red wine vinegar
⅓ cup honey
2 tablespoons brown sugar
1½ teaspoons black pepper
1 tablespoon orange juice
pinch of salt
1 cup olive oil

Salad:
4 to 5 cups of ripe watermelon,
 cut 2-inch square chunks
¼ large red onion, sliced vertically
 into ¼ inch slivers
4 cups mixed baby greens (include
 some bitter greens in the mix)
pepper

Dressing:
Mix the wine vinegar, honey, brown sugar, black pepper, orange juice, and salt in a deep-sided bowl. Drizzle the olive oil into the mixture to emulsify. Set aside.

Salad:
Mix the watermelon and red onion together in a large bowl. Pour the dressing over the melon, turning to coat all sides. Let the melon stand for 20 to 30 minutes. Layer the field greens on a small dinner plate. Place the chunks of watermelon and the onion in the center of the greens. Grind pepper to taste over the salad.

Note: *This serving size is a main-course salad. If you plan to serve it as a side salad, the chunks of watermelon may be cut a little smaller; the dish would then serve 4.*

Cranberry Holiday Salad
8 Servings

1 12-ounce package fresh cranberries
2 cups sugar
1 pound seedless red grapes, halved
1 cup chopped pecans, toasted
1 cup whipping cream, whipped

Process cranberries in processor until coarsely chopped, about 20 seconds. Combine cranberries and sugar in a bowl; cover and chill 8 hours. Drain cranberries for 2 hours, reserving liquid for other uses. Combine cranberries, grapes, and chopped pecans. Fold in whipped cream. Chill until ready to serve.

Frozen Fruit Salad
4 Servings

2 6-ounce cans frozen lemonade (thawed)
1 6-ounce can frozen orange juice (thawed)
1½ cups sugar
1 (No. 2½) can fruit cocktail with juice
1 can pineapple tidbits with juice
1 jar maraschino cherries with juice, cut in half
1 pint 7UP soda
2 cups fresh or frozen strawberry slices (thawed, if frozen)
4 firm bananas, sliced

Stir together lemonade, orange juice, sugar, fruit cocktail, pineapple, cherries, 7UP, and strawberries, adding bananas last. Freeze. Before serving, thaw to slush stage. (Usually takes a few hours or it can be softened by a few seconds in the microwave and breaking up with a large spoon). May be refrozen if not used in first serve. You can also add green grapes, melon balls, bing cherries, or any fresh fruit in season.

Sandwiches

Best Meatball Sandwich
8 Servings

2 pounds ground beef, pork, or veal
  (any combination)
2 eggs, beaten
6 cloves garlic, finely chopped, plus
  3 cloves garlic, chopped
1 cup seasoned breadcrumbs
1 teaspoon kosher salt
1 teaspoon freshly ground
  black pepper

½ cup grated Parmesan cheese
½ cup milk
1 cup flour
½ cup (or more) olive oil (for frying)
33 ounce (or more) jar of store
  bought or homemade
  tomato/spaghetti sauce
submarine rolls
mozzarella cheese slices

Combine ground meat in a large mixing bowl. Beat the eggs and add them to the meat along with 6 cloves finely chopped garlic, the breadcrumbs, salt, pepper, Parmesan cheese and milk. Mix this together with your hands. Roll this mixture into 2-inch balls. Pour flour in pie pan. Roll meatballs in the flour. Shake off excess. Heat at least ½ cup olive oil in a large skillet. Add 3 cloves of chopped garlic in oil and sauté until golden brown. Remove the garlic with a slotted spoon. Add the meatballs and sauté over medium-high heat, turning them until they are brown all over.

Place cooked meatballs in an oven-safe dish. Pour sauce over meatballs. Cook, covered, at 350°F for 15 to 20 minutes. As soon as you can pick the meatballs up with a fork, they are ready. You don't want them to be well done. If the meatball slides off the fork when you pick it up, it needs to cook a little longer.

While the meatballs are cooking, slice the submarine rolls in half. Scoop out some of the bread to make a well on each side. Place on baking sheet. When the meatballs are finished, remove from oven. Place several meatballs and sauce in the well on one side of the submarine roll. Top with a slice of mozzarella cheese. Put some sauce in the well on the other side of roll. Do this for each sandwich you make. Place back in oven until cheese is melted.

Note: *These sandwiches are best eaten with a knife and fork. Serve with a salad and enjoy a terrific lunch or dinner!*

Italian Beef Sandwiches
6 to 8 Servings

1 3- to 4-pound chuck arm roast
3 cups hot water
3 beef bouillon cubes
1 teaspoon salt

½ teaspoon pepper
1 teaspoon oregano
1 teaspoon basil
1 clove garlic, minced

Score meat with knife and place in roaster pan. Bake at 450°F for 30 minutes. Reduce oven to 300° and add remaining ingredients. Cover and bake 4 to 5 hours until meat is very tender and breaks apart easily. Remove meat from pan and shred while meat is still hot. Skim grease off of juice left in roaster. Return meat to juices. Serve on rolls.

Note: *Great served on rolls with yellow marinated pepper rings. It's also good as a Naked Burrito; serve it on lettuce with white rice, beans, cheese, and salsa. Really yummy, and easy to reheat. Can be made ahead and freezes well. Great for large groups as the recipe can be doubled or tripled.*

Shredded Pork Sandwiches
12 Servings

1½ teaspoons garlic powder
1½ teaspoons onion powder
1½ teaspoons ground black pepper
1 teaspoon celery salt
3-pound boneless pork shoulder roast
2 large onions, cut into thin wedges

½ cup water
2 cups shredded broccoli
  slaw mix
1 cup light mayonnaise
  dressing or salad dressing
barbecue sauce of your choice
12 sandwich buns

Stir together garlic powder, onion powder, pepper, and celery salt. Trim fat from the meat. Sprinkle pepper mixture over meat and rub with fingers. (Meat can be cut into smaller sections to fit in slow cooker). Place onion in bottom of slow cooker and place meat on top. Add water. Cover and cook in a crock pot on low for 8 to 10 hours, or high from 4 to 5 hours. When finished cooking, place meat on cutting board and allow to cool slightly. Using 2 forks pull the meat apart, discarding fat pieces. Toss the broccoli slaw mix with the dressing. Put some of the pulled pork on a bun, add barbecue sauce (if desired), and top with a spoonful of the broccoli slaw.

Havana Burgers
4 Servings

2 pounds ground chuck
salt and freshly ground black pepper
½ cup mayonnaise
3 cloves roasted garlic, puréed
¼ cup Dijon mustard

4 hamburger buns
8 slices Swiss cheese
4 slices thinly sliced smoked ham
2 dill pickles, sliced ¼-inch thick

Form the meat into 4 burgers. Season the meat with salt and pepper on both sides. Grill on high heat for 2 to 3 minutes on both sides for medium. When the burgers are done, remove from the heat and reduce heat to medium low.

Meanwhile, combine the mayonnaise and roasted garlic in a small bowl and season with salt and pepper, to taste. Spread both sides of each bun with the roasted garlic mayonnaise and the mustard. Place a slice of cheese on the bottom portion of each bun, place the burger on top of the cheese, then top the burger with a slice of ham and another slice of cheese, and finally, the pickle slices. Place the top of the bun over the pickles, wrap the burgers in aluminum foil, and place them on the grill. Using a heavy pan or a brick wrapped in foil, press down on the burgers for about 30 seconds to 1 minute. Lower the lid on the grill and continue grilling for 1 to 2 minutes or until the cheese has melted and the bun has become pressed and firm.

Gourmet Meatball Sliders
Makes 18 Sliders

½ pound ground beef
½ pound ground pork
½ pound ground veal
½ cup panko breadcrumbs
½ cup water
8 tablespoons freshly grated Pecorino
  Romano cheese, divided
1 large egg
1 large egg yolk
¼ cup plus 2 tablespoons
  chopped fresh parsley
1 teaspoon salt
½ teaspoon pepper

Tomato Sauce:
¼ cup vegetable oil
2 tablespoons olive oil
1 cup chopped onion
6 cloves garlic, chopped
¼ cup fresh basil leaves, packed
1½ teaspoons fennel seeds
1 28-ounce can whole peeled
  tomatoes
1 14.5-ounce can whole peeled
  tomatoes

18 small soft rolls, split horizontally
arugula leaves

Mix all meats, panko, ½ cup water, 6 tablespoons cheese, egg, egg yolk,
¼ cup parsley, 1 teaspoon salt, and ½ teaspoon pepper in large bowl.
Form 18 2-inch meatball patties. Heat vegetable oil in large skillet over
medium heat. Working in small batches, fry meatballs until brown all
over. Transfer to plate. Pour off drippings from skillet and reduce heat to
medium.

Add olive oil to skillet. Add onion, garlic, basil, and fennel seeds. Sauté
until onion begins to brown, about 5 minutes. Add all tomatoes with
juices. Bring to a boil, scraping up browned bits. Reduce heat to low,
cover and simmer about 30 minutes, stirring occasionally.

Purée sauce in processor until almost smooth. Return to same skillet and
add meatballs. Cover with lid slightly ajar and simmer until meatballs are
cooked through, stirring occasionally, about 30 minutes. Place meatball
slider on a bun and drizzle with sauce and remaining cheese. Add some
arugula leaves if desired.

Grilled Steak and Onion Sandwich
4 Servings

1 teaspoon Dijon mustard	1 pound skirt steak
1 tablespoon plus ½ teaspoon balsamic vinegar	1 red onion, sliced into ½-inch thick rounds
2 tablespoons plus 1 teaspoon extra-virgin olive oil	8 slices crusty bread
coarse salt and ground pepper	arugula
	Parmesan shavings

In a large baking dish, whisk together Dijon mustard, 1 tablespoon balsamic vinegar, and 2 tablespoons olive oil. Season with coarse salt and pepper. Add skirt steak and turn to coat, allowing to marinate for 15 minutes at room temperature. Heat a grill pan or cast-iron skillet over medium-high heat. Drizzle sliced red onion with 1 teaspoon oil and season with salt and pepper. Grill steak and onions until steak is medium rare and onions are tender, 5 to 7 minutes, flipping once. Let steak rest 5 minutes before thinly slicing against the grain.

Meanwhile, in a food processor, process the onions until finely chopped then mix with ½ teaspoon vinegar. Season with salt and pepper to taste. Spread onion mixture on 4 slices crusty bread. Top with steak, arugula, Parmesan shavings, and 4 more slices of bread.

Salmon Burgers
4 Servings

1 14.75-ounce can salmon
1 egg slightly beaten
2 tablespoons finely chopped onion
2 tablespoons flour
2 tablespoons lemon juice
¼ teaspoon salt
⅛ teaspoon pepper

2 tablespoons chopped parsley
1 teaspoon Worcestershire sauce
¼ cup Italian breadcrumbs
1 to 2 tablespoons olive oil

Drain and remove salmon from can. Carefully remove the black skin and circle bones, discard. Place flaked salmon in a large bowl, add egg, onion, flour, lemon juice, salt, pepper, parsley, Worcestershire sauce, and breadcrumbs. Mix together until well blended. Form into patties and sprinkle each side with more breadcrumbs as burgers will be moist. In a large skillet, heat 1 to 2 tablespoons olive oil and cook over medium heat until both sides are brown and heated through. Serve with or without your favorite sandwich rolls.

Classic Chicken Salad Sandwiches
4 to 5 Servings

2 large chicken breasts
good-quality olive oil
salt and pepper
¾ cup good-quality mayonnaise
1¼ tablespoons chopped fresh tarragon

1 cup diced celery
8 to 10 slices whole grain bread
salad mix

Place chicken breasts on a baking sheet and rub with olive oil. Sprinkle with salt and pepper. Roast at 350°F for 35 to 40 minutes until chicken is cooked through. Set aside to cool. When cool, remove the chicken skin and pull the chicken off the bone. Dice the chicken and place into a bowl. Add the mayonnaise, tarragon, celery, salt, and pepper to taste. Toss well. To assemble the sandwiches, spread additional mayonnaise on the bread, top with the chicken salad and lettuce, and cover with remaining bread.

Greek Salad Sandwich
4 Servings

1 cup canned chickpeas, rinsed and drained
2 tablespoons fresh lemon juice, divided
2 tablespoons plus 2 teaspoons extra-virgin olive oil
¼ cup fresh parsley leaves
½ small red onion, thinly sliced

coarse salt and pepper
3 ounces feta cheese
8 slices rustic bread or olive bread
½ medium cucumber, thinly sliced
1 tomato, thinly sliced

In a food processor, pulse chickpeas, 1 tablespoon lemon juice, 1 table-spoon olive oil, and parsley leaves until finely chopped. In a small bowl, stir together red onion, 1 tablespoon lemon juice, and 2 teaspoons oil. Season with salt and pepper. In another small bowl, mash feta with 1 tablespoon oil. Spread chickpea mixture on 4 slices of crusty bread. Top with cucumber, tomato, and onion mixture. Season with salt and pepper. Spread feta mixture on 4 more slices of bread and place on top of sandwiches.

Summer Tomato Sandwich
4 Servings

8 slices favorite bread—sourdough, Italian, etc.
butter
8 slices Havarti cheese

2 tomatoes
1 bunch basil
2 tablespoons honey

Spread butter on one side of each piece of bread. Place four pieces of bread, buttered side down on heated griddle or skillet. Place one slice Havarti cheese on each. Top with tomato slices and basil leaves. Drizzle with honey. Place another slice of Havarti cheese and second piece of bread. Grill until golden on both sides.

Mozzarella, Raspberry, and Brown Sugar Panini
6 Servings

12 ½-inch thick slices bakery-style white bread
⅓ cup olive oil
¾ cup raspberry jam
3 teaspoons chopped fresh rosemary

12 ounces fresh mozzarella cheese, sliced and patted dry
3 tablespoons light brown sugar

Preheat panini press or grill pan on a stove top to medium heat. Using a pastry brush, paint the bread on both sides with oil. Spread one side of each slice with jam. Sprinkle rosemary over the jam.

Cut mozzarella into 12 slices. Place 2 slices each on 6 pieces of bread. Season cheese with a pinch of salt. Place remaining slices of bread on top, jam side down. Sprinkle tops with brown sugar. Grill panini for 3 to 5 minutes until cheese is melted and bread is golden and crispy. Cut in half and serve.

Note: *If you don't have a panini press, use a foil-wrapped brick or a heavy cast iron skillet on top of the sandwiches to press them down. Grill for 2 to 3 minutes to brown, flip the sandwich, replace the weight and grill for another 2 to 3 minutes.*

Goat Cheese and Strawberry Grilled Cheese
3 Servings

1 4-ounce goat cheese log, softened
6 whole grain bread slices
4½ teaspoons red pepper jelly
¾ cup sliced fresh strawberries

6 large fresh basil leaves
1½ cups fresh watercress or arugula
salt and pepper

Spread goat cheese on 1 side of 3 bread slices. Spread pepper jelly on 1 side of remaining bread slices: layer with strawberries, basil leaves, and watercress. Sprinkle with salt and pepper. Top with remaining bread, goat cheese sides down. Grill sandwiches in a large, lightly greased skillet over medium heat 2 to 3 minutes on each side or until golden brown.

Entrees

Whenever possible, the surgical teams at Cardinal Glennon Children's Medical Center perform minimally invasive surgery. These procedures involve incisions smaller than a keyhole, which means less pain, less recovery time, less scarring, and less worry for parents.

Beef

Prime Pepper Pot
Makes 5½ Quarts

Paul V. Frintrup, *CCC, is a St. Louis native who began his career as a cook at Two Nice Guys and The Seventh Inn. Paul is the Executive Chef at the* Country Club of St. Albans. *He currently resides in Webster Groves with his wife and son.*

6 ounces diced smoked bacon	1 bay leaf
7 ounces diced yellow onion	1 pound beef or pork loin,
3½ ounces diced celery	cooked and diced
4½ ounces diced bell peppers	2 ounces chopped chipotle
(mixed colors)	peppers
4 ounces whole butter	1 cup heavy cream
4 ounces flour	1 teaspoon dried thyme
5 cups beef broth	salt and pepper
12 ounces diced potatoes	

In skillet, render bacon until crisp and then add onion, celery, and peppers. Sauté until vegetables are translucent; add butter and melt. Once the butter is melted, whisk in flour and cook until a blonde roux is formed. Pour stock in and bring to a soft boil. Simmer for 10 to 15 minutes; add potatoes and bay leaf and return to a simmer until the potatoes are just tender.

Next, add in beef, chipotle peppers, cream, and thyme. Bring back up to a simmer. Disard bay leaf. To finish, season with a salt and pepper blend to your liking.

Pastrami-Rubbed Certified Angus Beef Tenderloin with Savoy Cabbage, Potato Purée, Butter Vegetables, and Port Wine Sauce
4 Servings

Chef Kevin Storm *is the Executive Chef at* Bellerive Country Club.

1 Certified Angus Beef tenderloin, rubbed with pastrami rub and cold smoked

Cabbage:
2 ounces diced slab bacon
⅓ cup chopped onion
1 tablespoon crushed garlic
1½ cups chicken stock
1 pound Savoy cabbage, cut ½-inch wide
¼ cup cream
3 tablespoons butter, divided
1 teaspoon salt
¼ teaspoon ground white pepper

Potato Purée:
4 medium-size potatoes
¼ pound butter, unsalted
2 cups cream
salt and pepper to taste

Pastrami Cure:
1 tablespoon coriander seeds
1 tablespoon mustard seeds
1 tablespoon black pepper, whole
½ teaspoon fenugreek, whole
1 tablespoon sea salt
1 tablespoon garlic
2 tablespoons brown sugar
1 teaspoon ginger

Port Wine Sauce:
2 tablespoons oil
2 shallots, finely minced
½ cup port wine
¾ cup veal stock (or 6 tablespoons of demi-glace)
¼ cup morels, optional

Cabbage:
Heat a medium saucepan over medium-high heat. Add bacon and cook until very lightly browned, about 5 minutes. Add onion and garlic, Reduce heat to medium low, cover and cook until onions soften, about 7 minutes. Drain off any fat.

Add chicken stock and bring to a boil over high heat. Cook until reduced to 1 cup, about 10 minutes. Remove pan from heat and let stand 20 minutes. Strain stock into medium bowl. Meanwhile, cook cabbage in boiling, salted water over high heat until barely tender, 3 to 4 minutes. Drain and shock in ice water. Squeeze out all excess moisture. Bring the chicken-bacon stock and cream to a boil in medium saucepan over high heat. Add cabbage and reserved bacon. Reduce heat to low and simmer for 10 minutes. Gently stir in 2 tablespoons of butter and season with salt and pepper.

Port Wine Sauce:
Sauté shallots in oil until translucent, add morel mushrooms (if desired), and cook on medium-low heat until tender. Add port wine and cook on low heat until reduced by half. Add veal stock and simmer until slightly thickened. Serve with sliced beef tenderloin.

Potato Purée:
Peel and cut potatoes into ½-inch pieces; put into pot and cover with water. Boil until fork tender, about 30 minutes. Strain and put into mixer with whip attachment. Bring cream and butter to simmer; add to mixer with potatoes and mix until smooth, about 3 minutes. Adjust seasonings. Cover and hold for service.

Pastrami Cure:
Roast coriander seeds, mustard seeds, black peppercorns, and fenugreek in warm dry skillet approximately 3 to 4 minutes until spices release their natural aroma. Let cool and add sea salt, garlic, brown sugar, and ginger to coffee grinder and grind until fine powder. Rub beef 2 hours before cooking and refrigerate until ready to use.

To cook tenderloin, sear in a pan on stove top or grill for about 3 minutes on each side on high heat. Place in the oven on a wire rack and bake at 350°F for about 30 to 40 minutes or until the internal temperature reaches 125°F. Remove from oven and let rest for 10 minutes.

Slice and serve.

Short Ribs Braised with Caramelized Onions, Port Wine, and Beef Stock
8 Servings

Chef Gregory Ziengnefuss *has been working in the catering industry for 30 years, and has been with* Butler's Pantry Catering *for 11 years. As executive chef, he specializes in creative food, design, and presentation. Though Greg is a native of St Louis, he has traveled the world in order to broaden his culinary knowledge.*

6 pounds beef short ribs,
  trimmed—about 2 or 3 ribs
2 tablespoons olive oil
3 large yellow onions, diced small
4 large garlic cloves, minced
1½ cups port wine
1 28- to 32-ounce can diced
  tomatoes in juice

2½ cups beef broth
8 ounces cremini mushrooms,
  quartered
¼ cup low-sodium soy sauce
2 teaspoons chopped fresh
  rosemary
2 teaspoons kosher salt

Pat ribs dry; season generously with salt and pepper. In a heavy 1½-gallon sauce pot, or rondeau pan, heat oil until almost smoking. Brown ribs, on both sides, in batches, transferring to a platter until all browned. Add chopped onions and cook over medium heat, stirring frequently, until golden brown and fragrant. Add garlic and stir to aroma, about one minute. Add the port and deglaze the pan. Add tomatoes, beef broth, mushrooms, soy sauce, rosemary, and salt, bring to a boil.

Add ribs and any juices from the platter, making sure the ribs are covered by the liquid. Reduce to a simmer, cover, and simmer for 1½ to 2 hours or until the ribs are fork tender. The ribs can be prepared to this point, cooled, and held for up to three days refrigerated. If serving immediately, transfer the meat to a platter and hold in a warm oven. Pour the braising liquid into a fat separator and pour the liquid into a clean sauce pot and reduce by half. Adjust seasoning if necessary with kosher salt and white pepper. If reheating, remove congealed fat from the top of the braising liquid. Place the ribs in a roasting pan with a small amount of the braising liquid, cover, and reheat at 350°F until hot, about 20 minutes. Transfer the braising liquid to a clean sauce pot and reduce to sauce consistency if necessary. Adjust seasoning with kosher salt and white pepper.

Holiday Beef Tenderloin
10 to 12 Servings

Seasoning Blend:
3 tablespoons dried thyme
2 tablespoons onion powder
1½ teaspoons ground cumin
1 tablespoon black pepper
1 teaspoon ground cloves
1 teaspoon garlic powder
3 bay leaves

1 cup port wine
1 cup soy sauce
½ cup olive oil
5 tablespoons seasoning blend
1 5- to 6-pound beef tenderloin,
 trimmed

Mix ingredients of seasoning blend and set aside. Combine wine, soy sauce, oil, and 3 tablespoons of seasoning blend and mix well. Place tenderloin in a 9×13 glass dish, pour wine mixture over top, and cover tightly. Refrigerate 8 hours and turn occasionally.

Uncover tenderloin, drain, and reserve marinade. Place tenderloin on a rack in a roasting pan and insert meat thermometer. Bake at 425°F for 45 to 60 minutes or until thermometer reads 125° for rare, 135° for medium rare, or 145° for medium. Baste with marinade occasionally.

Fillets Boursin
6 Servings

2 tablespoons soy sauce
6 beef fillets mignon,
 1½- to 2-inches thick
2 tablespoons olive oil
1 package frozen puff pastry, thawed

¼ cup breadcrumbs
15-ounce package herb
 Boursin cheese
1 egg lightly beaten with 1
 teaspoon water

Rub soy sauce on both sides of the fillets. Heat oil over medium-high heat and sauté fillets 2 minutes on each side. Remove from pan and cool. Roll out pastry sheets and cut into a total of six squares. Sprinkle breadcrumbs in center of each square. Place fillet on top and dot cheese evenly on each fillet. Be generous. Gather pastry and pinch closed, totally enclosing fillet. Place, topknot side up, in a shallow glass baking dish. Brush with egg mixture. Bake at 400°F for 18 to 20 minutes, until golden brown. Meat will be medium rare.

Beef Wellington
8-10 Servings

1 whole filet of beef (4 to 5 pounds),
   trimmed
beef suet
melted butter or oil

Marinade:
1½ cups dry red wine
1 tablespoon Worcestershire sauce
juice of 1 lemon
several grinds of fresh black pepper

Madeira Sauce:
pan juice from roasted meat
½ cup canned beef consommé
½ cup Madeira wine
salt and pepper
2 teaspoons arrowroot or cornstarch
cold water

Stuffing:
2 tablespoons butter
1 to 1½ pounds fresh mushrooms,
   finely diced
5 shallots or green onions, very
   finely minced
½ cup Madeira wine
4 or 5 ounce can pâté de foie gras

Pastry:
3 cups flour
2 teaspoons salt
14 tablespoons chilled butter
4 tablespoons vegetable shortening
¾ cup iced water
1 egg, lightly beaten with 1
   teaspoon water

Start two days before you want to serve. The beef should be marinated
for 24 hours before baking, and baked a day before serving. When you
buy your tenderloin, ask the butcher to give you a large strip of beef suet.

Marinade:
Mix the 1½ cups dry red wine, 1 tablespoon Worcestershire sauce, juice
of 1 lemon, and several grinds of black pepper; pour over beef tenderloin. Cover and refrigerate for 24 hours, turning occasionally.

Roast Beef:
Remove meat from refrigerator, drain off marinade, and reserve. Dry
meat. One end of the meat slopes off to a thin "tail." Fold that end
down under meat and tie with twine, forming a uniformly thick strip. Rub
meat with oil or melted butter. Cut suet in half lengthwise. In shallow
baking pan layer one piece of suet, then the beef, and then the other strip
of suet. Bake at 425°F for 30 minutes, turning meat once and replacing
the suet over the top. Remove the meat from the pan; untie the meat, let
cool, and refrigerate until the next day.

Madeira Sauce:

Make the day before. Skim off fat from the pan and discard. Put remaining juices in a small saucepan; add beef consommé, Madiera wine, and salt and pepper to taste. Add a few tablespoons of reserved marinade; allow to cook down for about 5 minutes. Taste for seasonings. Dissolve 2 teaspoons arrowroot or cornstarch in a few tablespoons cold water and add to the sauce. Stir over low heat until slightly thickened. Refrigerate until time to reheat.

Stuffing:

Make stuffing the day before serving. Heat butter in a skillet and sauté mushrooms and shallots or green onions. Sauté about 8 to 10 minutes, until mixture seems quite dry. Stir in Madeira wine; boil down until wine has practically evaporated. Season with salt and pepper, and blend in pâté de foie gras. Cover and refrigerate.

Pastry:

Make pastry the day before serving. Put flour and 2 teaspoons salt in a bowl. Cut in butter and shortening. Sprinkle in iced water, a little at a time, tossing all the while, until the dough holds together. Wrap in waxed paper and refrigerate.

To Assemble:

About 3 to 4 hours before serving, remove meat and stuffing from the refrigerator and allow to reach room temperature. Time your cooking schedule so beef will be ready no more than 30 minutes before serving. Preheat oven to 425°F. Roll out pastry in a rectangle about 9×14 inches and ¼-inch thick, large enough to cover the meat. Stir the stuffing to soften it and spread over the pastry, leaving the borders uncovered. Place the meat in center of pastry with the side down that you want eventually to be up. Fold pastry over meat and seal seam and ends with water. Place, seam-side down, on a buttered cookie sheet and brush top and sides with an egg lightly beaten with a teaspoon of water. With a very sharp knife make hash marks in a herringbone pattern over the top of pastry. Prick with fork on sides. Place in preheated oven; after 15 minutes, decrease temperature to 375° and bake 30 minutes more. The beef should rest in a warm spot about 20 minutes before carving. When ready to carve, remove carefully with two spatulas to heated serving platter. Slice into 1½-inch servings. Serve with the reheated Madeira sauce.

Note: *If meat must wait to be served, it will hold for about 30 minutes in the oven set at its lowest temperature—about 120°F, if possible.*

Boliche-Cuban-Style Roast
6 to 8 Servings

4 pounds eye of round roast
1 carrot
5 teaspoons crushed garlic
½ teaspoon dried oregano
salt
black pepper

1 cup orange juice
½ cup lemon juice
½ cup lime juice
2 large onions, sliced
2 bay leaves
1 cup dry sherry
3 cups beef broth

With a long, thin knife, poke a hole in the center of the roast, then twist to leave enough room for the carrot to go through. Insert the carrot (it helps to use the counter to help push the carrot).

With a knife, slash beef in several places. Combine crushed garlic and oregano. Fill the slashes with the garlic-oregano mixture. Any leftover mixture should be rubbed over the surface of the roast. Rub salt and pepper liberally on the roast.

Mix the orange, lemon, and lime juices. Pour over the roast and marinate for 3 hours or overnight.

To Cook:
Add the onions, bay leaves, sherry, and beef broth to slow cooker or pressure cooker. Add the roast with marinade. Cook in a slow cooker for 4 to 5 hours or in a pressure cooker for 1½ to 2 hours. The meat will be very tender and flavorful.

Steak Modiga
4 Servings

Lemon-Wine Sauce:
2 tablespoons lemon juice
2 tablespoons chicken base
½ cup white wine
2 cups water
3 tablespoons butter
¼ cup flour
3 cloves garlic, finely chopped
¼ teaspoon ground white pepper

Steaks:
4 strip sirloin steaks, about 10 ounces each
½ cup butter, melted
2 cups Italian-seasoned dry breadcrumbs
16 mushrooms, sliced
1½ cups shredded provel cheese

Sauce:

Combine lemon juice, chicken base, wine, and water in a pot. Bring to a boil then reduce to a simmer. Make a roux by melting butter in a small skillet. Whisk flour into butter until no lumps remain. Slowly whisk roux into lemon mixture. Stir in garlic and pepper; let simmer for 5 to 10 minutes, stirring frequently. If not using immediately, set aside to cool, stirring occasionally. Store in refrigerator.

Steaks:

Trim fat from steaks. Dip steaks in melted butter, coat lightly with Italian breadcrumbs. Cook on grill or under broiler to desired doneness. Just before steak is done, add mushrooms to warm sauce. When steak is done, top with shredded cheese. Let cheese melt over steak, then top with sauce.

Braised Short Ribs
6 Servings

3 pounds bone-in beef short ribs, well trimmed of fat and cut into 3-inch lengths
¾ teaspoon salt, divided
¼ teaspoon freshly ground pepper
1 tablespoon olive oil
2 medium onions, halved and sliced
2 large carrots, diced
1 tablespoon minced garlic
1 14-ounce can chicken broth
½ cup dried tart cherries
½ cup dry red wine
½ teaspoon dried thyme
1 bay leaf
1 tablespoon Dijon mustard
1 tablespoon prepared horseradish

Sprinkle ribs with ½ teaspoon salt and the pepper. Heat oil in a large Dutch oven over medium-high heat. Brown ribs on all sides. Set ribs aside; discard drippings in pot. Reduce heat to medium low. Add onions, carrots, and garlic; cook 10 minutes, until softened.

Return ribs to pot. Add broth, cherries, wine, thyme, bay leaf, and remaining ¼ teaspoon salt. Bring to a boil and cover pot. Transfer to oven and bake at 350°F for 2 hours, or until very tender and meat falls off the bone. Check occasionally; you may have to add more liquid.

Transfer ribs to a large, deep serving platter and cover. Skim fat, discard bay leaf and any bones that have fallen off. If sauce is too thin, bring to a boil and cook 5 minutes to reduce slightly; you should have about 2½ cups. Whisk in mustard and horseradish. Pour sauce over ribs and serve.

Flat Iron Steak with Spice Rub
4 Servings

Steak Spice Blend:
4 tablespoons kosher salt
1 tablespoon ground black pepper
1 tablespoon onion powder
1 tablespoon garlic powder
½ tablespoon crushed red pepper
½ tablespoon dried thyme
½ tablespoon dried rosemary
½ tablespoon dried coriander or cilantro

1 flat iron steak, 1 to 1¼ pound
2 teaspoons steak spice blend
1 large Vidalia onion, sliced
1 tablespoon vegetable oil

Mix the steak spice blend ingredients together and set aside.

Allow flat iron steak to come to room temperature, approximately 15 minutes. Rub 1 teaspoon of steak spice blend over each side of the steak; let rest on plate. Store remaining steak spice blend for future use.

Spray a large nonstick skillet with cooking spray; sauté onion slices over medium high heat, stirring often. Remove onions to a bowl when they are soft and browned. Re-spray skillet; add 1 tablespoon oil. Heat over medium-high heat. Add flat iron steak to skillet, cut into 2 equal pieces if it is too big for the skillet; cook 5 minutes per side for medium rare. Remove to platter; let stand for 5 minutes before slicing thinly across the grain. Serve with the onions.

Note: *Be prepared to use your vent hood and clean your skillet, but this recipe is worth it!*

Pacific Rim Glazed Flank Steak
6 Servings

1 cup prepared teriyaki marinade	1 large clove garlic, crushed
½ cup chopped onion	pepper
⅓ cup honey	1 beef flank steak 1½ to 2
⅓ cup fresh orange juice	pounds
1 tablespoon chopped fresh rosemary	orange slices and rosemary
1 tablespoon dark sesame oil	sprigs

In medium shallow dish, whisk together marinade, onion, honey, orange juice, chopped rosemary, oil, garlic, and pepper as desired until blended. Remove and reserve 1 cup for basting. Using sharp knife, lightly score both sides of steak in a crisscross pattern. Turn to coat in marinade. Marinate, covered, in refrigerator for 30 minutes, turning once. Remove steak from marinade; discard marinade.

Grill over medium coals 17 to 21 minutes for medium rare to medium doneness, basting occasionally with reserved marinade and turning once. Carve steak diagonally across grain in thin slices. Arrange on platter. Warm remaining basting liquid and spoon over beef. Garnish with orange slices and rosemary sprigs.

Chutney Pepper Steak
4 Servings

4 center-cut beef fillet steaks about 1¼ inches thick and six ounces each
2 tablespoons unsalted butter
¼ cup mango chutney, Major Grey's brand preferred
2 teaspoons cracked black pepper
3 ounces Armagnac brandy

In large skillet, sauté fillets in melted butter over medium-high heat. Cook 3 minutes per side for rare, or until desired temperature. Top with chutney, then pepper. Flambé with Armagnac.

Note: *Use caution when flaming brandy. Armagnac should be warmed before flaming, but not boiled. Pour Armagnac in a large spoon. Gently heat bottom of spoon with stick lighter until Armagnac ignites and carefully pour over meat.*

Beef Stir Fry

4 Servings

2 tablespoons white wine
1 pound beef tenderloin or sirloin,
  cut into 3-inch strips
3 tablespoons cooking oil
1 clove garlic, minced
1 teaspoon salt
⅛ teaspoon pepper
½ head broccoli, cut into florets
3 medium carrots, thinly sliced
1 medium red bell pepper, seeds
  and ribs removed, cut into ¾-inch pieces

1 cup snow peas or sugar
  snap peas
1 cup sliced mushrooms
1½ teaspoons freshly grated
  ginger
1 8-ounce can water
  chestnuts, sliced
3 cups cooked rice
soy sauce or bottled stir fry
  sauce

Pour wine over the meat strips, stirring to coat lightly. Heat oil and garlic in frying pan or wok. Brown meat quickly in hot oil. Remove from pan and season with ½ teaspoon salt and the pepper. Keep warm.

Add vegetables to pan, cover and steam partially, stirring frequently. Cook until tender, but still crisp. Season with remaining ½ teaspoon salt. Stir in steak strips and heat the mixture thoroughly.

German Beef Burgundy Stew
4 Servings

1½ pounds beef stew meat
2 tablespoons cooking oil
1 large apple, pared and shredded,
   approximately 1 cup
1 medium carrot, shredded,
   approximately ½ cup
½ medium yellow onion, sliced
½ cup water
½ cup Burgundy wine
½ teaspoon anchovy paste
1 clove garlic, minced
2 beef bouillon cubes

1 small bay leaf
⅛ teaspoon crushed dried
   thyme
4 teaspoons cornstarch
¼ cup cold water
½ teaspoon Kitchen Bouquet
4 cups medium noodles,
   cooked and drained
¼ teaspoon poppy seeds,
   optional
8-ounce package fresh
   mushrooms

Cut beef cubes in equal sizes. Brown meat in hot oil. Add apple, carrot, onion, the ½ cup water, wine, anchovy paste, garlic, bouillon cubes, bay leaf, and thyme. Cover and cook over low heat for 1½ hours. Slice and then add mushrooms; cover and continue cooking an additional ½ hour. Remove bay leaf.

Combine cornstarch and the ¼ cup cold water; add to beef mixture. Cook and stir until thickened. Stir in Kitchen Bouquet; use enough so that beef mixture is a rich brown color. Serve over hot noodles sprinkled with poppy seed.

Note: *This may also be served over rice if preferred.*

Pork

Smoked Pepper Grilled Pork Chops
4 Servings

Located in the Washington Avenue loft district, Lucas Park Grille *offers a variety of New American cuisine in both small and large plates.* Lucas Park Grille *is proud to support local farmers who practice responsible animal stewardship and agriculture. Executive Chef* Kyle Patterson *offers a classically influenced menu including the best of local and seasonal cuisine with creative ingredients, both familiar and adventurous, to create a harmonious palate.*

2 ounces smoked peppercorns
4 pork chops
kosher salt
1 pound new potatoes
4 ounces butter, divided
1 small onion, diced
green beans
white wine

Tomato Basil Jam:
1 quart diced tomatoes
3 ounces minced shallots
1 teaspoon ground black pepper
1 ounce lemon juice
1 teaspoon kosher salt
¾ cup sugar
¼ ounce (weight) basil, chiffonade (roll and cut into strips)

Process smoked pepper in a spice grinder to a rough grind. Season pork chops with ground pepper and salt, and grill until done. Quarter and boil potatoes until done, but still fork firm. Sauté in 2 ounces butter with onions, season with salt and pepper to taste, and sauté until golden brown.

Sauté green beans in the remaining butter and season. Deglaze with white wine and cover to finish.

Tomato Basil Jam:
Combine tomatoes, shallots, black pepper, lemon juice, salt, and sugar in a heavy bottom pot. Cook on low heat until mixture begins to thicken, stir frequently. When finished, remove from heat and add basil.

To Plate:
Top pork chops with warmed tomato basil jam, potato hash, and green beans.

Braised Greenwood Farm Pork Cheeks with Greens, Turnips, Stone-Ground Grits, and Jus
6 Servings

For nearly a quarter of a century, Sidney Street Café *has been the crown jewel of Benton Park. Chef* Kevin Nashan *and his wife, Mina, bought the restaurant in 2003, and have added a contemporary flair to the restaurant's old-school charm. Nashan grew up working in his family's restaurant, La Tertulia, in Santa Fe, New Mexico. After graduating from Saint Louis University, he attended the Culinary Institute of America, and spent the next six years traveling and working in restaurants around the world.*

Pork Cheeks:
6 pork cheeks (can purchase
    from butcher, local farm, or
    farmer's market)
oil
8 ounces mirepoix (medium diced
    onions, carrots, celery)
2 ounces crushed garlic
2 ounces minced ginger
2 ounces tomato paste
4 thyme sprigs
4 ounces white wine
4 ounces apple cider
16 ounces veal stock
16 ounces chicken stock
salt and pepper

Grits:
4 ounces cream cheese
1 quart heavy cream
1 quart water
16 ounces milk
16 ounces stone-ground grits
salt

Turnips:
2 dozen turnips (cleaned,
    stemmed)
6 ounces butter
2 ounces water
salt to taste

Greens:
1 yellow onion, julienned
4 ounces roasted garlic
1 to 2 bunches greens (collards,
    turnips tops, beet tops, etc.)
4 ounces white wine
6 ounces chicken stock
2 ounces Tabasco
2 ounces Steen's vinegar
2 ounces Steen's syrup
salt and pepper to taste

Jus:
32 ounces braise liquid (reduce
    by half, strain, and reserve)

Dredge the seasoned cheeks in flour. Heat a braising pan, add oil and sauté until brown. Remove the cheeks and sauté the vegetables with the garlic and ginger. Add tomato paste, thyme, and white wine simmering on a low heat until half the liquid remains. Add rema... liquid and bring to a boil; add the cheeks and put into a 325°F oven for 2 hours. The cheeks are ready when you can easily pierce them with a knife. Reserve for jus.

Grits:

In a pot, heat the cream cheese and all liquid for the grits. Bring to a boil, season, and slowly whisk in the grits. Bring them back to a boil, cover, and slowly cook the grits for about 30 minutes on low heat. Season to taste.

Turnips:

In a sauté pan, heat the butter and add the turnips, deglazing with water. Season and cook the turnips until tender.

Greens:

In a braising pan, heat and slowly sauté onions. Add garlic and all cooking greens. Deglaze with white wine and add remaining liquids for the greens. Season and cover. Cook until soft, stirring occasionally for 30 to 40 minutes.

Apricot-Glazed Pork Medallions
4 Servings

1 pork tenderloin, cut crosswise into ½-inch thick rounds
salt and ground pepper
2 teaspoons sesame oil

1¼ cups apricot preserves
¼ cup soy sauce
1 tablespoon chopped fresh ginger

Season both sides of pork with salt and pepper. Heat oil in large skillet over medium-high heat. Add pork and sear 2 minutes per side. Add apricot preserves, soy sauce, and ginger; bring to a simmer. Simmer 5 minutes, until pork is cooked through and sauce thickens and reduces.

Note: *Serve with rice and steamed broccoli for a healthy and easy weeknight dinner.*

Bacon-Wrapped Pork Tenderloin
6 to 8 Servings

½ cup soy sauce
1 to 3 tablespoons grated onion
1½ teaspoons white vinegar
¼ cup sugar
1 tablespoon garlic salt

1 tablespoon seasoned salt
1 teaspoon black pepper
2 pork tenderloins
6 slices bacon

Combine soy sauce, onion, vinegar, sugar, garlic salt, seasoned salt, and pepper to make marinade. Wrap tenderloins in bacon, securing with wooden toothpicks. Place in shallow baking dish and cover with marinade. Refrigerate up to 4 hours or overnight.

Bake at 300°F for 1½ hours. Turn during last half hour to crisp bacon.

Simply Roasted Pork
10 Servings

⅓ cup apricot or peach preserves
1 teaspoon salt
1 teaspoon dried oregano
¾ teaspoon garlic powder

½ teaspoon freshly
　ground pepper
2 or 3 pork tenderloins

Melt preserves in saucepan over low heat; keep warm. Combine salt, oregano, garlic powder, and pepper; rub over pork. Place pork on a cooking rack coated with cooking spray.

Bake at 425°F for 30 minutes. Brush half of the melted preserves over the pork. Bake 10 additional minutes. Brush second half of preserves over pork; bake another 10 minutes. If using a meat thermometer, bake until 155°F. Let stand 10 minutes before slicing.

Grilled Pork Tenderloin
with Molasses and Mustard
4 to 6 Servings

¼ cup mild-flavored light molasses or Karo syrup
3 tablespoons apple cider vinegar, divided
2 tablespoons Dijon mustard
2 tablespoons coarse-grained mustard
1 pork tenderloin

Whisk molasses, 2 tablespoons vinegar, and both mustards in small bowl to blend. Place pork in heavy-duty re-sealable plastic bag. Cover with marinade. Seal tightly and refrigerate about 4 hours. Drain marinade into heavy saucepan. Sprinkle pork with salt and pepper. Grill pork over medium-high heat until the thermometer inserted into center registers 145°F, turning occasionally with tongs, about 20 minutes. Transfer pork to serving platter; let rest 5 minutes.

Meanwhile, add 1 tablespoon vinegar to pan with marinade and boil until thickened to sauce consistency, about 1 minute. Cut pork crosswise on slight diagonal into ½-inch-thick slices. Arrange pork slices on platter; drizzle sauce over and serve.

Honey-Herb Pork
6 Servings

1 cup beer or ginger ale
1 tablespoon oil
1½ teaspoons crushed dried rosemary
1 teaspoon garlic powder
½ cup honey mustard
2 tablespoons onion powder
1 teaspoon salt
¼ teaspoon pepper
2 pork tenderloins

In a small bowl, combine the beer or ginger ale, oil, rosemary, garlic powder, honey mustard, onion powder, salt and pepper. Pour 1 cup marinade into a large re-sealable bag; cover and refrigerate the remaining marinade to use for basting. Add the pork tenderloins to the bag and turn to coat. Refrigerate for at least 1 hour up to 24 hours. Grill, basting occasionally with reserved marinade until meat registers 160°F. Let meat stand 10 minutes before slicing.

Hoisin and Bourbon-Glazed Pork Tenderloin
8 Servings

1 cup hickory wood chips
⅓ cup hoisin sauce
2 tablespoons seasoned rice vinegar
2 tablespoons bourbon
2 tablespoons maple syrup
1½ teaspoons grated, peeled
   fresh ginger
1½ teaspoons fresh lime juice

½ teaspoon chili paste
   with garlic
1 garlic clove, minced
2 pork tenderloins, trimmed
½ teaspoon salt
½ teaspoon freshly ground
   black pepper

Soak wood chips in water 30 minutes; drain well. Combine hoisin sauce, rice vinegar, bourbon, maple syrup, ginger, lime juice, chili paste, and garlic in a small bowl; stir with a whisk. Slice pork lengthwise, cutting to, but not through, other side. Open halves, laying pork flat. Sprinkle pork with salt and pepper. Add wood chips to grill. Place pork on grill rack coated with cooking spray; cook on medium heat for 5 minutes. Turn and baste pork with hoisin mixture; cook 5 minutes. Turn and baste pork with hoisin mixture; cook 5 minutes or until pork reaches 155°F or desired degree of doneness. Let stand 5 minutes; cut pork into ½-inch slices.

Chinese Sweet and Sour Pork
4 Servings

1 beaten egg
½ teaspoon salt
½ cup flour
4 tablespoons water
1 pound pork shoulder, cubed
oil for frying
1 cup pineapple chunks, drained
1 green pepper, cut diagonally in 1-inch strips

½ cup vinegar
¼ cup brown sugar
¾ cup water
1 tablespoon molasses
½ carrot, thinly sliced
2 tablespoons cornstarch
¼ cup water

Make batter with beaten egg, salt, flour, and 4 tablespoons of water. Salt and pepper pork cubes and coat each cube with batter. Fry cubes in deep oil until golden brown, drain and set aside. In a large pan mix pineapple, green pepper, vinegar, brown sugar, ¾ cup water, molasses, and carrot; heat to boiling. Mix cornstarch with ¼ cup water, add to boiling mixture, lower heat and stir gently until thickened. Add reserved fried pork, mix well. Serve at once with rice or fried noodles.

Fall Pork
8 Servings

1½ teaspoons salt
1½ teaspoons ground allspice
1½ teaspoons sage or thyme
1½ teaspoons fresh ground pepper

3 to 3½ pounds boned pork roast (tenderloin or pork chops also work well)
1 tablespoon light oil
1 tablespoon coarse kosher salt

Combine the salt, allspice, sage or thyme, and pepper. Trim excess fat off meat, leaving ⅛ inch on the outside. Set the meat fat side down and make several lengthwise slashes in the thickest part of the meat to even it out. Rub the spices over the meat and then rub with the oil. Cover and refrigerate overnight or at least for a few hours. For a more intense flavor, it can sit for 2 days in the refrigerator.

Place the meat in a shallow roasting pan and place on the middle rack of a 375°F oven. Roast for 1 hour, or until the internal temperature reads 140°, basting every 20 minutes with accumulated juices. Lastly, turn the meat over and rub the coarse salt into the fat side. Continue roasting for 20 minutes or until internal temperature reaches 160°. Remove from oven and let rest for 10 minutes before carving.

Note: *This dish is best served with roasted root vegetables such as butternut squash, rutabaga, and parsnips. Roasted Brussels sprouts with butter and toasted sesame seeds are also a good complement.*

Pork Chops Gruyere
4 Servings

4 loin pork chops, about 1¼ pounds
salt and freshly ground pepper to taste
1 tablespoon vegetable oil
1 cup grated Gruyere cheese
2 tablespoons Dijon mustard
1 tablespoon heavy cream

½ teaspoon finely chopped garlic
1 tablespoon finely chopped chives
1 egg yolk
2 tablespoons dry white wine

Sprinkle the chops with the salt and pepper. Heat oil in a heavy skillet and add the chops. Cook on medium-high heat until browned, about 10 minutes. Turn and continue cooking until browned. While the chops are cooking, blend the Gruyere cheese, mustard, cream, garlic, chives, and egg yolk. Remove the chops from the skillet and place on oven-proof serving dish. Smear the cheese mixture on one side of the chops and smooth it over. Broil the chops until topping is browned. Meanwhile, pour off the fat from the skillet and add the white wine. Stir and scrape the browned bits until dissolved. Pour over cooked chops.

Strawberry Pork Chops
4 to 6 Servings

salt and pepper to taste
4 to 6 pork chops, ½-inch thick
3 tablespoons olive oil, divided
1 large sweet onion, chopped

2 cloves garlic, minced
½ cup balsamic vinegar
2 cups sliced strawberries

Sprinkle salt and pepper over both sides of pork chops. Heat 2 tablespoons oil in a large skillet over medium-high heat. Place pork chops in skillet, turning only once to sear both sides. When done, place pork chops on a plate to rest. Add a tablespoon of oil to skillet and warm over medium heat. Place chopped onions and garlic into skillet and cook until caramelized. Be sure to stir onions often so they do not burn. Once onions are to desired color, pour in balsamic vinegar and reduce for 5 to 8 minutes. Once reduced, turn heat to low, add sliced strawberries, and cook for 2 minutes. Return pork chops to skillet and allow to soak up juices, approximately 2 minutes. Place pork chops on a serving platter and top with strawberry-onion marmalade.

Honey-Mustard & Honey Glazed Ribs
6 Servings

Honey-Mustard Glaze:
½ cup apple cider vinegar
2 tablespoons light brown sugar
⅓ cup honey
3 heaping tablespoons Dijon mustard
salt and freshly ground black pepper

2 racks St. Louis style/country
  style pork ribs (12 ribs each)
4 tablespoons canola oil
salt and freshly ground black
  pepper
1 cup soy sauce
4 cups water
2- to 3-inch piece ginger, skin-
  on and sliced

Honey-Mustard Glaze:
Combine the vinegar and brown sugar in a small saucepan over high heat and cook, stirring occasionally, until the sugar is completely dissolved and mixture reduces slightly, about 5 minutes. Remove from the heat and whisk in the honey, mustard, and salt and pepper to taste. Let cool to room temperature.

Brush the pork racks on both sides with canola oil and season with salt and pepper.

In a saucepan over medium-high heat, combine the soy sauce, water, and ginger; bring to a boil. Pour the mixture into the bottom of a roasting pan, fitted with a rack, and arrange the ribs on the rack. Wrap the pan with foil and roast at 500°F until the ribs are tender, about 1½ hours.

Remove the ribs from the oven and transfer to baking sheets lined with foil. Turn on the broiler and let heat for 3 to 5 minutes. Brush the ribs heavily on the top side with some of the glaze, put under the broiler and broil until golden brown and a crust has formed. Remove from the oven to a cutting board and brush with more of the glaze. Let rest 10 minutes before slicing. Arrange the ribs on a serving platter and serve.

Veal

Veal Cynthia
4 Servings

Chef Joseph Mueller, *CEC, is the Executive Chef at the* Racquet Club Ladue. *Joe earned a degree in Culinary Arts and Hotel/Restaurant Management from St. Louis Community College at Forest Park and has also attended continuing education classes at the Culinary Institute of America in both New York and California. Joe won the 2010 Chef of the Year competition with this Veal Cynthia recipe, which is named after his wife.*

Veal Rib Eye:
1 veal rack
2 tablespoons fennel spice blend
1 ounce whole butter (Vermont)
2 garlic cloves, crushed
1 shallot, cut into fourths
2 thyme sprigs
salt and pepper to taste
clarified butter
6 pieces bacon

Veal Roulade:
1 cap from veal
1 tablespoon roasted garlic butter
1 tablespoon fine herbs
salt and pepper
stock from Madeira wine sauce
butcher's twine
1 tablespoon fine herbs to finish

Chanterelle Ragout:
12 white pearl onions
½ ounce bacon, diced very small
2 ounces chanterelle mushrooms
1 ounce sherry wine
4 ounces veal glaze
1 tablespoon fine herbs
½ ounce whole butter, cubed
1 teaspoon minced shallot
1 teaspoon sherry vinegar

Potato Foam:
10 ounces Yukon Gold potatoes,
    peeled and cryovac (or keep in
    cold water)
¾ cup 2% milk, warmed
1 ounce butter, cubed
truffle salt and black pepper

Candied Orange:
1 orange: zest, juice, segment
4 ounces orange juice
4 ounces simple syrup
Marcona almonds

Carrot:
4 carrots, peeled
1 ounce butter
1 teaspoon sugar
4 ounces stock: 2 ounces
    vegetable, 2 ounces chicken
4 mint stems
2 thyme sprigs
salt and pepper
nutmeg, fresh grated, to taste
20 chervil plucks, for plate up

Pickled Red Pearl Onions:
4 red pearl onions, peeled and sliced
½ cup red wine vinegar
¼ cup water
2 tablespoons sugar
kosher salt to taste

Corn Silk:
3 corn on the cob
1 tablespoon minced shallot
butter, to sauté
4 ounces corn milk
1 ounce white beans (canned)
1 pinch dried tarragon
½ pinch cayenne pepper
salt and pepper, to taste
butter

Brussels Sprouts:
14 Brussels sprouts leaves
7 each Brussels sprout hearts
1 tablespoon bacon fat
2 teaspoons minced shallots
¼ teaspoon ground caraway seed
salt and pepper
2 ounces vegetable stock
2 ounces butter

Grape Tomatoes:
15 grape tomatoes, peeled
1 tablespoon extra-virgin olive oil
1 teaspoon red wine vinegar
½ tablespoon honey
parsley, chopped
kosher salt and pepper as needed

Madeira Wine Sauce:
veal scrap
3 cups veal stock
4 ounces Madeira wine
2 ounces veal glacé
1 lemon wrap
1 ounce butter, to finish
3 ounces mirepoix (onion, carrot, and
  celery), medium diced
1 thyme sprig, bay
  leaf and parsley stem
2 whole black peppercorns

Veal Rib Eye:
Break down loin and trim to appropriate size. Rub loin with clarified butter and season. Sear loin until golden brown on all sides; baste loin with butter, garlic, shallot, and thyme while searing. Wrap in bacon and place on bones to roast. Roast at 325°F to internal temperature of 135°. Hold hot for service.

Veal Roulade:
Cut cap from veal rack and clean. Pound veal until uniform thickness and appropriate size. Trim as needed. Season with salt and pepper; rub with roasted garlic butter and herbs. Roll and tie the veal with the twine. Liberally season with fine herbs. Sear on all sides and finish cooking in veal stock. Slice to order. Hold hot for service.

Chanterelle Ragout:
Roast pearl onions until golden brown. Add diced bacon and render until brown. Add mushrooms and cook until tender. Add sherry wine and reduce until dry. Add veal glaze and simmer. Finish with herbs, butter, and vinegar as needed. Hold hot for service.

Potato Foam:
Simmer peeled potatoes in salted water until tender. Remove from water and set to dry. Peel and rice. Wisk in warm milk and butter to the proper consistency. Season as needed. Place in ISI gun and fill with charges. (Home cooks can use a cookie gun.) Hold hot for service.

Candied Orange:
Peel and segment orange. Small dice skins with pith attached, and blanch 3 times cold to hot. Cover zest with simple syrup and orange juice. Cook until tender and candied. Thin with water as needed.

Carrot:
Caramelize carrot in butter and sugar until light golden brown. Season with salt and pepper. Add stock, mint stems, and thyme; simmer until carrot is tender and stock reduced. Finish with fresh grated nutmeg. Hold hot for service.

Pickled Red Pearl Onions:
Thin slice onions into rings. Combine vinegar, water, sugar, salt, and pepper. Bring pickling solution to a boil and pour over onions. Let sit at room temperature to pickle.

Corn Silk:
Grate corn on a box grater to remove kernels, reserving kernels and corn milk. Scrape cob with back of knife to remove all milk from cob. Sauté shallot in butter until tender; add corn and cook. Add corn milk, beans, tarragon, cayenne pepper, salt, and pepper. Cook until corn is tender and liquid is reduced. Blend corn until smooth. Finish with butter; strain as needed. Hold hot for service.

Brussels Sprouts:
Blanch sprouts and leaves in salted water until tender. Shock in ice bath. Sauté sprouts in bacon fat until tender and lightly caramelized. Add shallots, caraway, and sprout leaves. Season with salt and pepper as needed. Deglaze pan with stock and finish with butter. Hold hot for service.

Grape Tomatoes:
Mix olive oil, vinegar, honey, and parsley. Toss tomatoes in dressing and season as needed. Cover and hold at room temperature for service.

Madeira Wine Sauce:
Sear loin in skillet and remove. Add scrap and cook until caramelized.

Add mirepoix and caramelize. Add aromatics and wine; reduc
Add ⅓ of the veal stock and reduce until set. Add ⅓ of the veal stock
at a time, in the same manner to create reduction. Finish with veal glace,
lemon juice, and butter as needed.

To Assemble:

This dish may be assembled and presented any way the preparer would
like. To somewhat resemble the dish presented by the chef: Put a line of
corn silk on side of each plate, then a small amount on which to place
veal rib eye. Put ladle of Madeira wine sauce under last slice of rib eye.
Put a grape tomato on each of three Brussels sprout leaves and place
around slices of rib eye. Lay carrot along top of plate; place candied
orange segments across carrot; finish with chervil and almonds. Ladle
serving of chanterelle mushroom ragout onto plate. Place slice of veal
roulade in center of ragout; surround with three Brussels sprouts, potato
foam, and one red pearl onion.

Note: *Each of these parts can be used on its own as an individual recipe.*

Veal Piccata
4 Servings

2 tablespoons olive oil, divided	2 tablespoons white wine
¼ pound fresh mushrooms, sliced	1 tablespoon fresh lemon
¼ cup flour	juice
¼ teaspoon salt	2 tablespoons minced fresh
pinch of pepper	parsley
1 pound thinly sliced veal scallops	½ lemon, thinly sliced

Heat 1 tablespoon olive oil in medium skillet. Add mushrooms and cook
over medium heat for 4 to 5 minutes. Remove mushrooms and set aside.
In a flat dish, combine flour with salt and pepper. Lightly coat each veal
slice with seasoned flour. Heat 1 tablespoon of the oil in same non-stick
skillet over medium-high heat. Cook half of the veal in hot oil for 2
minutes per side. Remove veal to warm platter and repeat cooking procedure with remaining slices. Return all veal to pan. Add wine, lemon juice,
and mushrooms; simmer for 2 minutes. Arrange veal on serving platter;
spoon mushroom sauce over veal and sprinkle with parsley. Place lemon
slices on top of veal. Serve immediately.

Ossa Bucco
4 Servings

Lombardo's Trattoria *is a family owned third generation Italian restaurant. They specialize in signature pastas, hand cut steaks and fresh seafood in an upscale atmosphere. Chef* Nick Angelou *emphasizes consistency and the use of the freshest ingredients available for every dish they prepare.*

2 tablespoons olive oil
2 tablespoons unsalted butter
flour
4 veal shanks weighing about a
   half pound each
½ cup dry sherry
1¼ cups broth (unsalted bouillon
   will be fine)

2 medium onions, julienned
4 sliced carrots or 1 pound
   baby carrots
4 sliced celery stalks
2 cups tomato sauce
salt and pepper to taste

Put the olive oil and butter in a roasting pan large enough for the shanks to lay flat in a single layer; heat the oil and butter over moderate heat. Flour the shanks, shaking off whatever doesn't stick to meat. Add the meat and cook several minutes, turning the shanks once or twice to brown on both sides. Salt the meat lightly, add the sherry, and cook over medium-high heat, shaking the pan occasionally to make sure the shanks do not stick to the bottom and burn.

In the meantime, heat the broth. When almost all of the sherry has evaporated, sprinkle the hot broth over the meat; add onions, carrots, celery, tomato sauce, salt, and pepper. Cover the pan tightly with a sheet of aluminum foil and transfer to the oven. Roast the shanks at 400°F for at least 2 hours; there should be no need to check them. Transfer the shanks and vegetables to a serving dish. Serve at once.

Note: *Suggest you serve with mushroom risotto or garlic mashed potatoes.*

Veal Scaloppine with Port Wine Sauce
4 Servings

Sauce:
2 cups port or other sweet red wine
¼ cup sherry vinegar
¼ cup sugar

Veal:
1 teaspoon olive oil
1 pound veal scallopine
¼ teaspoon salt
¼ teaspoon pepper
cooking spray

Sauce:

Combine the port, vinegar, and sugar in a medium saucepan. Bring wine mixture to a boil, and cook 35 minutes or until reduced to ½ cup.

Brush oil over veal and sprinkle with salt and pepper. Prepare grill or broiler. Place veal on grill rack or broiler pan coated with cooking spray, and cook 1½ minutes on each side until done. Top with port wine sauce. Great served over a bed of mashed potatoes.

Summer Veal Cutlets
4 Servings

Lemon Vinaigrette:
3 tablespoons lemon juice
3 tablespoons olive oil
1 tablespoon water
1½ teaspoons sugar
⅓ teaspoon salt

4 veal cutlets
2 tablespoons butter
1 tomato, sliced
1 avocado, peeled and sliced
1 cup shredded Monterrey
   Jack cheese (4 ounces)
red leaf lettuce

In small saucepan, combine all lemon vinaigrette ingredients and heat until warm; set aside. On a cutting board, pound each veal cutlet to about ⅓-inch thickness. In a large skillet, sauté cutlets in melted butter, a few at a time until browned on both sides, 3-4 minutes. Arrange cooked cutlets in skillet in single layer. Top with tomato slices, avocado slices, and then cover with shredded cheese. Cover skillet and cook over low heat until cheese melts. To serve, arrange cutlets on lettuce leaves on platter. Pour lemon vinaigrette over all.

Veal Bauletto
4 Servings

8 veal cutlets, 2- to 3-ounces each
4 thin slices prosciutto
4 slices Monterrey Jack cheese
salt and pepper
⅓ cup flour
3 tablespoons olive oil
1 pound fresh mushrooms, sliced
¼ cup chopped shallots
　or onion
1 cup canned chicken broth
½ cup Chablis or other dry
　white wine
2 tablespoons chopped
　fresh parsley
¼ cup butter, softened

Place cutlets between 2 sheets of wax paper; flatten to ⅛-inch thickness, using a meat mallet or rolling pin. Place a slice of prosciutto and a slice of cheese on 4 veal cutlets; top with remaining cutlets. Place between 2 sheets of wax paper; flatten slightly; using a meat mallet or rolling pin. Sprinkle with salt and pepper; dredge in flour.

Cook cutlets in oil in a large skillet until browned on both sides. Remove cutlets to a serving platter, reserving drippings in skillet. Set cutlets aside, and keep warm.

Sauté sliced mushrooms and chopped shallots in drippings in skillet until vegetables are tender. Add chicken broth, wine, and chopped fresh parsley. Bring to a boil; cook 5 minutes or until mixture is reduced by half. Add butter, stirring with a wire whisk until sauce is blended. Spoon warm sauce over cutlets on serving platter.

Lamb

Pesto Crusted Lamb Chops
with Raspberry Sauce
4 to 6 Servings

Matthew Unger, *CSW, is the Executive Chef at the* Missouri Athletic Club West.

Pesto:
4 ounces sweet basil
1 ounce fresh garlic
1 ounce toasted pine nuts
1 ounce spinach
¾ cup olive oil
¼ cup Parmesan cheese

Raspberry Sauce:
1 cup fresh raspberries
1 cup Pinot Noir
¼ cup sugar
1 tablespoon cold water
1 tablespoon corn starch

16 French lamb chops (2 racks)

Pesto:
Purée the basil, garlic, pine nuts, spinach, olive oil, and Parmesan cheese in a blender or food processor.

Lamb:
Rub each chop with pesto and refrigerate for 8 hours. Grill for 3 to 4 minutes on each side over medium heat (this is for a temperature of medium rare). Drizzle with raspberry sauce before serving.

Raspberry Sauce:
Put raspberries, wine, and sugar into a sauce pot. Cook until reduced by half. Add water and corn starch to thicken. Bring to a boil. Drizzle over lamb chops. Serve.

Note: *Serve these with roasted potatoes and mushrooms and, of course, the rest of the Pinot Noir. Enjoy!*

Shepherd's Pie
4 Servings

Chris Desens *is currently the program director for the* Culinary Institute at Hickey College. *He has thirty years of varied industry experience, including both national and international culinary competitions. He is a certified culinary judge through the American Culinary Federation, a Certified Executive Chef, and a member of the American Academy of Chefs.*

Dough for Shepherd Pie:
24 ounces flour
½ ounce salt
12 ounces cold butter
ice water as needed
1½ egg
3 egg yolks
chives, thyme, rosemary as needed

Duchesse Potatoes:
9 russet potatoes
½ pound butter
4 ounces cream
3 egg yolks
3 tablespoons chives
salt, pepper, and nutmeg to taste

Shepherd's Pie Filling:
1½ pounds lamb leg, small diced into ½-inch cubes
3 cups flour
4 ounces celery root, diced into ½-inch cubes
4 ounces carrot, diced into ½-inch cubes
4 ounces onion, diced into ½-inch cubes
1 cup Madeira wine
½ gallon lamb stock
2 tablespoons rosemary
2 tablespoons thyme
4 tablespoons parsley
bouquet garni

Filling procedure:
Coat meat lightly in flour; sear each side at a time or until evenly browned. Take meat out, add celery root, carrot, and onion, and sweat off. Add seared meat back with vegetables and deglaze with Madeira. Scrape bottom of pot and add stock. Simmer stew until meat is tender; add bouquet garni. If sauce not thick, strain meat and reduce the sauce. Add meat, herbs, seasoning; set aside to cool.

Dough procedure:
Pulse flour, salt, and cold butter in processor to consistency of corn meal; add ice water slowly until dough comes together (30 seconds). On floured surface, gently form into rectangle ½-inch thick. Cover with floured cloth, chill until firm, remove from cooler, roll out thinly, and cut to size.

Dock dough (by pricking holes in dough with the tines of a fork approximately 1 inch apart) and place in mold. Add lamb filling. Top with dough; prick twice with fork. Bake in preheated 350°F for approximately 15 to 20 minutes until golden crisp. Add egg wash towards end of baking for color and flavor. Remove from oven; hold till service.

Duchesse Potatoes:
Simmer potatoes in salted water; melt butter and cream; once done, food mill the potatoes and add cream. Mix in egg, chive, and seasoning; store in cloth pastry bag with star tip and pipe on plate to serve.

Note: *Serve with Duchesse Potatoes, steamed carrots, and beets.*

Rack of Lamb
4 to 6 Servings

1½ tablespoons kosher salt
2 tablespoons minced fresh
   rosemary leaves
3 garlic cloves, minced

½ cup Dijon mustard
1 tablespoon balsamic vinegar
2 racks of lamb, French cut

In the bowl of a food processor fitted with a steel blade, process the salt, rosemary, and garlic until they are finely minced. Add the mustard and balsamic vinegar and process for 1 minute.

Place the lamb in a roasting or sheet pan with the ribs curving down and coat the tops with the mustard mixture. May be refrigerated at this point. Allow to stand for 1 hour at room temperature.

Roast the lamb at 450°F for 25 to 30 minutes for medium rare. Remove from oven and cover with foil. Allow to sit 10 minutes, then cut into individual ribs and serve.

Note: *"Frenching" refers to scraping the meat off the tips of the bones. Ask your butcher to leave ⅛ inch of fat on the meat.*

Roasted Lamb Chops
with Charmoula and Asparagus
4 Servings

Charmoula:
1 tablespoon cumin seeds
1½ cups fresh Italian parsley leaves, lightly packed
½ cup fresh mint leaves, lightly packed
½ cup fresh cilantro leaves, lightly packed
2 large garlic cloves
3 teaspoons sweet smoked paprika or sweet Hungarian paprika
1 teaspoon coarse kosher salt
¼ teaspoon cayenne pepper
6 tablespoons extra-virgin olive oil, divided
1 tablespoon fresh lemon juice

8 lamb loin chops, about 3 pounds

1 tablespoon butter
1 tablespoon extra-virgin olive oil
1½ pounds thin asparagus, trimmed, peeled, tops cut into 3-inch-long
   pieces, stalks cut into ½-inch pieces
3 tablespoons chopped shallot
1 teaspoon finely grated lemon peel

Charmoula:
Heat small skillet over medium heat. Add cumin seeds and toast until ar-
omatic and slightly darker, stirring occasionally, about 2 minutes. Transfer
to processor. Add parsley, mint, cilantro, garlic, paprika, salt, and cayenne
pepper to processor. Pulse until coarse paste forms. With machine running, gradually add 4 tablespoons oil. Transfer 2 tablespoons charmoula
to small bowl; whisk in lemon juice and remaining 2 tablespoons oil.
Cover and chill to serve with lamb.

Lamb:
Transfer remaining charmoula to large re-sealable plastic bag. Add lamb
chops; seal bag and turn to coat well. Chill at least 4 hours and up to 24
hours. Let lamb and charmoula sauce in bowl stand at room temperature
1 hour.

Line rimmed baking sheet with foil. Place rack on prepared baking sheet. Place lamb on rack and sprinkle with salt and pepper. Roast at 500°F until thermometer inserted into center registers 130° for medium rare, about 13 minutes. Transfer lamb to platter. Tent with foil and let rest 5 minutes. Meanwhile, melt butter with 1 tablespoon oil in heavy large skillet over high heat. Add asparagus and sauté until tender, stirring often, about 3 minutes. Add shallot and lemon peel. Sauté 1 minute. Season to taste with salt and pepper.

Place 2 lamb chops on each of 4 plates. Divide asparagus among plates. Drizzle lamb and asparagus with charmoula sauce, passing remaining sauce alongside.

Roasted Rosemary Lamb
6 to 8 Servings

1 leg of lamb, 6 to 6½ pounds
½ cup minced fresh parsley
2 tablespoons minced fresh rosemary
¼ cup vegetable oil, divided

4 cloves garlic, finely chopped
½ teaspoon ground cardamom
salt and pepper to taste
1 cup Chablis or other dry white wine

Make several deep slits on outside of lamb; set aside. Combine parsley, rosemary, 1 tablespoon oil, garlic, and cardamom. Stuff slits with herb mixture. Brush outside of lamb with 1 tablespoon of oil and sprinkle with salt and pepper. Place lamb in roasting pan; bake at 450°F for 5 to 10 minutes. Combine remaining 2 tablespoons oil and wine; set aside. Reduce heat to 350°; bake lamb for 2½ hours, or until meat thermometer reaches 160°, basting occasionally with wine mixture. Let stand 10 minutes before carving.

Rosemary-Orange Lamb Chops
4 Servings

½ cup olive oil
¼ cup red wine
1 tablespoon brown sugar
½ teaspoon minced garlic

¼ cup fresh orange juice
2 tablespoons chopped fresh
  rosemary
4 to 8 lamb chops

In a small bowl, combine olive oil, wine, brown sugar, garlic, orange juice, and rosemary. Pour over lamb chops. Cover and marinate in refrigerator at least 6 hours, turning occasionally. Grill or broil at medium heat for 5 minutes per side for medium rare.

Grilled Lamb Shish Kebab
6 Servings

Marinade:
½ cup wine vinegar
1½ cups vegetable oil
¾ cup low-sodium soy sauce
¼ cup Worcestershire sauce
2 tablespoons dry mustard
2 teaspoons salt
2 teaspoons chopped parsley
1 tablespoon black pepper
1 clove garlic, crushed
⅓ cup lemon juice
1 teaspoon chopped lemon rind

3 pounds lamb, cubed
1 red onion, cut into wedges
1 red pepper, cut into squares
1 yellow pepper, cut into
  squares

Blend marinade ingredients in blender for 5 to 8 minutes. Pour marinade over meat in baking dish and refrigerate for 4 hours. Place meat and vegetables, alternating, on kebabs. Grill over medium heat for 15 to 20 minutes until cooked through.

Moussaka
12 to 14 Servings

2 large eggplants, about 3 pounds
1 cup butter, melted
1 cup Italian seasoned breadcrumbs
2 large onions, chopped
1 large clove garlic, crushed
¼ cup olive oil
2 pounds ground lamb or chuck
1 28-ounce can Italian-style tomatoes, not drained and chopped
1 15-ounce can tomato sauce
2 teaspoons salt
1 teaspoon dried whole oregano
½ teaspoon dried whole basil
¼ teaspoon dried whole thyme
¼ teaspoon freshly ground pepper
salt and pepper
Béchamel sauce
½ cup Parmesan cheese, grated

Béchamel Sauce:
½ cup butter, melted
½ cup flour
4 cups half-and-half
¼ teaspoon salt
¼ teaspoon ground white pepper
4 egg yolks

Peel eggplants, and cut into ¼-inch thick slices. Brush eggplant slices with butter; dredge in breadcrumbs. Place on a rack in a broiler pan; broil 4 inches from heat 2 minutes on each side or until golden brown. Set aside. Sauté onion and garlic in oil in a large skillet until tender. Add meat, and cook until browned, stirring to crumble meat. Drain well; return meat mixture to skillet. Add tomatoes, tomato sauce, salt, oregano, basil, thyme, and freshly ground pepper. Bring to a boil; cover, reduce heat, and simmer 2 hours, stirring occasionally. Place one-third of reserved eggplant slices in buttered 15×11×2½-inch baking dish or two 11×7×1½-inch baking dishes. Sprinkle with salt and pepper. Cover eggplant slices with half of meat sauce. Repeat layers, ending with eggplant slices. Top with Béchamel Sauce. Sprinkle with Parmesan cheese. Bake at 350° for 35 to 45 minutes or until golden brown. Serve immediately.

Béchamel Sauce:
Combine butter and flour in a large pot. Cook over medium heat, stirring constantly, until roux is caramel colored, 20 to 30 minutes. Gradually stir in half-and-half, cook, stirring constantly, until mixture thickens. Add salt and pepper. Add egg yolks, one at a time, stirring with a wire whisk. Cook 1 minute, stirring constantly. Yields 4½ cups sauce.

Ɪꞷultry

Chicken Marsala
2 Servings

Giuseppe's Restaurant *has been serving Italian specialties to St. Louisans for more than 80 years. Originating downtown in 1927 as Rosario's, and then Roses's, the restaurant was moved to its current location on Grand and Meramec and changed its name to Guiseppe's. It remains a favorite dining spot, as well as offering full catering services.*

2 boneless, skinless chicken breast
   halves (about 6 ounces each)
⅓ cup plus 1½ tablespoons
   flour, divided
6 tablespoons butter

¾ cup Marsala wine
½ cup beef broth
1¼ cups sliced mushrooms
salt, a pinch
ground black pepper

Pound chicken between sheets of plastic wrap until uniformly thick, about ⅓ inch. In a shallow bowl or plate, dredge chicken in ⅓ cup flour, shaking to remove excess flour.

In a large skillet over medium-high heat, melt butter. Be careful not to burn the butter. Add chicken to the pan. Sprinkle the remaining 1½ tablespoons flour into the butter, around the chicken; use a fork or small whisk to gently stir in flour. Cook chicken until golden brown, about 2 minutes per side. Add Marsala wine and bring liquid to a boil; cook until it has reduced by half, about 4 minutes. Add beef broth and cook 5 to 6 minutes more, turning chicken once. Add mushrooms, reduce heat to medium low and continue cooking until mushrooms are cooked through and sauce has thickened, 3 to 4 minutes. Season to taste with salt and pepper.

Arrange chicken on serving plates; pour sauce and mushrooms over chicken.

Chicken with Tarragon Cream
6 Servings

1 14½-ounce can chicken broth
1¼ cups water
3 sprigs tarragon
1 sprig parsley
4 large, skinless, boneless chicken
   breast halves, about 1½ pounds
2 tablespoons butter
2 tablespoons flour

1 cup whipping cream
¾ cup milk
¼ teaspoon fresh ground
   pepper
⅛ teaspoon salt
1 egg yolk, beaten
2 tablespoons grated
   Parmesan cheese
2 tablespoons snipped fresh
   tarragon

In a large skillet, bring broth, water, tarragon, and parsley sprigs to boiling. Add chicken. Reduce heat and simmer, covered, about 12 minutes. Remove chicken and cool slightly. Discard cooking liquid. Chop chicken and transfer to a medium bowl. Meanwhile, in a medium saucepan, melt butter and stir in flour. Add whipping cream and milk. Cook and stir until slightly thickened and bubbly. Add about half of the mixture, plus salt and pepper to chicken. Stir to blend. Spread chicken mixture evenly in an oven-safe 1½-quart au gratin dish. Gradually stir remaining cream mixture into beaten egg yolk. Stir in cheese and snipped tarragon. Spread evenly on chicken mixture. Bake, uncovered, at 500°F for 12 minutes or until top is brown and bubbly around the edges.

Ente Mit Kirschen (Duck with Cherries)
4 to 6 Servings

1 5-pound duck
1 15-ounce can pitted bing cherries
1 cup red wine

½ cup orange juice
1 ounce kirsch
2 tablespoons cornstarch

Season duck lightly and place on a rack in an open roasting pan. Roast breast side up at 325°F for 2½ to 3 hours, or until flesh on leg feels tender to the touch. Remove to a hot platter and keep warm. Pour off all but 3 tablespoons of fat from the pan. Add cherries, wine, orange juice, and kirsch and blend well. Combine 2 tablespoons of cornstarch with a little cold water and add to the cherry mixture. Cook and stir until smooth and thickened. Serve the sauce alongside the duck.

Chicken and Artichoke Hearts
6 Servings

6 skinless, boneless chicken breasts
1 teaspoon salt
½ teaspoon pepper
½ teaspoon paprika
8 tablespoons butter or margarine
3 cups sliced mushrooms

2 tablespoons flour
1 teaspoon tarragon
½ cup dry sherry
1 14-ounce can chicken stock
9 ounces marinated artichoke
    hearts, drained
chopped parsley for garnish

Pat chicken dry. Sprinkle with salt, pepper, and paprika. Sauté in 4 tablespoons butter until browned. Transfer chicken to a 9×13-inch pan. Sauté mushrooms in 4 tablespoons butter. Sprinkle on flour and tarragon. Add sherry and chicken stock. Bring to a boil. Simmer 3 to 4 minutes, stirring constantly. Arrange artichoke hearts around chicken in pan. Pour sauce over chicken and bake at 350°F for 40 to 45 minutes until chicken is done. Sprinkle with parsley and serve.

Chicken Enchiladas
4 to 6 Servings

1 rotisserie chicken, shredded or 4 to
    5 boneless chicken breasts,
    cooked and shredded
1 10½-ounce can cream of
    chicken soup
1 8-ounce container sour cream
1 package taco seasoning

½ package of frozen spinach,
    thawed (optional)
½ 15-ounce can corn (optional)
1 15-ounce can enchilada sauce
10 to 12 flour tortillas
1 8-ounce package of shredded
    Mexican style cheese

Filling:
Combine chicken in a bowl with soup, sour cream, taco seasoning, and if using, spinach and corn.

Assembling the Enchiladas:
Pour enough enchilada sauce to coat the bottom of 9×13-inch pan. Spoon filling evenly into tortillas and roll. Place tortillas in pan and repeat until filling is gone. Pour the rest of the enchilada sauce evenly over the rolled tortillas. Evenly sprinkle the cheese over the enchiladas. Cover with aluminum foil and bake at 375°F for 30 to 35 minutes until cheese is melted.

Stir-Fry Chicken and Broccoli
4 to 6 Servings

2 tablespoons vegetable oil
1¼ pounds skinless boneless chicken
 breasts, cut into 1-inch pieces
2 cups broccoli florets
½ pound fresh mushrooms, sliced
4 scallions, cut into 1-inch pieces

3 tablespoons soy sauce
3 tablespoons dry sherry
½ teaspoon ground ginger
1 teaspoon cornstarch dissolved
 in 2 tablespoons water
1 teaspoon sesame oil

In a large frying pan or wok, heat oil over medium-high heat. Add chicken and stir-fry for 3 minutes, until chicken becomes opaque. Remove with a slotted spoon and set aside. Add broccoli, stir-fry 1 to 2 minutes. Add mushrooms, scallions, soy sauce, sherry, ginger, and sesame oil. Stir-fry 2 more minutes. Add dissolved cornstarch and reserved chicken. Cook until heated through and sauce has thickened. Serve over rice.

Greek Chicken
6 Servings

Sauce:
½ cup olive oil
⅓ cup lemon juice
1 garlic clove, crushed
½ teaspoon oregano
pepper
½ teaspoon salt

honey
orange slices
6 to 8 boneless, skinless
chicken breasts

Mix sauce ingredients together. Marinate chicken in the sauce for at least 6 hours. Drain off marinade and bake at 350°F for 40 to 45 minutes. Drizzle generously with honey and top with orange slices in the last half of cooking.

Grecian Chicken Bundles
4 Servings

4 boneless, skinless chicken
  breast halves
½ cup dry white wine
2 tablespoons olive oil
2 cloves garlic, minced
½ teaspoon grated lemon zest
2 tablespoons fresh lemon juice
½ teaspoon dried dill weed
½ teaspoon ground white pepper

1 sheet puff pastry, thawed, or 12
  sheets phyllo dough, thawed
4 to 6 tablespoons butter,
  melted (only for phyllo)
2 tablespoons dry bread
  crumbs (only for phyllo)
4 ounces crumbled herbed
  feta cheese
1 egg lightly beaten with 1
  tablespoon water (only for
  puff pastry)

Pound each chicken breast to ½ inch thick. In a large re-sealable plastic bag, mix together wine, olive oil, garlic, lemon zest and juice, dill and white pepper. Place pounded chicken into bag; seal and refrigerate for several hours. Heat large skillet over medium heat and spray with non-stick cooking spray. Remove chicken from marinade and cook in skillet for 3 minutes per side or until lightly browned. Remove from skillet and drain on paper towels. Allow to cool slightly.

If Puff Pastry is used:
On a flat, floured surface, roll out one sheet of puff pastry into a 12-inch square. Cut into four 6-inch squares with a pizza wheel, sharp knife, or kitchen scissors. Brush with egg wash to seal pastry. Place 1 tablespoon feta cheese in center of pastry, top with a chicken breast, and then another tablespoon of feta. Brush edges of pastry square with egg wash. Join 4 points of pastry over chicken and pinch to seal seams well. Place on parchment-paper lined baking sheet. Brush tops with remaining egg wash. Cover tightly with plastic wrap. Refrigerate for at least 30 minutes or as long as overnight. Bake at 375°F for 25 to 30 minutes or until golden brown and puffed.

If Phyllo Dough is used:
On flat surface, layer 3 phyllo sheets, brushing each with melted butter and sprinkling breadcrumbs between each layer. Place 1 tablespoon feta cheese in center of pastry, top with a slightly cooled chicken breast, and then another tablespoon of feta. Enclose chicken in phyllo by twisting the top like the end of a candy wrapper or folding like a package and placing seam-side

down on a parchment-paper lined baking sheet. Repeat procedure with remaining phyllo dough, chicken, and cheese to make 4 bundles. Bake at 375°F for 23 to 25 minutes or until phyllo is golden brown. Cool slightly before serving. To prepare these ahead, brush tops liberally with butter and wrap tightly with plastic wrap before refrigerating.

Note: *Great for dinner parties!*

Slow Cook French Chicken
4 to 5 Servings

2 carrots, sliced
2 onions, sliced
2 celery stalks with leaves, cut in
 1-inch pieces
1 3-pound broiler/fryer chicken,
 or chicken pieces

1 teaspoon salt
½ teaspoon coarse black pepper
½ cup white wine or chicken
 broth
½ teaspoon dry basil

In a Crockpot, add ½ cup water. Add carrots, onion, and celery. Add chicken. Top with salt, pepper, and liquid. Sprinkle basil over top. Cook on low for 8 to 10 hours or on high for 3 to 5 hours.

Swiss Chicken Casserole
4 to 6 Servings

4 cups chicken or turkey cooked,
 cut into pieces
1 medium onion, chopped
3 to 4 ribs celery, chopped
2½ cups seasoned croutons
2 cups grated Swiss cheese

1½ cups mayonnaise
1 cup sour cream
1 package dry buttermilk ranch
 dressing mix
½ cup toasted slivered
 almonds

Combine chicken, onion, celery, croutons, and Swiss cheese in bowl. In a separate bowl, combine mayonnaise, sour cream, and ranch mix. Combine with chicken mixture and mix well. Spoon mixture into a 2-quart oblong dish. Bake at 325°F for 40 minutes then sprinkle top with almonds and bake additional 10 minutes.

Chilaquiles
4 Servings

4 boneless, skinless chicken breasts	*Tomato Sauce:*
1 onion, quartered	2 onions, small dice
2 cloves of garlic	1 garlic clove, small dice
	1 tablespoon olive oil
4 round corn tortillas	12 tomatoes peeled, seeded,
1 cup vegetable oil	and puréed
	1 tablespoon cilantro, minced
1 cup sour cream diluted with	2 tablespoons Tabasco sauce,
small amount of water	optional
½ pound Manchego cheese	salt and pepper to taste
½ pound mozzarella cheese	

Cook chicken with a little water, pinch of salt, the quartered onion, and 2 cloves of garlic. Cover and slowly cook over medium heat. Cook until the chicken is cooked through and tender. Put chicken on plate to cool. Shred it into very small pieces with your hands or a fork.

Tomato Sauce:
Sauté the chopped onion and garlic in the olive oil. When the onion is translucent, add the tomatoes, cilantro, and optional Tabasco sauce. Cook over medium heat for 10 minutes. Season with salt and pepper.

Add the shredded chicken to the sauce, lower heat, and cook for a few minutes so the shredded chicken can absorb some of the flavors from the tomato sauce. Don't let the sauce cook too long or the chicken will be dry.

Cut the tortillas into ½-inch strips. Slice the cheeses into thin slices. Fry the corn tortillas in ½ inch vegetable oil over medium-high heat in skillet. When they are crisp, remove and place on sheets of paper towels to remove excess oil.

Assemble the chilaquiles like a lasagna: a layer of tortillas, a layer of chicken in sauce, a few dollops of the sour cream, and a layer of cheese. Repeat all layers again and finish with cheese and some sour cream. Bake at 325°F for approximately 45 minutes.

Note: *Muy Bueno!*

Duckling with Green Peppercorn Sauce
4 Servings

1 5- to 6-pound duckling, dressed
½ teaspoon salt
⅛ teaspoon pepper
1 onion, peeled
6 fresh parsley sprigs

Green Peppercorn Sauce:
1 tablespoon minced shallots
  or onion
2 tablespoons butter, melted
⅓ cup cognac
½ cup whipping cream
1 tablespoon whole green
  peppercorns
1 tablespoon Dijon mustard

Remove giblets from duckling. Rinse duckling with cold water and pat dry. Prick skin with a fork at 2-inch intervals. Sprinkle cavity with salt and pepper. Stuff with onion and parsley.

Place duckling, breast side up, on a lightly greased rack in a roasting pan. Insert meat thermometer in thigh, making sure it does not touch bone.

Bake at 450°F for 20 minutes. Shield wings and drumsticks with aluminum foil to prevent excessive browning. Reduce heat to 325°, and bake 2 hours and 15 minutes, or until thermometer reaches 185°. If duckling starts to brown too much, cover loosely with foil. Remove duckling to a serving platter. Serve with green peppercorn sauce.

Green Peppercorn Sauce:
In a small saucepan sauté shallots in butter over medium heat until tender. Place cognac in a small long-handled saucepan; heat until warm, do not boil. Remove from heat. Ignite with long match. When flames subside, add whipping cream and stir well. Cook over medium heat 3 minutes or until slightly thickened. Stir in sautéed shallots, peppercorns, and mustard; reduce heat and simmer 1 minute.

Seafood

Grilled Lemongrass Prawns with Garlic Noodles
2 Servings

Recipe provided by P.F. Chang's China Bistro.

Lemongrass Sauce:
1 stick butter, unsalted
1 ounce olive oil
1 tablespoon minced fresh
   lemongrass
½ teaspoon Shaoxing rice wine
   (can substitute dry sherry)
½ teaspoon minced fresh ginger
1 teaspoon minced fresh garlic
½ tablespoon seeded and
   minced jalapeno
1 teaspoon soy sauce
1 scallion, green part only,
   finely chopped
½ teaspoon sesame oil
½ teaspoon lemon zest
1 teaspoon sea salt

Prawns:
I pound large prawns, shell on,
   split down back side
   (butterfly), and deveined
1 lemon wedge (for garnish)

Garlic Noodles:
2 tablespoons butter, unsalted
1 ounce olive oil
½ teaspoon minced fresh garlic
½ teaspoon minced fresh shallot
8 ounces Chinese egg noodles
   (can substitute linguine pasta
   and follow directions on package)
kosher salt and black pepper

Lemongrass Sauce:
Combine all sauce ingredients in a small saucepan, and simmer on low heat for 1 minute. Let cool slightly; pour half the sauce over prawns and let marinate for 1 hour. Reserve remaining sauce to drizzle over grilled prawns.

Garlic Noodles:
Place butter, olive oil, garlic and shallots in a small saucepan and simmer for 3 minutes on very low heat. Reserve. Place Noodles in boiling water and boil for 2 minutes until just done. Drain well; do not rinse. Add seasoned butter to the noodles and toss well. Add kosher salt and black pepper to taste.

Prawns:
On a hot grill, place prawns flesh (butterfly) side down for 1 minute. Turn over the prawns and cook on other side until just done.

Place garlic noodles on serving dish. Place grilled prawns over garlic noodles and pour remaining lemongrass sauce over grilled prawns. Garnish with lemon wedge.

Margarita Shrimp
4 Servings

Rob Marbs *is the Executive Chef at* Glen Echo Country Club. *Chef Ron began his culinary career as a teenager and quickly progressed as a chef in his twenties. In his career, he has prepared meals for a wide variety of events and people, including two former presidents of the United States, the president of Ireland, and the president of Poland.*

12 jumbo shrimp	½ chipotle pepper, minced
olive oil	(optional; will add heat)
1 teaspoon minced garlic	1 tablespoon chopped cilantro
2 ounces tequila, to deglaze	2 limes, squeezed
1 tomato, seeded and diced	1 avocado, diced
¼ red onion, diced	shredded lettuce

Sauté shrimp in olive oil on medium heat until opaque and cooked through. Add garlic, sauté for 30 seconds. Pull skillet off heat (for safety reasons), and add tequila. Put back on the burner and flambé tequila. Set aside to cool. Put shrimp, tomato, onion, chipotle pepper, cilantro, and lime juice in a bowl. Toss and let marinate for 15 minutes. Gently fold in avocado and serve in bowl or glass on a bed of shredded lettuce.

Paella Mixta
4 to 6 Servings

Chef Grace Dinsmoor *is passionate about Spanish cuisine, and this is one of her favorite recipes. Celebrating ten years in business,* Modesto *is known for its delicious tapas, attentive service, and fun atmosphere.*

2 cups strong chicken broth
1 whole chicken, cut into pieces
salt
6 tablespoons olive oil
2 green peppers, chopped
1 onion, chopped
2 cloves garlic, minced
2 fresh tomatoes, skinned and chopped
2 pimentos, homemade or imported, chopped
3 teaspoons paprika

¼ teaspoon saffron
2 cups bomba rice
1½ pounds chorizo, sliced
1½ cups dry white wine
freshly ground pepper
6 to 10 clams
1 pound shrimp, deveined and peeled to tail
1 tablespoon minced parsley for garnish

In a small saucepan over medium heat, warm the chicken broth until very hot. Sprinkle the chicken pieces with salt. Heat the oil in a paella pan and fry the chicken until golden on all sides. Remove to a warm platter.

Add the green peppers, onion, and garlic and sauté until the green pepper is tender. Stir in the tomatoes and pimentos and cook, uncovered, 10 minutes more. Add the paprika and saffron. Add the rice and chorizo, and stir to coat well with the oil. Add the hot broth and the wine, and season to taste with salt and pepper. Boil over medium heat, uncovered and stirring occasionally, for about 7 minutes until the rice is no longer soupy, but not very dry.

Arrange the chicken pieces, the clams, and the shrimp over the rice and place in the oven, uncovered. Bake at 425°F for 15 minutes or until the liquid is absorbed but the rice is still al dente. Remove from the oven and let sit, lightly covered with foil, for 5 minutes more. Sprinkle with the parsley and serve.

Pan Roasted Alaskan Halibut Fillet with Morels, Spring Vegetables, and Morel Jus
1 Serving

Oceano Bistro *is St Louis' premiere fresh fish bistro that partners with fisherman, farmers, and food artisans to bring fresh, innovative and enticing foods to St. Louis. Executive Chef* Jon Lowe *has been a chef for about 13 years and describes his cuisine as upscale comfort food.*

Halibut:
4 to 6 ounces halibut
2 tablespoons olive oil
⅛ cup morel mushrooms, fresh or
  rehydrated
1 ounce green beans, blanched
  and sliced
1 ounce yellow wax beans,
  blanched and sliced
1 ounce asparagus, blanched and sliced
2 tablespoons English peas, shucked and blanched
2 ounces vegetable stock
1 tablespoon unsalted butter
1 ounce morel jus
salt and pepper to taste

Morel Jus:
⅛ cup morel mushrooms
3 tablespoons vegetable stock
2 fresh thyme sprigs
1 teaspoon sliced garlic
2 tablespoons olive oil
salt and pepper to taste

Halibut:
Heat a sauté pan until almost smoking; season fish with salt and pepper. Add 1 tablespoon olive oil to the pan and carefully add fish; sauté until brown and then turn and continue to cook approximately 2 to 3 minutes total; remove when medium (the fish should be white, flaky, and moist throughout). In the same pan, add the remaining oil and mushrooms, beans, asparagus, and peas; sauté briefly and then add stock and butter. Reduce heat to low and season with salt and pepper.

Morel Jus:
Roast ingredients in 350°F oven for 8 to 10 minutes. After roasting, purée in blender with olive oil and season with salt and pepper. Serve fish over vegetables with the jus around.

Pan Seared Sea Scallop with Fava Bean Ravioli, Tomato Jam, and Micro Greens
10 Servings

Chef Kevin Storm *is the Executive Chef at* Bellerive Country Club.

Sea Scallops:
10 dry pack U-10 sea scallops
fresh ground black pepper
sea salt
olive oil

Fava Bean Ravioli:
1 pound fava beans, blanched
   and cleaned
2 tablespoons olive oil
¼ cup chopped onion
2 tablespoons chopped shallot
1 teaspoon chopped garlic
1 cup chicken or vegetable stock
½ cup 40% cream
fresh grated nutmeg to taste
fresh ground black pepper to taste
sea salt to taste

Pasta Dough for Ravioli:
2 cups flour
1 egg
6 egg yolks
1 tablespoon milk
2 tablespoons olive oil

Parsley Oil:
4 bunches parsley, cleaned,
   blanched and shocked in
   ice water
2 cups olive oil

Tomato Jam:
5 tomatoes concasse
   (peeled, seeded, and chopped)
1 tablespoon chopped tarragon
½ cup rice wine vinegar
1 tablespoon sugar
1 tablespoon chopped shallot
½ teaspoon chopped garlic
1 tablespoon olive oil
fresh ground black pepper
sea salt to taste

Corn Sauce:
3 ears of sweet corn, cut off cob
1 branch basil
½ cup corn or vegetable stock
¼ cup fish fumet
2 ounces 40% cream
½ ounce butter
fresh ground black pepper to taste
sea salt to taste

Micro Greens:
⅛ pound micro greens
1 teaspoon fresh lemon juice
1 teaspoon olive oil
sea salt fresh ground black
   pepper to taste

Sea Scallops:
Clean the scallops and lay on paper towels to pat dry. Season to taste with salt and pepper. Heat pan until smoking; add scallops and sear for about 2½ minutes per side.

Fava Bean Ravioli:
Sweat onions, shallots, and garlic until translucent. Add fava beans, cook for 2 minutes, then add stock, cooking until reduced until ½. Remove ½ of the fava beans, add cream, and reduce until thick sauce consistency; then purée. Add seasonings along with the other half of the fava beans. Adjust seasonings; cool and use for filling ravioli.

Pasta Dough for Ravioli:
Mix dough and let rest for 1 hour. Roll out to desired shape and cook in boiling salted water.

Tomato Jam:
Sweat shallot and garlic with olive oil. Add tomatoes, sugar, rice wine vinegar, and tarragon and simmer slowly until all liquid is gone and tomatoes have jam-like consistency. Adjust seasonings.

Corn Sauce:
Take corn, basil and stock—simmer and reduce by ½. Remove basil; then purée. Add fumet and reduce by ½ again. Add cream and reduce to sauce consistency. Mount with butter and adjust seasonings. Strain through fine chinoise (or very fine mesh strainer).

Parsley Oil:
Blend in blender. Let set one day before use.

Micro Greens:
Toss greens, lemon juice, olive oil, and salt and pepper together.

To Plate Dish:
Place ravioli in center of warm bowl. Place seared sea scallop on top of ravioli. Add 1 teaspoon of tomato jam of top of scallop. Place sauce around ravioli. A small bunch of tossed micro greens on top to finish. Drizzle parsley oil around edge of sauce.

Scallops with White Risotto, VerJus Reduction, and Micro Greens
6 to 8 Servings

Robust Wine Bar *creates an enjoyable and enriching food and wine experience that educates each guest, and encourages you to explore and rediscover a passion for life through truly experiencing what wine, food and hospitality are all about.* Chef Kris Janik *believes that being true to ingredients is important, and that one can be adventurous and traditional.*

VerJus Reduction:
2 bottles red verjus
2 sprigs fresh thyme
2 bay leaves
5 black peppercorns
1 quart cream

scallops (3-4 per serving)

White Risotto:
2 yellow onions
4 parsnips
4 ribs celery, preferably inner
    ribs (lighter in color
    and much sweeter)
olive oil
1 kilo arborio rice (see note)
(approximately) 3 cups white
    wine
3 quarts or so chicken
    stock, hot

VerJus Reduction:
In a sauce pot combine verjus, thyme, bay leaves, and peppercorns. Reduce by at least half over medium-high heat. When reduced, add the cream and reduce again by half. Strain, cool, and set aside.

White Risotto:
Peel the onions and parsnips and wash the celery. Small dice the onions, celery, and parsnips. In a rondeau, (see note), heat a good amount of the olive oil and sweat the vegetables for a few minutes—no color, just softening them. Add the rice, and more olive oil if needed to coat the rice, and continue to cook while stirring until the rice becomes a bit opaque. This helps even out liquid absorption so that the outside of the rice doesn't overcook, leaving the middle undercooked. Add the white wine and cook, stirring from time to time, until much of it has been absorbed. Add a ladle or two of chicken stock and continue cooking until it is absorbed. Keep doing this until the chicken stock is used up. If you are going to serve

this right away, go ahead and cook the rice until you are satisfied with the texture, roughly 18 minutes; season with salt and mound with butter. If you are serving this dish later, only cook the rice for about 12 minutes and wait to season and do not add the butter; spread it out on a sheet tray and let cool.

Scallops:
Clean the scallops of the smooth muscle located on the side of the abductor. It is about an inch long, and looks similar to the rest of the scallop, but is indeed not too great to eat. It gets very rubbery, but is great to throw in a pot with other fish bones. Or discard. Lightly pat dry; this helps with the Maillard reaction (see note) to give you a nice crispy texture. Season; I prefer salt only, but feel free to use pepper. Heat a heavy-bottom skillet that will comfortably fit the amount of scallops, or cook in batches or two pans. You want a good amount of residual heat stored so that when the scallops hit the pan, the pan can bounce back from the cold and cook—or you could end up with a scallop with no textural contrast and poor color. Heat a few tablespoons of extra-virgin olive oil until you see just a bit of smoke, put the scallops in, and cook for about a minute. I prefer to finish them by either putting a good pat of butter in the pan and basting, or adding the butter then placing in a hot oven for just a couple minutes; do not turn them.

To Assemble:
Take a few tablespoons of the verjus reduction and a couple tablespoons cream and heat in a saucepan. Let this reduce a bit then turn the heat down very low, just enough to keep it warm. With a whisk, slowly add butter and (probably 2 or 3 tablespoons total, but just a bit at a time) all the while whisking until the shade turns from a sort of bright purple to a pastel light magenta and it has a nice sheen to it. Season with salt. For the risotto, add as much as you'd like or need to a deep-sided skillet and heat gently, adding enough stock to loosen it all up, and cook until the rice is done but still has a nice tooth to it, or cook to your liking. Season with salt and mound with butter. In a warmed bowl put some of the risotto in, some of the sauce around the rice. Carefully remove the scallops with a fish spatula (not tongs!) and place atop rice. Place greens on top of the scallops and enjoy.

Note: *A kilo is approximately 2.2 pounds. A rondeau is a large, round, relatively shallow pan that allows steam to disperse quickly, usually stainless steel with two loop handles. The Maillard reaction is similar to caramelization and is a form of non-enzymatic browning. It is important in the preparation and presentation of many foods.*

Roasted Corn Crab Cakes
10 to 12 Servings

Matthew Unger, *CSW, is the Executive Chef at the* Missouri Athletic Club West.

½ ounce cilantro
½ ounce celery leaf
1 ounce small diced red bell pepper
1 tablespoon lemon or lime juice
¼ cup Dijon mustard
2 cups mayonnaise
1 teaspoon Old Bay Seasoning

2 cups breadcrumbs
1 cup corn (fire roasted off of the cob is preferred, otherwise use frozen corn roasted in a broiler for 5 minutes)
2 pounds lump crab meat

Mix cilantro, celery leaf, bell pepper, juice, mustard, mayonnaise, Old Bay seasoning, breadcrumbs, and corn into a large bowl. Gently fold in crab meat. Portion into 2-ounce discs. Cook in nonstick pan for 3 to 4 minutes on each side over medium heat.

Note: *These can be served with a number of different sauces. Tartar, cocktail, and rémoulade are some obvious choices, but you may want to try salsa as well. We serve ours with our Chipotle Ranch Sauce.*

Seafood Paella
6 Servings

Bernard Pilon, *CEC, was a chef in Montreal and Maryland before arriving in St. Louis in 1995. He has been the Executive Chef at* Norwood Hills Country Club *since 2000, and won the Chef of the Year Award in 2007. His family includes his wife Stephanie, his daughter Olivia, and his son Brian.*

1 pound shrimp (about 16 to 20)	½ pound firm white fish
2 medium tomatoes, chopped	⅛ teaspoon saffron
small bunch parsley	½ medium onion
3 sprigs of thyme	3 garlic cloves
½ pound squid, cut into rings	1½ cups short grain rice
1 pound mussels	salt and pepper

Peel and devein shrimp. Put shrimp shells in pot with tomatoes, parsley, thyme, and water to cover (about 8 cups). Simmer 30 minutes. Strain.

Cook squid in simmering broth 30 minutes. Remove.
Cook mussels in simmering broth 5 minutes. Remove.
Cook shrimp in simmering broth 5 minutes. Remove.
Cook fish in simmering broth 5 minutes. Remove.
Stir saffron into broth.

Cook onions and garlic in paella pan. Add rice and stir for 2 to 3 minutes. Add 6 cups broth to pan and simmer on stove. Put all seafood in pan. Cover and bake at 300°F for 15 to 20 minutes.

Seared Tuna with Oriental Citrus Sauce
6 Servings

Chef Jeffrey Conner is the executive chef at Bogey Hills Country Club. He has enjoyed the culinary field for seventeen years, and takes great pleasure in bringing enjoyment to people through food. He has been happily married for twelve years, and is the proud father of a great seven-year-old boy.

Sauce:
2½ cups fresh orange juice
3 tablespoons fresh lemon juice
2 tablespoons fresh lime juice
¾ cup soy sauce
1 tablespoon balsamic vinegar
1 tablespoon Asian sesame oil
⅓ cup chopped peeled fresh
   ginger root

3 tablespoons vegetable oil
6 6-ounce tuna steaks
   (1-inch thick)
2 cups sesame seeds

In a large saucepan, combine orange juice, lemon juice, lime juice, soy sauce, balsamic vinegar, sesame oil, and ginger root. Simmer for 15 minutes. Pour sauce through a fine sieve into a bowl and set aside.

In a large non-stick skillet, heat vegetable oil over moderately high heat until hot, but not smoking. Coat 2 tuna steaks with sesame seeds and sear 1 minute on each side, transferring to a baking sheet. Coat and sear remaining 4 tuna steaks in batches in same manner.

Cook tuna in middle of oven at 400°F, 3 minutes for medium rare. Cut each tuna steak into 4 slices and arrange slices, cut side up, on 6 plates. Pour about ¼ cup sauce over tuna on each plate.

Tilapia with Beurre Blanc Aux Champignon
6 Servings

The Crossing *is an upscale French-American restaurant located in Clayton, Missouri. The setting is intimate and the eclectic menu features anything from game to pasta to seafood.* Jim Fiala *is the chef and owner of* The Crossing, *and his top priority is quality control; he believes that every meal should be a great meal.*

1 large shallot, peeled and sliced
10 button mushrooms, sliced
2 large portobello mushrooms, sliced
10 shiitake mushrooms, sliced
¼ bottle of dry vermouth

1 bottle of Chablis
¾ pound butter
salt and pepper to taste
extra-virgin olive oil as needed
6 tilapia fillets, fresh or frozen

In a 4-quart saucepot over low heat, sweat the sliced shallot with virgin olive oil. When the shallot is soft, turn the heat to high, add the mushrooms and stir. Cover mushrooms with a lid and stir every minute until the volume of mushrooms reduces by half. Be very careful not to burn the bottom of the pot. Season with a couple pinches of salt and pepper. Add the vermouth and Chablis. Reduce the wine to 75% of the starting volume.

Turn heat to medium, enough to keep mix hot while adding the butter. Cut the butter into small pieces. While the pot is on the medium flame, whisk butter gradually into the hot, but not boiling, wine. If the butter is added too quickly, the temperature of the sauce will fall too low and the sauce will "break." (If the sauce temperature is to high, 190°F and above, the sauce will "break." As long as there is a balance between the stream of butter and level of flame on the pot the sauce will hold). The sauce can be held for a couple of hours on a warm range top.

Cook the tilapia in the fashion you please. Take the completed sauce and ladle over the cooked tilapia.

Baja Fish Wrap/Tacos
Makes one wrap or 3 small tacos (corn or flour tortillas)

Alexander Pille *is chef at* Crescent Farms Golf Club.

¼ cup frozen corn
1 tablespoon sugar
1 tablespoon black pepper
8-ounce grouper, cod, tilapia or any
  white fish (skinless, boneless)
1 12-inch flour tortilla or 3 6-inch corn
  or flour tortillas
1 cup shredded lettuce
¼ cup diced tomato
¼ cup shredded Monteray
  Jack cheese
3 tablespoons sour cream

Creole Seasoning:
1 tablespoon paprika
1 tablespoon chili powder
1 tablespoon sugar
1 tablespoon seasoned salt
1 tablespoon black pepper
1 tablespoon thyme
pinch of onion powder, granulated
  garlic, cayenne

Spread corn on greased 9×9 pan and dust with 1 tablespoons each of
sugar and black pepper. Bake at 350 degrees for about 10 minutes. Cut
fish fillet into small strips and coat in Creole Seasoning. Sauté fish in
small amount of vegetable oil until brown on both sides. Warm tortilla
shells on grill or in microwave. Top each tortilla with lettuce, tomato,
cooked corn, cheese, sour cream, and fish. Wrap and serve.

Tilapia Provencale
4 Servings

Bernard Pilon, *CEC, was a chef in Montreal and Maryland before arriving in St. Louis in 1995. He has been the Executive Chef at* Norwood Hills Country Club *since 2000, and won the Chef of the Year Award in 2007. His family includes his wife Stephanie, his daughter Olivia, and his son Brian.*

4 Roma tomatoes	½ ounce capers
2 ounces kalamata olives	4 garlic cloves, minced
4 7-ounce Tilapia fillets	1 medium lemon
3 ounces olive oil	2 ounces white wine
½ medium zucchini, diced	salt, pepper, parsley to taste

Dice tomatoes, zucchini, and kalamata olives. Season tilipia with salt and pepper. Sear on medium heat. Cook 4 minutes on each side. In a separate pan, sauté in olive oil in this order: zucchini, garlic, tomato, kalamata olives, and capers for 2 to 3 minutes. Add wine and cook for 1 to 2 minutes. Add salt, pepper, and parsley, and serve.

Trout with Almonds
8 Servings

1 cup coarsely chopped,	1 teaspoon salt
blanched almonds	8 trout fillets, 8 to 10 ounces
¼ cup plus 2 tablespoons butter,	each
melted	¾ cup butter, divided
1½ tablespoons fresh lemon juice	lemon wedges
1 cup flour	fresh parsley

Sauté almonds in ¼ cup plus 2 tablespoons melted butter in a large skillet over medium heat until golden brown. Stir in lemon juice. Remove from heat and set aside. Combine flour and salt; dredge fillets in flour mixture. Melt ¼ cup plus 2 tablespoons butter in a large skillet over medium-high heat. Add half of fillets; cook 5 minutes on each side or until fish flakes easily when tested with a fork. Remove to a serving platter and keep warm. Repeat procedure with remaining ¼ cup plus 2 tablespoons butter and fillets. Sprinkle with reserved almond mixture. Garnish with lemon wedges dipped in minced parsley.

BBQ Shrimp
4 Servings

Creole Seasoning:
2 tablespoons salt
2 tablespoons pepper
1 tablespoon garlic powder
1 tablespoon onion powder
1 teaspoon dried thyme
¼ cup Hungarian sweet paprika
¼ teaspoon cayenne pepper
3 bay leaves, finely crushed

Shrimp:
15 to 20 large shrimp, peeled and deveined
2 tablespoons vegetable or peanut oil
1 to 2 tablespoons Creole seasoning, to taste
¼ cup Worcestershire sauce
1 bunch green onions, finely chopped

Seasoned Butter:
2 tablespoons paprika
¼ bunch parsley, minced
⅛ teaspoon dried thyme
1 tablespoon ground black pepper
1½ teaspoons white pepper
⅛ teaspoon cayenne pepper
2 dashes Tabasco sauce
2 tablespoons freshly squeezed lemon juice
1 tablespoon Worcestershire sauce
1 pound unsalted butter, softened

French bread for serving

Creole Seasoning:

Mix all Creole seasoning ingredients in a small bowl. Use 1 to 2 tablespoons for this recipe and store the rest in a sealed container.

Seasoned Butter:

Combine paprika, parsley, thyme, black pepper, white pepper, and cayenne pepper in a food processor and process until very fine. Combine dry ingredients with Tabasco sauce, lemon juice, Worcestershire sauce, and softened butter with an electric mixer on low speed until well blended. Place in refrigerator until very cold.

To prepare the shrimp, heat a large sauté pan over high heat and add oil. While pan is heating, season shrimp liberally with the Creole seasoning. Add shrimp to hot pan; do not move shrimp for 30 to 40 seconds. Stir shrimp constantly until almost cooked through, about 2 minutes. Add Worcestershire and green onions; remove from heat. Add seasoned butter to taste, using at least half, but up to the entire recipe amount, a little at a time, stirring quickly after each addition. Serve 4 or 5 shrimp per serving with warm French bread.

Creamed Grits with Sautéed Shrimp and Thyme
4 to 6 Servings

2 tablespoons olive oil
1 Vidalia onion, sliced, about 2 cups
1¼ cups whole milk
½ cup instant white grits
½ cup heavy whipping cream
4 tablespoons butter
24 uncooked large shrimp, peeled
  and deveined

¼ cup lager beer
3 tablespoons fresh lemon
  juice
6 garlic cloves
1 tomato, peeled, seeded, and
  chopped
2 teaspoons chopped fresh
  thyme

Heat 1 tablespoon oil in medium skillet over medium-high heat. Add onion; sauté until golden, stirring frequently, about 15 minutes. Season with salt and pepper. Bring milk and grits to boil in heavy medium saucepan, whisking constantly. Reduce heat and simmer until tender, stirring frequently, about 5 minutes. Mix in cream and 2 tablespoons butter. Season to taste with salt and pepper.

Meanwhile, heat remaining 1 tablespoon oil in heavy large skillet over medium-high heat. Add shrimp and sauté 1 minute. Add beer, lemon juice, and garlic; simmer until shrimp is just opaque in center and sauce is slightly reduced, about 2 minutes. Mix in tomato, thyme, and remaining 2 tablespoons butter. Season to taste with salt and pepper. Divide grits among 4 plates. Top with onion, then shrimp and sauce.

Greek Shrimp Scampi
4 to 6 Servings

4 garlic cloves, minced
1 pound shrimp, shelled and deveined
2 tablespoons olive oil
2 tablespoons butter
2 cups diced fresh tomatoes

1 cup feta cheese
½ cup fresh lemon juice
2 tablespoons dried oregano
salt and pepper

Sauté garlic and shrimp in olive oil and butter. Cook over medium heat for one minute. Add tomatoes, feta, lemon juice, and oregano. When shrimp are pink, add salt and pepper. Serve over rice or pasta.

Asian Shrimp & Sugar Snap Peas
4 Servings

1 large garlic clove, minced
2 teaspoons fresh ginger root, grated
1 small red onion, thinly sliced
2 cups sugar snap peas
1 pound large frozen shrimp, thawed,
  drained, peeled and deveined
1 cup chicken broth, divided
1½ teaspoons cornstarch

2 tablespoons low-sodium
  soy sauce
¼ teaspoon crushed red
  pepper flakes, or to taste
½ teaspoon unpacked brown
  sugar
2 cups cooked brown rice

Heat oil in large nonstick skillet over medium-high heat. Add garlic, ginger and onion; cook, stirring frequently, 1 minute. Add sugar snap peas; cook until crisp-tender, stirring frequently, about 3 minutes. Add shrimp; cook until shrimp are almost cooked through and turn pink; about 3 minutes.

Meanwhile, in a small bowl, mix together ¼ cup broth and cornstarch; stir well to blend. Add remaining ¾ cup broth and soy sauce.

Pour broth mixture into skillet, scraping up any browned bits with a spoon; stir in red pepper flakes and sugar. Reduce heat to low and simmer until sauce thickens and shrimp are completely cooked, about 2 minutes. Serve over rice. Yields about 1 cup shrimp-vegetable mixture and ½ cup rice per serving.

Note: *Thinly sliced broccoli or asparagus spears are also tasty in this recipe.*

Shrimp Étouffée
6 Servings

½ cup chopped onion
½ cup chopped celery
½ cup chopped green pepper
2 cloves garlic, crushed
½ cup butter, melted
½ teaspoon thyme
½ teaspoon chili powder
½ teaspoon dried basil
2 tablespoons flour

1 teaspoon tomato paste
½ cup seafood stock
½ cup dry white wine
1 cup cream of mushroom
　soup
2½ cups peeled raw shrimp
½ cup chopped green onion
¼ cup chopped parsley
¼ teaspoon Creole seasoning
½ teaspoon hot sauce

Sauté onion, celery, green pepper, and garlic in butter until tender. Add thyme, chili powder, dried basil, flour, and tomato paste. Stir often and cook for 15 minutes. Add stock and wine and cook 10 minutes. Add soup and shrimp, cover and simmer 15 to 20 minutes. Add green onion, parsley, Creole seasoning, and hot sauce. Cover and cook 5 minutes. Remove and let stand 15 minutes before serving. Serve over rice.

Honey Mustard Salmon
6 Servings

6 salmon fillets
salt and pepper
4 tablespoons Dijon mustard
4 tablespoons melted butter
3 tablespoons honey

⅓ cup panko breadcrumbs
⅓ cup finely chopped pecans
2 tablespoons fresh parsley
lemon slices

Sprinkle salmon with salt and pepper; place salmon skin side down in a lightly greased 9×13 baking dish. Combine mustard, butter, and honey in a small bowl and spread over salmon. Combine breadcrumbs, pecans, and parsley and spoon over fish. Bake at 450°F for approximately 10 minutes or until cooked through.

Marinated Salmon with Dill Sauce
6 Servings

Salmon Marinade:
⅓ cup low-sodium soy sauce
½ cup canola oil
¼ cup lemon juice
1 tablespoon Dijon mustard
1 clove garlic, minced

Dill Sauce:
¼ cup Dijon mustard
2 teaspoons dried dill weed
3 tablespoons olive oil
3 tablespoons lemon juice
⅛ teaspoon black pepper

6 salmon filets

Mix marinade ingredients and marinate salmon for up to 6 hours. Combine the dill sauce ingredients and set aside.

Grill salmon in a foil pan with some of the marinade until flaky, turning once, or bake at 375°F for approximately 15 minutes. Serve with dill sauce on the side.

Mustard Glaze Salmon Steaks
4 Servings

4 salmon steaks, 1 inch thick, about 7 ounces each
¼ cup light brown sugar
¼ cup Dijon mustard

Line a rimmed baking sheet with nonstick foil. Place salmon on top. Whisk together the brown sugar and mustard. Spread evenly on top of salmon. Bake at 425°F for 15 minutes or until cooked through. Broil 4 inches from top for 2 minutes or until golden brown.

Salmon in Wine and Aromatic Vegetables
6 to 8 Servings

1 large carrot, diced
1 large onion, diced
3 tender celery stalks, diced
2 tablespoons unsalted butter
dash salt

dash freshly ground pepper
dash dried tarragon
2-pound skinless fillet of
    salmon
1½ cups dry white French
    vermouth
parchment paper

Simmer the carrots, onions, and celery very carefully in the butter until tender, not brown, approximately 10 minutes. Add the seasonings and stir to combine. Rub your fingers carefully on the fish to detect and remove any small bones. Score the skin side of the fish. Dust with salt and pepper and place best side up in baking dish. Spread the cooked vegetables over the fish and pour ¼-inch vermouth around it. Cover the fish with parchment paper.

Bake at 350°F on the middle rack for 12 to 15 minutes. Baste the fish with the liquid in the dish several times. When fish is springy to the touch, remove from oven. Carefully drain the juices from the dish into a saucepan. Keep fish warm. Rapidly boil down juices until syrupy. You may add 3 to 4 tablespoons of butter to the sauce if you wish. Pour over fish and serve.

Mustard Roasted Fish
4 Servings

4 white fish fillets, about 8 ounces each
8 ounces crème fraîche
3 tablespoons Dijon mustard
1 tablespoon whole grain mustard

2 tablespoons minced shallots
2 teaspoons drained capers
1 teaspoon salt
½ teaspoon pepper

Place fillets skin side down in oven safe dish. Combine crème fraîche, mustards, shallots, capers, salt, and pepper. Spoon sauce over fish to cover. Bake at 425°F for 10 to 15 minutes until flakes easily.

Grilled Tuna with Rosemary Beurre Blanc
6 Servings

½ cup fresh lemon juice
6 cloves garlic, minced
1 teaspoon cracked black pepper
½ teaspoon salt
¼ cup olive oil
6 fresh albacore or yellow fin
    tuna steaks, about 6 ounces each
6 sprigs fresh rosemary for garnish

Rosemary Beurre Blanc:
1½ tablespoons chopped shallots
¾ cup dry white wine
dash of lemon juice
pinch of white pepper
1 tablespoon heavy cream
2 tablespoons fresh rosemary,
    chopped
1 cup butter

Combine ½ cup lemon juice, garlic, pepper, salt, and olive oil to make a marinade and marinate the tuna for 1 hour, no more. Remove the tuna from the marinade and grill the fish until it is medium rare to medium, about 8 minutes.

Rosemary Beurre Blanc:
Combine the shallots, white wine, lemon juice, pepper, heavy cream, and rosemary in a heavy saucepan and reduce over medium heat until the liquid has almost disappeared. Turn off the heat and whisk in the butter 1 tablespoon at a time. Strain the sauce, discarding solids. Adjust seasonings to taste.

Serve the tuna with Rosemary Beurre Blanc adding a small sprig of rosemary to each plate.

Grilled Swordfish with Tomato-Feta Relish
4 Servings

1 medium tomato, seeded and chopped
1 green onion, sliced
¼ cup olive oil
¼ cup crumbled feta cheese
1 tablespoon fresh lemon juice
2 teaspoons chopped fresh dill weed
freshly ground pepper to taste
¼ cup extra-virgin olive oil

¼ cup Dijon mustard
2½ tablespoons red wine
 vinegar
1 teaspoon garlic powder
1 teaspoon ground oregano
½ teaspoon salt
4 swordfish steaks, 6 to 8
 ounces each

Combine tomato, green onion, ¼ cup olive oil, feta cheese, lemon juice, dill weed, and freshly ground pepper in a medium bowl; stir well, and set aside. Combine ¼ cup olive oil, mustard, vinegar, garlic powder, oregano, and salt; stir well. Brush both sides of swordfish steaks with half of mustard mixture. Grill fish over hot coals 6 to 8 minutes on each side, or until fish flakes easily when tested with a fork, basting frequently with remaining mustard mixture. Serve fish with tomato-feta relish.

Baked Red Snapper
6 Servings

1 teaspoon sugar
2 pound whole red snapper
⅛ teaspoon salt
dash of pepper
1 clove garlic
1 red pepper pod
1 onion, finely minced
2½ cups tomatoes

1 tablespoon Worcestershire
 sauce
½ cup olive oil
1 tablespoon vinegar
2 pounds small potatoes,
 halved or quartered
1 cup sliced mushrooms

Brown sugar in oven-proof pan over medium heat. Sprinkle red snapper with salt and pepper; place garlic and pepper pod inside fish. Place onion and red snapper in pan with sugar. Cover with tomatoes; add Worcestershire sauce, olive oil, vinegar, and potatoes. Bake at 350°F for 15 minutes. Add mushrooms and bake 15 minutes longer or until fish and potatoes are tender.

Catfish Parmesan
6 Servings

⅔ cup freshly grated Parmesan cheese
¼ cup flour
½ teaspoon salt
¼ teaspoon pepper
1 teaspoon paprika

1 egg, beaten
¼ cup milk
6 catfish fillets, 2 to 2½ pounds
¼ cup butter, melted
⅓ cup sliced almonds

Combine cheese, flour, salt, pepper, paprika and mix well. Combine egg and milk, stir well. Dip fillets in egg mixture and dredge in flour mixture. Arrange fillets in a lightly greased 13×9×2-inch baking dish. Drizzle butter and sprinkle almonds evenly on top of fish. Bake at 350°F for 35 to 40 minutes or until fish flakes easily when tested with a fork.

Vegetable Smothered Fish
6 Servings

3 pounds sole fillets
4 tablespoons olive oil
1 tablespoon minced garlic
4 cups chopped cauliflower
1 cup sliced red pepper
1 cup sliced yellow pepper
2 cups sliced mushrooms
½ cup dry sherry

¼ cup lemon juice
1 teaspoon salt
2 teaspoon dried basil or 1 teaspoon chopped fresh basil
1 teaspoon black pepper
4 dashes hot pepper sauce
½ cup grated Parmesan cheese

Brush 9×13-inch baking dish with 1 tablespoon olive oil. Place sole fillets on top. In large saucepan, sauté garlic, cauliflower, peppers, and mushrooms in 2 tablespoons olive oil until crisp-tender. Spoon vegetable mixture over fish. Combine sherry, lemon juice, salt, basil, pepper, and pepper sauce and pour over fillets.

Bake at 350°F, uncovered, for 30 minutes. Remove vegetables and fish to a platter. Pour pan juices over fish and vegetables and sprinkle with Parmesan cheese.

Fish Tacos with Mango Salsa
4 Servings

Mango Salsa:
1 ripe yet firm mango, peeled
  and diced
½ cup halved grape tomatoes
½ cup diced cucumber
¼ cup minced red onion
1 teaspoon sugar
¼ teaspoon kosher salt
¼ teaspoon ground cumin
juice of one lime
1 ripe avocado

Fish:
4 tilapia fillets, about 4 ounces
  each, halved
3 teaspoons flour
3 tablespoons yellow cornmeal
1 teaspoon chili powder
1 teaspoon kosher salt
¼ teaspoon cayenne pepper

8 7-inch corn tortillas
1 head Napa cabbage, thinly sliced

Creamy Chipotle Sauce:
¼ cup plain low fat yogurt
¼ cup mayonnaise
2 teaspoons sugar
1 to 2 chipotle chilies in adobe
  sauce, minced
juice of ½ lime

Mango Salsa:
Combine all ingredients except avocado. Set aside to allow flavors to mingle. Just before serving, dice avocado and add to the salsa.

Creamy Chipotle Sauce:
Stir together all ingredients and chill until ready to serve.

Marinate tilapia fillets in lime juice for 10 minutes, turning once to coat. Place 2 baking sheets in a 500°F oven and preheat for 5 minutes. Blend flour, cornmeal, and seasonings in a shallow bowl. Coat fish on both sides with mixture. Remove hot pans from oven and spray with non-stick spray. Place coated fillets on hot pan and roast for 5 minutes. Turn and roast for another 3 to 4 minutes. Remove from oven and keep warm. Spray both sides of the tortillas with non-stick spray. Oven toast the tortillas just until they are lightly toasted, about 3 to 4 minutes. Assemble tacos using tortillas, fish, cabbage, mango salsa, and chipotle sauce.

Cioppino
6 Servings

4 tablespoons olive oil
1 green pepper, chopped
1 medium onion, chopped
4 tablespoons chopped fresh parsley
2 cloves garlic, minced
2 16-ounce cans diced tomatoes
1 6-ounce can tomato paste
¼ teaspoon crushed dried basil
1 large bay leaf
½ teaspoon grated lemon rind

1 teaspoon salt
dash black pepper
1 pound fish fillets, cut in
  2-inch pieces (haddock,
  bass, pike, etc.)
1 pound fresh raw shrimp,
  boiled, shelled, and cleaned
8 ounces canned or frozen
  crab meat
hot cooked rice

Heat oil in large saucepan and sauté green pepper, onion, parsley, and garlic until tender, but not brown. Stir in tomatoes, tomato paste, basil, bay leaf, lemon rind, salt, and pepper. Cover and simmer for 30 minutes.

Add fish fillets and cook slowly for 15 minutes. Do not overcook; fish pieces should remain whole and not cook to shreds. Add shrimp and crab meat, simmer for 10 minutes, stirring gently now and then. Discard bay leaf. Serve Cioppino in large soup plate with mound of rice in center.

Paella
6 Servings

10 small to medium chicken
 drumsticks
½ cup olive oil
2 cups medium shrimp, enough
 for about 5 per person
1 medium Spanish onion, finely diced
½ cup ripe tomatoes, puréed
1 teaspoon kosher salt
1 teaspoon saffron threads
2 tablespoons sweet pimentón
 (Spanish smoked paprika)

4 quarts chicken stock
2 cups bomba or other short-
 grain rice
1 pound Manila clams,
 scrubbed
1 cup freshly shucked peas
10 spears pencil asparagus,
 stalks cut on the diagonal
 into ¼-inch thick slices
1 pound sausage, cut into
 1-inch pieces

Place the drumsticks on a baking sheet and season all over with salt and olive oil. Bake at 400°F for 20 to 22 minutes and set aside. In the meantime, heat a 14- to 18-inch paella pan over medium-high heat. Add the oil and heat until smoking. Add the sausage and cook until browned on both sides, about 3 minutes per side. Transfer to a plate and set aside. Add the shrimp and cook until no longer pink, about 1 minute per side. Transfer to a plate and set aside. Add the onion to the pan and cook until soft, about 8 minutes. Push the onions into the center of the pan and sprinkle 2 tablespoons of the salt around the edges of the pan.

Add the tomato purée, stirring it into the onions, and cook for 3 minutes. Add the remaining salt, saffron, and pimentón; cook, stirring, for 5 minutes. Add chicken stock, bring to a boil, and cook for 5 minutes. Add the rice and stir well to distribute it evenly. Add clams, drumsticks, arranging them nicely throughout the pan. Then add the peas and asparagus and bring the stock back to a boil, and cook without stirring for 10 minutes. Taste for salt and add it if needed, then cook, again without stirring, for 10 more minutes, or until the liquid is almost completely absorbed and the pan starts to make a crackling noise (don't worry, this is what you want).

Add the sausage and shrimp back into the pan. Combine. Remove from the heat and let rest for 10 minutes before serving.

Vegetarian

Eggplant Rollatini
4 Servings

white of 1 large egg
¾ cup non-fat or part-skim ricotta
cheese, 1 tablespoon reserved
½ cup coarsely grated
provolone cheese
4 tablespoons chopped fresh
parsley, divided
¼ teaspoon freshly ground
black pepper

1 large eggplant, about 1½
pounds, cut into 12 length
wise slices
¼ cup red wine vinaigrette
1 cup good quality marinara
sauce
12 large fresh basil leaves or 1
tablespoon dried
2 fresh parsley sprigs

In small bowl, using fork, beat egg white lightly. Stir in all but 1 table-spoon ricotta, provolone, 2 tablespoons parsley, and pepper; mix well. Set filling mixture aside.

Arrange 6 eggplant slices in single layer on rack in broiler pan; brush with vinaigrette. Broil on a rack positioned 4 inches from heat source, for 3 to 4 minutes until speckled with brown. Turn slices; brush again with vinaigrette; broil 3 to 4 minutes longer until browned and tender. Remove eggplant to plate; repeat with remaining eggplant and vinaigrette. Spoon marinara sauce over bottom of 10-inch round shallow baking dish; set aside.

Place reserved broiled eggplant slices flat on work surface. Spread each slice with 2 tablespoons filling mixture; top with one fresh basil leaf, if using, or sprinkle with ¼ teaspoon dried basil. Roll eggplant slices up, jelly-roll style, from bottom end.

Dip each roll in sauce in baking dish to coat all over, then arrange, seam side down, in dish. Bake at 400°F, covered with foil, 35 minutes until rolls are heated through and sauce is bubbling.

Sprinkle eggplant with reserved 1 tablespoon grated provolone and re-maining parsley. Serve garnished with parsley sprig.

Pasta, Rice, & Beans

Cardinal Glennon Children's Medical Center was the first Level 1 Pediatric Trauma Center in St. Louis. Twenty-four hours a day, there are fully trained neuro and trauma surgeons on staff and certified transport teams ready for any type of trauma situation.

Pasta

Black Pepper Fettuccine with Morels, Asparagus, and Country Ham Tossed in Goat Cheese Cream
4 Servings

Chris Desens *is currently the program director for the* Culinary Institute at Hickey College. *He has thirty years of varied industry experience including national and international culinary competitions. He is a certified culinary judge through the American Culinary Federation, a Certified Executive Chef, and a member of the American Academy of Chefs.*

2 tablespoons olive oil	½ cup goat cheese
1 tablespoon shallots, minced	2 tablespoons julienned basil
1 cup morel mushrooms, cleaned	1 tablespoon chopped parsley
¼ cup white wine	1 tablespoon snipped chives
2 cups heavy cream	2 teaspoons chopped tarragon
¼ cup country ham	¼ cup whole butter
2 tablespoons roasted garlic	salt
1 tablespoon lemon zest	pepper

Pasta:

1 cup flour	1 teaspoon olive oil
1 egg	½ teaspoon coarse ground
3 egg yolks	black pepper

Pasta:
Combine all ingredients and knead well. Let rest for half hour. Roll out in pasta maker and cut into fettuccine. Cook in boiling water until al dente; set aside. Heat pan and add oil, shallots, and morel mushrooms. Sauté and add wine and reduce. Add remaining ingredients except pasta and continue to reduce to sauce consistency. Add pasta, toss well, and serve when fully heated through. Taste for seasoning; adjust if necessary.

Note: *This is an appetizer we feature every spring when Missouri morel season hits. It can easily be presented as an appetizer or an entrée. This recipe draws inspiration from great Missouri producers of country ham, goat cheese, and the local flavors of morels and asparagus.*

Gnocchi with Braised Chicken, Broccoli Rabe, and Peppadew Peppers
6 Servings

Kirk Warner *is the chef and owner of* Chef Kirk's Traveling Kitchen.

5 to 6 cups gnocchi pasta
olive oil
2 pounds boneless chicken thighs
salt
pepper
2 tablespoons porcini powder, optional, divided
3 cups chicken stock, preferably homemade
1 bunch broccoli rabe, coursely cut

1½ cups coursely cut Peppadew peppers
1 cup pasta water, from cooked pasta
¾ cup Peppadew Pickle Brine (or juice from peppers)
3 tablespoons unsalted butter
4 ounces Parmesan cheese, reserving 4 tablespoons for topping

Cook prepared pasta in boiling, salted water according to package directions until tender but firm. Drain and reserve 1 cup water. Keep gnocchi moist and warm.

In a heavy-bottomed braising pan, heat enough olive oil to cover bottom of pan. Toss chicken with salt, pepper, and half the porcini powder. Brown the chicken for approximately 10 to 15 minutes. Chicken may start to fall apart. When the chicken is browned, remove from pan and drain the pan. Return the chicken to the pan and add the chicken stock. Cook the chicken over low heat for 15 to 20 minutes, stirring occasionally. Add the broccoli rabe, peppers, pasta water, remaining porcini powder, and pickle brine. Raise the heat and cook 5 minutes. Add the pasta, butter, and cheese, tossing carefully. Season with salt and pepper to taste and top with remaining cheese.

Bowtie Pasta with Smoked Salmon
4 to 6 Servings

This recipe is a favorite at Soulard's Restaurant, *which is known for fine dining in a friendly atmosphere since 1977.*

¼ pound plus 1 tablespoon butter
2 tablespoons minced garlic
3 tablespoons Creole
seasoning (recipe follows)
1 teaspoon salt
1 tablespoon pepper
8 ounces heavy cream
2 tablespoons chopped green onion
4 ounces Parmesan cheese
¼ pound smoked salmon, chopped
¼ pound shiitake mushrooms, sliced
1 pound bow tie pasta, cooked and drained

Creole Seasoning:
2½ tablespoons paprika
2 tablespoons salt
2 tablespoons garlic powder
1 tablespoon black pepper
1 tablespoon onion powder
1 tablespoon cayenne pepper
1 tablespoon dried leaf oregano
1 tablespoon dried leaf thyme

In sauce pan, add ¼ pound butter, garlic, Creole seasoning, salt, and pepper. Cook for 5 minutes, add cream, green onions, two ounces Parmesan cheese, and smoked salmon. Cook for 2 minutes. Meanwhile, sauté mushrooms in remaining tablespoon butter. Toss pasta and sautéed mushrooms into sauce and serve topped with remaining 2 ounces Parmesan cheese.

Creole Seasoning:
Combine paprika, salt, garlic powder, black pepper, onion powder, cayenne pepper, oregano, and thyme thoroughly and store in an airtight jar or container.

Note: *Instead of using smoked salmon, use a big piece of salmon and put the Creole seasoning and some olive oil on it and bake it for 15 minutes or so—just as good and not as expensive to make! You can use half-and-half instead of cream to reduce the fat and leave out the mushrooms if you choose.*

˙nd Fresh Basil Linguini

4 Servings

Culinary Institute of America graduate Sherrill Gonterman *started* LaChef Catering *30 years ago with her mother.* LaChef *specializes in healthy, creative cuisine for residential and corporate clients.*

½ cup lemon zest
1 pound linguine
¼ cup lemon juice
1 stick butter
½ cup olive oil
2 tablespoons minced garlic

½ cup shredded fresh basil
½ cup chopped fresh parsley
1 teaspoon salt
½ teaspoon fresh black pepper
½ cup Parmesan cheese, grated

Blanch lemon zest in boiling water for 1 minute. Cook linguine to al dente according to package directions. Combine linguine, lemon zest, lemon juice, butter, olive oil, garlic, basil, parsley, salt, pepper, and Parmesan together. Toss and serve.

Note: *Great Mother's Day brunch entree.*

Layered Gnocchi Casserole

6 Servings

¾ cup part skim ricotta cheese
¼ cup thinly sliced fresh basil
½ cup grated
  reduced-fat mozzarella, divided
2 tablespoons grated
  Parmesan cheese

1 egg, lightly beaten
3 cups basic tomato sauce
1 16-ounce package potato
  gnocchi
2 cups spinach leaves, thinly
  sliced

In a small bowl, combine ricotta, basil, ¼ cup mozzarella, Parmesan, and egg. Stir until blended. Set aside. Spread a thin layer of the tomato sauce in a lightly greased 1½-quart casserole or gratin dish. On top of the sauce, layer half of the gnocchi and then half of the spinach. Using half of the ricotta mixture, place small dollops on top of the spinach. Cover with another thin layer of sauce. Repeat the process, ending with sauce. Sprinkle on the remaining ¼ cup of mozzarella. Bake for 40 minutes at 400°F or until the top is bubbly and the cheese is lightly browned. Let stand for 15 minutes before serving.

Brown Butter Gnocchi with Spinach
4 Servings

1 16-ounce package vacuum packed gnocchi
2 tablespoons butter
2 tablespoons pine nuts
2 garlic cloves, minced
1 10-ounce package fresh spinach, torn

¼ teaspoon salt
¼ teaspoon freshly ground black pepper
¼ cup finely shredded Parmesan cheese

Cook gnocchi according to package directions, omitting salt and fat; drain. Heat butter in a large nonstick skillet over medium heat. Add pine nuts to pan; cook 3 minutes or until butter and nuts are lightly browned, stirring constantly. Add garlic to pan; cook 1 minute. Add gnocchi and spinach to pan; cook 1 minute or until spinach wilts, stirring constantly. Stir in salt and pepper. Sprinkle with Parmesan cheese.

Seafood Pasta
6 Servings

1 quart heavy cream
10 ounces chopped shallots
1 pound large shrimp, raw, shelled and deveined
1 pound bay scallops, raw
1 pound fresh snow peas

3 cups frozen green peas
salt and pepper
arrowroot (if needed)
1 pound linguini
2 tablespoons chopped parsley

Place heavy cream and shallots in a large, heavy saucepan. Boil for 5 minutes. Add raw shrimp and boil for 4 minutes. Add raw scallops, snow peas, and green peas, and boil for 4 minutes. Add salt and pepper to taste, but sauce should be peppery. The sauce may be thickened with arrowroot. Cook pasta according to package directions. Serve sauce over pasta and garnish with a little parsley.

Note: *Great "red and green" dish for Christmas.*

Angel Hair Pasta with Lobster Sauce
4 Servings

2 5-ounce lobster tails, fresh or
  frozen, thawed
16 ounces angel hair pasta
⅔ cup sliced mushrooms
3 tablespoons chopped green onions
2 tablespoons unsalted butter, melted
2 tablespoons flour
1 cup plus 2 tablespoons half-and-half
2 tablespoons dry white wine

2 tablespoons drained and
  chopped pimientos
¼ teaspoon salt
¼ teaspoon dry mustard
dash red pepper
dash paprika
2 tablespoon grated
  Parmesan cheese
sprigs of fresh parsley

In a large pot heat 2 quarts of water. Add lobster tails. Cover, reduce heat, and simmer 6 minutes. Drain; rinse with cold water. Drain again. Split and clean tails. Cut meat into ¼-inch pieces. Cook pasta according to package directions. Drain, toss with small amount of olive oil, and keep warm.

Sauté mushrooms and onions in butter until tender. Add flour, stirring until smooth. Cook 1 minute, stirring constantly. Gradually add half-and-half. Cook over medium heat, stirring constantly until thick and bubbly. Stir in wine, pimiento, salt, mustard, red pepper, and lobster meat. Cook over low heat, stirring constantly until thoroughly heated. Serve sauce over pasta. Sprinkle with paprika and Parmesan cheese. Garnish with parsley.

Spaghetti with Tuna and Capers
4 Servings

1 pound spaghetti
⅓ cup olive oil
3 cloves garlic, peeled and smashed
1 medium yellow onion, diced
2 cloves garlic, minced
1 tablespoon chopped capers
½ teaspoon red pepper flakes

1 can Arroyabe or Ortiz brand
   Bonito del Norte tuna in olive
   oil, drained
sea salt
pepper
flat leaf parsley for garnish,
   roughly chopped
½ lemon

Bring a large pot of water, seasoned with enough salt to make it taste of the sea, to a boil. Add the spaghetti and cook until al dente.

Meanwhile, place the olive oil in a large sauté pan over high heat. When the oil is hot, add the smashed garlic and cook until lightly brown to flavor the oil. Remove the smashed garlic from the pan and discard. Reduce the heat to medium high and add the onion and minced garlic. Sauté until tender and caramel in color. Add the capers, pepper flakes, and tuna. Season with a pinch of sea salt and pepper to taste. Sauté for several minutes, stirring to combine the ingredients.

Drain the spaghetti and add it to the sauté pan, tossing to coat the pasta with the sauce. Add the parsley and a squeeze of lemon juice.

Note: *The tuna listed in this recipe is white, different from other common canned tuna found in the grocery store. Bonito del Norte tuna can be found at specialty stores in the area.*

Tuna Pasta
4 Servings

1 pound spaghetti pasta
⅓ cup olive oil
2 cloves garlic, minced
2 crowns of broccoli

2 cans tuna in water
8 ounces of cherry or grape
    tomatoes
salt and pepper to taste

Cook pasta in salted boiling water. Heat deep skillet over medium heat and place olive oil in pan. Add garlic to pan and allow garlic to infuse flavor. Add broccoli and tuna and cook for approximately 7 minutes, stirring occasionally. Add tomatoes and cook for 4 minutes, until tomatoes are hot. Drain pasta and place in bowl. Add tuna, broccoli, and tomato mix to pasta; mix and serve.

Bowtie Sausage Pasta
4 to 6 Servings

12 ounces bowtie pasta
1 to 1½ pounds ground Italian sausage
2 tablespoons olive oil
½ cup diced onion
3 garlic cloves, minced
½ teaspoon dried red pepper flakes
1 28-ounce can Italian plum
    tomatoes, chopped

1 cup whipping cream
½ teaspoon salt
3 tablespoons chopped fresh
    parsley
freshly grated Parmesan
    cheese

Cook pasta according to package directions. In large saucepan, brown sausage; drain off fat. Remove sausage and set aside. Add olive oil, onion, garlic, and red pepper flakes to pan. Sauté until onions are tender. Add sausage and tomatoes. Simmer for 10 minutes. Add whipping cream and salt. Stir and simmer 5 minutes. Pour sauce over cooked pasta; garnish with parsley and grated Parmesan cheese to taste.

Penne with Radicchio, Spinach, and Bacon
6 Servings

1 whole head of garlic
6 teaspoons olive oil
1 pound penne
8 to 10 slices bacon, cut in ½-inch chunks
2 cups chopped onion
1 cup low sodium chicken broth
6 cups packed (about 2 medium heads) radicchio leaves, torn

3 cups packed (about 10 ounces) baby spinach leaves, torn in half
1 cup packed fresh basil leaves, torn in half
1 cup Parmesan cheese, freshly grated
¼ teaspoon dried crushed red pepper

Peel away the outer layers of skin of the garlic bulb, leaving the skins of the individual cloves intact; leave garlic bulb whole. Using a sharp knife, slice ½ inch off of the pointed end of the garlic bulb, exposing the individual cloves of garlic. Put the garlic head in a small ovenproof dish. Pour ½ teaspoon olive oil over the top of bulb and let it sink in between the cloves. Place on a baking sheet and cover with aluminum foil. Cover and bake at 375°F for approximately 45 to 60 minutes or until cloves are browned at the exposed end and soft throughout. Remove from oven, cool, and squeeze garlic into small bowl.

Cook pasta in large pot of salted water according to package directions until al dente. Drain, return to pot, set aside.

Cook bacon and onion in large skillet over medium-high heat until golden brown, stirring occasionally Add chicken broth, 5½ teaspoons olive oil, and roasted garlic. Bring mixture to a simmer, stirring occasionally. Add radicchio, spinach, and basil. Stir to combine. Simmer until radicchio and spinach wilt, about 1 minute. Add radicchio and spinach mixture to pasta. Add 1 cup Parmesan cheese and crushed red pepper; toss to coat. Season with salt and pepper to taste. Garnish with additional Parmesan cheese.

Savory Red and Green Sausage Pasta
6 to 8 Servings

1 roll of Jimmy Dean's medium
  pork sausage
1 teaspoon fennel seed
1 teaspoon dried oregano
1 green pepper, julienned

1 red pepper, julienned
3 Roma tomatoes, chopped
1 package linguine pasta
½ cup freshly grated
  Parmesan cheese

Brown sausage, fennel seed, and oregano. Add peppers. Add tomatoes and let simmer until sausage is cooked through and vegetables are cooked to desired texture. Cook pasta as directed on box. Drain and combine with sausage mixture. Serve warm and top with freshly grated Parmesan cheese.

Note: *This hearty and colorful meal includes carbs, veggies, and protein all in one dish. It's great served with garlic bread and an Italian salad.*

Cheesy Sausage Mac
8 to 10 Servings

2 links andouille sausage
2 links chorizo sausage
5 strips bacon
1 large sweet or yellow onion, chopped
5 cloves of garlic, 2 cracked and
  3 minced
1 sprig fresh thyme, removed from
  stem and finely chopped
1 tablespoon butter
1 tablespoon flour

2 cups half-and-half or 2%
  milk
2 fresh sprigs of thyme
1 pound elbow macaroni
1½ cups shredded white
  American cheese
1½ cups shredded white
  Gouda, such as Blarney
  Castle by Kerrygold
1½ cups shredded Parmesan
  cheese

In a large skillet, sear sausage links over medium high, cover, and cook until cooked all the way through, about 10 minutes. Once sausage is cooked, put aside to rest. Cook bacon in same skillet. Remove bacon and set aside. Add onion, 3 cloves garlic, and thyme to skillet. Cook until onions caramelize. While sausage is cooking, in large pot add butter and flour, stirring constantly for 1 minute. Add half-and-half or milk and stir to combine. Add 2 cracked cloves of garlic and 2 sprigs of thyme to milk and let simmer over low heat. Cook macaroni in large pot of salted water.

While onions and garlic are cooking, remove thyme sprigs and cracked garlic from milk. Slowly add cheeses to milk mixture, stirring frequently to prevent burning. Slice sausage thinly and crumble bacon.

Once cheeses are melted, add onion mixture, cooked macaroni, sausage and bacon. Stir and place in serving dish. If desired, sprinkle an additional ½ to 1 cup shredded cheese over macaroni and bake until a golden crust develops, about 10 minutes.

Note: *If you do not have fresh thyme, substitute 1 teaspoon dried for each sprig. A variety of cheeses can be substituted, try using Asiago or cheddar for variety.*

Sicilian Tomato Meat Sauce
12 Servings

3 tablespoons extra-virgin olive oil
1 small yellow onion, minced
½ pound coarsely chopped crimini
  or other white mushrooms
¾ pound ground beef
½ pound ground pork
1 tablespoon tomato paste
⅔ cup water
1 tablespoon sugar
½ teaspoon red pepper flakes

¼ cup loosely packed
  chopped fresh basil
4 cloves garlic, chopped
2 28-ounce cans crushed
  Italian plum tomatoes
1 teaspoon salt
¼ teaspoon freshly ground
  black pepper

Heat oil in a large, heavy-bottomed pot over medium-low heat. Add onion and cook, stirring frequently, until soft, about 20 minutes. Increase heat to medium high, stir in mushrooms and cook for 5 minutes. Add beef and pork, breaking up lumps with a wooden spoon, and brown for 8 minutes. Drain fat if desired.

Combine tomato paste with ⅔ cup water in a small bowl. Over medium heat, add tomato paste mixture to meat and cook, stirring for 1 minute.

Stir in sugar, red pepper flakes, basil, garlic, and tomatoes. Reduce heat to medium low, season with salt and pepper, and gently simmer, uncovered, stirring frequently, for 40 minutes. Adjust seasoning to taste. Serve with your favorite pasta.

Note: *To store sauce, cool to room temperature. Store covered in refrigerator for up to 1 week, or frozen for up to 1 year.*

Fettuccine with Chicken and Mushrooms
4 Servings

12 ounces fresh or 8 ounces
dried fettuccine
4 tablespoons butter
1 8-ounce boneless and skinless
chicken breast, cut into
¾-inch pieces
12 ounces mushrooms, cut into
¼-inch slices (mixture of white
button, shiitake—tough stems
discarded, and oyster)

½ cup chopped scallions
1 garlic clove, minced
½ cup heavy cream
1 14½-ounce can chopped
tomatoes, drained
1 cup frozen tiny peas
½ teaspoon salt
dash of black pepper
2 tablespoons finely chopped
parsley
grated Parmesan cheese

Cook the fettuccine in salted water according to package directions until al dente. Drain; set aside.

Heat butter in a large, heavy skillet. Add the chicken; sauté until edges are golden, about 5 minutes. Add mushrooms to the chicken, sauté until tender, about 5 minutes. Add the scallions and garlic; sauté 2 minutes.

Add the heavy cream and tomatoes; heat to boiling over medium-high heat; reduce heat to low and simmer until sauce is thickened. Add the peas, salt, and pepper. Heat, stirring until peas are tender.

Place the fettuccine in a large serving bowl; top with chicken and mushroom mixture and toss. Sprinkle with parsley and grated Parmesan cheese.

Chicken and Asparagus Lasagna
10 Servings

6 tablespoons butter or margarine
6 tablespoons flour
2 cups chicken broth
1 cup half-and-half or whipping
  cream (can be made richer by
  adding extra whipping cream)
½ teaspoon each salt and pepper
dash of nutmeg
1 teaspoon marjoram
1½ cups sliced and sautéed
  mushrooms

9 lasagna noodles, cooked
  and dry
4 chicken breast halves,
  cooked and shredded
1 pound asparagus, cut into
  1-inch pieces, blanched and
  drained
8 ounces shredded mozzarella
  cheese
8 ounces shredded cheddar
  cheese
1 cup grated Parmesan
  cheese, divided

Melt butter in saucepan and add flour, cook 1 minute. Whisk in chicken broth and half-and-half or whipping cream. Cook until very thick. If still too thin, add a bit more flour dissolved in water and bring to boil to thicken. Add salt, nutmeg, pepper, marjoram, and mushrooms.

To assemble, grease or spray a 9×13 pan and spoon a bit of the sauce to cover bottom. Arrange 3 of the noodles on the bottom. Layer in half of the chicken and asparagus, and sprinkle with half of the mozzarella, cheddar, and ½ cup grated Parmesan cheeses. Spoon half of the sauce over layer. Arrange 3 more noodles on top and again repeat layering and sprinkling with remaining ½ cup grated Parmesan on top of sauce. Can be done 2 days ahead and kept refrigerated.

Bake at 350°F for about 1 hour (tent loosely with aluminum foil for half of the baking time). If chilled, add 15 minutes to baking time.

Southern Spaghetti Dinner
8 to 10 Servings

1 pound spaghetti
1 to 2 pounds chicken
  breasts, skinned
3 cups chopped celery
1 cup chopped onion
1 cup chopped green pepper
1 10¾-ounce can cream of
  mushroom or cream of chicken soup
1 10¾-ounce can tomato soup

1 10-ounce can diced tomatoes
  with green chilies
  (optional, for more heat)
1 teaspoon chili powder
1 tablespoon Worcestershire
  sauce
½ teaspoon hot sauce
  (optional)
1 pound Velveeta, cubed
Parmesan cheese

Cook spaghetti in salted water according to package directions. Drain; set aside.

Place chicken in a Dutch oven pot (or larger) and cover with water. Boil until almost tender. Add celery and onion; continue cooking until chicken is tender. Add green pepper. Remove chicken (reserve broth) to cool and cut into bite-sized pieces. For crunchier vegetables, cook chicken first then strain. Add vegetables and boil until they begin to soften.

Adjust broth in pan to 2 cups. Add cream soup, tomato soup, tomatoes with green chilies (if using), chili powder, Worcestershire sauce and hot sauce if using. Add the cubed cheese, stirring occasionally until cheese is melted. Stir in chicken and spaghetti. Serve with Parmesan cheese if desired.

Note: *Can also be made with leftover Thanksgiving turkey.*

Spaghetti with Roasted Butternut Squash
8 Servings

½ cup chopped walnuts
1 2-pound butternut squash,
  peeled and cut in 1-inch pieces
1 bulb garlic, separated into cloves
  and peeled (halve the large cloves)
3 tablespoons olive oil
¼ teaspoon salt
¼ teaspoon pepper
1 14- to 16-ounce package dried
  multigrain, whole wheat, or regular
  spaghetti

¼ cup butter
3 slices bacon, crisp cooked
  and crumbled
½ teaspoon freshly grated
  nutmeg or ¼ teaspoon
  ground nutmeg
⅓ cup shredded Pecorino
  cheese
green onion, sliced (optional)

Toast walnuts in small dry skillet over moderate heat until lightly browned. Set aside. In 15×10×1-inch baking pan, toss together squash, peeled garlic cloves, oil, salt, and pepper. Evenly spread squash in pan. Bake at 425°F for 15 to 18 minutes, or until squash is tender and lightly browned.

Meanwhile, cook spaghetti according to package directions. Drain; keep warm. In small saucepan heat butter over medium heat until it turns light brown, stirring frequently.

In serving bowl toss spaghetti with about half the browned butter. Toss squash, garlic, bacon, nuts, and nutmeg with remaining browned butter. Serve squash mixture over spaghetti. Sprinkle with cheese and green onions.

Sun-Dried Tomato and Escarole Linguini
6 to 8 Servings

1½ pounds linguini
½ cup extra-virgin olive oil
1 large onion or 2 to 3 green onions, diced
1 red bell pepper, julienned
¾ cup pine nuts
¾ cup coarsely chopped sun-dried tomatoes

2 medium heads escarole, finely chopped
2 tablespoons finely diced garlic
¼ cup dry white wine
½ cup vegetable broth
salt
freshly ground black pepper
3 tablespoons butter

Cook pasta according to package directions until al dente. Drain; set aside. Heat oil in large saucepan. Add onions and red peppers; sauté until onions are translucent. Stir in pine nuts, sun-dried tomatoes, and escarole. Sauté until escarole is wilted, 2 to 3 minutes. Add garlic, cook 1 minute. Add wine and vegetable broth; simmer 2 to 3 minutes. Add salt and pepper to taste. Add butter, heat thoroughly. Add pasta and toss.

Pasta with Tomatoes, Basil, and Smoked Cheese
4 to 6 Servings

1 pound penne or mostaccioli pasta
1 28-ounce can Italian style whole tomatoes, drained well and chopped, or 2 pounds fresh tomatoes, chopped
1 cup loosely packed chopped fresh basil leaves

1 cup (4 ounces) smoked Gouda or any other smoked cheese, cubed
1 to 2 cloves garlic, minced
¼ cup olive oil
salt
pepper

In a bowl large enough to hold the cooked pasta, combine tomatoes, basil, cheese, garlic, and olive oil. Add salt and fresh ground pepper to taste and stir until just combined. The sauce may be made several hours in advance; keep cool and covered. In a large pot of boiling water, cook pasta according to package directions. Drain pasta and add to bowl, stirring quickly to coat. Add salt and pepper to taste; serve.

Pasta Primavera
4 to 6 Servings

4 to 6 quarts water	1 pound linguini
½ cup coarsely chopped broccoli	3 tablespoons chopped onion
½ cup peeled and diced carrots	¼ cup olive oil
3 large mushrooms, diced	2 tablespoons chopped garlic
10 fresh green beans, diced	3 plum tomatoes, peeled,
½ medium, slender zucchini, diced	seeded, and coarsely chopped
1 handful spinach leaves, each leaf	splash of white wine
quartered	salt
	fresh basil, chopped

Bring 4 to 6 quarts of water to a boil in a large pan. Add broccoli, carrots, mushrooms, green beans, zucchini, and spinach; boil vegetables about 2 minutes. Add pasta and boil until pasta is cooked al dente.

Meanwhile, in a large skillet, sauté onion in olive oil until onion is light golden brown. Add garlic and sauté several minutes. Add tomatoes and cook until tomato liquid evaporates, about 2 minutes. Add a splash of wine, salt, and basil to taste.

Drain pasta and vegetables, saving some cooking liquid. Toss pasta and vegetables into skillet with tomato mixture. Add a little cooking liquid if needed to make the sauce moist. Adjust seasoning, add basil, and serve immediately.

Wild Mushroom Cannelloni with Basil Alfredo Sauce
6 Servings

12 uncooked cannelloni shells
1 teaspoon margarine
butter flavored cooking spray
1 tablespoon minced shallots
1 garlic clove, minced
1 pound assorted wild mushrooms, coarsely chopped
1 cup sliced green onions
1 cup bottled roasted red bell peppers, chopped
2 tablespoons balsamic vinegar
3 tablespoons chopped fresh flat leaf parsley
1 teaspoon chopped fresh oregano, or ¼ teaspoon dried oregano

1 teaspoon chopped fresh thyme, or ¼ teaspoon dried thyme
1 cup (4 ounces) shredded part-skim mozzarella cheese
1 10-ounce container light Alfredo sauce
2 tablespoons chopped fresh basil, or 2 teaspoons dried basil
2 cups diced plum tomatoes (about ½ pound)
2 tablespoons grated Parmesan cheese
flat leaf parsley sprigs (optional)

Cook cannelloni shells according to package directions. Drain and rinse under cold water. Drain well; set aside.

Over medium-high heat, melt margarine in a large nonstick skillet coated with cooking spray. Add shallots and garlic; sauté 1 minute. Add mushrooms, and cook 5 minutes or until liquid almost evaporates. Add green onions, bell peppers, and vinegar; sauté 2 minutes. Remove mushroom mixture from heat, and stir in chopped parsley, oregano, and thyme. Cool. Stir in mozzarella cheese. Spoon about ⅓ cup mushroom mixture into each cannelloni shell. Arrange stuffed shells in a 13×9 dish.

Combine Alfredo sauce and basil, and pour over stuffed shells. Cover shells with foil, and bake at 325°F for 20 minutes or until thoroughly heated. Sprinkle tomatoes and Parmesan cheese over shells, and garnish with parsley sprigs, if desired.

Vegetarian Lasagna
8 to 10 Servings

1 large butternut squash
3 medium delicata squash
(or acorn squash)
1 12-ounce package lasagna noodles
½ cup cashews
½ cup vegetable stock
1 teaspoon vinegar
¼ to ½ cup lemon juice
2 tablespoons chopped sage

1 tablespoon chopped
marjoram
salt to taste
pepper to taste
2 28-ounce jars of your favorite
tomato pasta sauce
1 cup shredded mozzarella
cheese
1 cup fresh breadcrumbs
1 tablespoon chopped Italian
parsley

Cut squash in half and remove seeds. Sprinkle salt and pepper on flesh of squash. Place squash face down on a greased sheet in roasting pan. Roast squash at 350°F for 30 to 40 minutes, or until tender. Allow squash to cool to room temperature. Bring 8 quarts of water and 2 tablespoons of salt to a rolling boil in a large saucepan. When the water boils, add lasagna noodles and cook until barely tender. Drain and separate the noodles. Keep in a bowl of ice water.

In mixing bowl or food processor fitted with metal blade, process cashews until they become a paste, and slowly add water, a little at a time, until the mixture takes on a thick creamy or buttery texture. Add the squash, vegetable stock, vinegar, lemon juice, sage, marjoram, salt, and pepper and process until smooth.

Lightly grease a 9×13×3 ovenproof dish or lasagna pan. Put a little pasta sauce on the bottom of the pan and cover it with a layer of noodles. Spoon a third of the squash mixture on top of the noodles, followed by a third of the sauce and then sprinkle a third of the mozzarella cheese. Continue layering until all the ingredients are used, finishing with mozzarella and a cup of fresh breadcrumbs.

Cover the lasagna with aluminum foil, and bake at 350°F for about 30 minutes. Uncover and continue to cook until golden and bubbly. Sprinkle the chopped fresh parsley on top. Let stand for 15 minutes before serving.

Peanutty Noodles
10 Servings

16 ounces dried linguini
2 carrots, peeled
1 tablespoon vegetable oil, divided
2 teaspoons peeled and grated
　fresh ginger
3 garlic cloves, minced
1 cup fat-free, low-sodium
　chicken broth
½ cup natural style peanut butter
¼ cup low-sodium soy sauce

3 tablespoons rice or white
　wine vinegar
1 teaspoon chili garlic sauce
¼ teaspoon salt
2 teaspoons oil
cooking spray
2 cups red bell pepper, cut in
　strips
1 pound snow peas, trimmed
½ cup chopped fresh cilantro

Cook linguini according to package directions. Drain, and set aside. Shave the carrots lengthwise into thin strips using a vegetable peeler; set aside.

Heat 1 teaspoon oil in a small saucepan over medium heat. Add the ginger and minced garlic; sauté 30 seconds. Add chicken broth, peanut butter, soy sauce, vinegar, chili garlic sauce, and salt; stir until well blended. Reduce heat; simmer 7 minutes, stirring occasionally. Remove from heat; keep warm.

Heat 2 teaspoons oil in large non-stick skillet coated with cooking spray over medium-high heat. Add bell pepper and snow peas; sauté 5 minutes or until tender. Remove from heat. Combine carrots, peanut butter mixture, vegetable mixture, and linguini in large bowl. Toss well; sprinkle with cilantro. Serve warm or at room temperature.

Thai Noodle Salad
4 to 6 Servings

1 bag #3 Chinese noodles
2 tablespoons sesame oil
¼ cup soy sauce
2 tablespoons rice wine vinegar
1 tablespoon hot chili oil
1 tablespoon sugar

1 teaspoon minced fresh ginger
1 bunch green onions,
   chopped
2 red bell peppers (optional)
1 16-ounce package sliced
   mushrooms, optional

Cook noodles according to package directions; drain. Mix oil, soy sauce, vinegar, hot chili oil, sugar, ginger, onions, bell peppers, and mushrooms into cooked and drained noodles. Can make ahead and serve either hot or cold.

Note: *#3 Chinese noodles refers to noodle size. They can be found at area specialty stores.*

Noodles Romanoff
6 to 8 Servings

6 ounces thin- or medium-width
   egg noodles
1 cup cottage cheese
1 cup sour cream
¼ cup finely chopped onion
1 clove garlic, minced

2 teaspoons Worcestershire
   sauce
dash of Tabasco
½ teaspoon salt
½ cup grated Parmesan
   cheese

Cook noodles according to package directions. In large bowl, mix noodles, cottage cheese, sour cream, onion, garlic, Worcestershire, Tabasco, and salt. Put in a greased 8×8 pan; sprinkle Parmesan on top. Bake at 350°F for 30 minutes.

Note: *Can be assembled in advance and refrigerated for a day. Bring to room temperature and bake as directed. This is a great side dish with meats.*

Gourmet Noodles
4 Servings

¼ pound butter
½ pound mushrooms, sliced
¼ cup chopped onion
¼ cup sliced almonds
1 clove garlic, minced

1 tablespoon lemon juice
1 10-ounce can beef
  consommé
4 ounces medium egg
  noodles, uncooked

Melt butter. Add mushrooms, onion, almonds, and garlic; cook about 10
minutes on low heat. Add lemon juice, consommé, and noodles; cook
until noodles are tender, about 10 minutes.

Note: *Great with steak or roast.*

Gourmet Macaroni and Cheese
6 to 8 Servings

16 ounces elbow macaroni
1 stick butter
2½ cups heavy whipping cream
2 eggs, beaten
2 ounces sharp cheddar cheese

2 ounces mild cheddar cheese
2 ounces Muenster cheese
2 ounces Monterey Jack
  cheese
4 ounces smoked Gouda
8 ounces Velveeta cheese

Cook macaroni according to package directions and drain. Spread into
a buttered baking dish. Melt butter. Add heavy whipping cream, eggs,
sharp cheddar, mild cheddar, Muenster, Monterey Jack, smoked Gouda,
and Velveeta cheese. Stir over low heat until cheeses are melted. Pour
cheese mixture over macaroni. Bake at 350°F for 30 minutes.

Mac and Cheese
8 to 10 Servings

1 pound elbow macaroni	4 cups whole milk
8 tablespoons butter	2 cups shredded cheddar
6 tablespoons flour	cheese
1 tablespoon dry mustard	2 cups cubed Velveeta cheese
1 tablespoon paprika	1 cup shredded provel cheese
1 teaspoon hot sauce	2 teaspoons salt

Cook macaroni according to package directions, drain, set aside. Melt butter, add flour, and make a roux. Add dry mustard, paprika, and hot sauce and cook about one minute. Add milk slowly to the roux, stirring constantly. Cook about 2 minutes or until thick. Add all the cheeses and salt, stir until melted. Combine cheese sauce and macaroni. Place in a buttered casserole dish. Bake at 350°F for 30 minutes.

Toasted Orzo Pilaf
6 Servings

1 tablespoon olive oil	½ teaspoon dried thyme leaves
¾ cup diced red onion	½ teaspoon salt
1⅓ cups orzo	¼ teaspoon ground black pepper
2¾ cups reduced sodium chicken broth	

In a skillet, heat olive oil over medium heat. Add red onion; cook covered for 3 minutes stirring occasionally. Increase heat to high. Add orzo and cook 3 to 4 minutes, stirring frequently. Slowly stir in broth. Add thyme, salt, and pepper and heat to boiling. Reduce heat to low. Cover skillet and cook 15 minutes or until liquid is absorbed and orzo is tender. Let orzo stand 5 minutes before serving.

Orzo with Artichokes and Pine Nuts
4 Servings

1½ cups orzo (10 ounces)
3 tablespoons pine nuts
¼ cup extra-virgin olive oil
2 tablespoons red wine vinegar
¾ teaspoon salt
½ teaspoon black pepper

1 14-ounce can whole
artichoke hearts, drained,
rinsed and chopped (not
marinated)
½ cup finely chopped fresh
flat-leaf parsley
1 teaspoon finely grated fresh
lemon zest

Cook orzo in a 4- to 5-quart pot of boiling water until al dente. Drain. While orzo cooks, lightly toast pine nuts in a dry small skillet over moderate heat, stirring, until lightly toasted. Remove from heat and cool 1 minute; coarsely chop. In a large bowl, stir together oil, red wine vinegar, salt and pepper. Add orzo, pine nuts, artichokes, parsley, and lemon zest. Toss to combine.

Orzo with Tomatoes, Olives, and Feta
6 Servings

1½ cups tri-color orzo
¼ cup pine nuts
3 tablespoons extra-virgin olive oil
2 tablespoons minced garlic
2 medium tomatoes, halved, seeded,
and chopped (about 2 cups) or
1 pint grape tomatoes, chopped
¾ cup pitted, whole kalamata olives

1 tablespoon grated or zested
lemon peel
¼ cup fresh lemon juice
1 cup crumbled feta cheese
2 tablespoons chopped fresh
basil
salt
freshly ground black pepper

Cook orzo according to package directions; drain, set aside. Lightly toast pine nuts in a dry, small skillet over moderate heat, stirring, until lightly browned. Set aside. In large skillet, heat olive oil over medium-high heat. Add garlic; cook until softened, about 1 minute. Add tomatoes, olives, zested lemon and juice; stir until well mixed. Add cooked orzo. Cook, stirring occasionally, until heated through, about 2 to 3 minutes. Transfer to large serving bowl. Sprinkle feta and basil over top, lightly toss until well combined. Season with salt and pepper. Sprinkle pine nuts over top. Serve warm or at room temperature.

Pasta Salads
Greek Orzo Salad
12 Servings

½ cup pine nuts
16 ounces orzo
4 cups chicken broth
2 cups water
2 tablespoons olive oil
½ cup chopped green onion
1 cup chopped fresh spinach
½ cup chopped basil
½ cup chopped red pepper
½ cup chopped yellow pepper
½ cup sliced kalamata olives
1 cup crumbled feta cheese

Dressing:
½ cup olive oil
3 tablespoons fresh lemon juice
½ teaspoon salt
½ teaspoon pepper

In small dry pan, toast pine nuts over moderate heat until lightly browned. Set aside. Cook orzo in chicken broth and water according to package directions, drain. In large bowl, toss orzo with olive oil to coat. Mix green onion, spinach, basil, red pepper, yellow pepper, olives, feta cheese, and pine nuts with orzo.

Dressing:
Whisk olive oil, lemon juice, salt, and pepper.

Combine orzo mixture and dressing. Refrigerate and serve cold.

Greek Pasta Salad
6 Servings

Pasta Salad:
2 medium zucchini, thinly
  sliced lengthwise
1 medium yellow pepper,
  halved lengthwise, seeded
2 tablespoons olive oil
ground black pepper, to taste
kosher salt, to taste
1 pound medium pasta shells
2 tablespoons salt for pasta water
1 pound medium cooked shrimp,
  halved lengthwise
8 ounces cherry or grape
  tomatoes, halved
¾ cup pitted coarsely chopped
  kalamata olives
1 cup crumbled feta (can use
  low fat or fat free)
½ small red onion, diced
2 teaspoons dried oregano

Dijon Vinaigrette:
¼ cup rice wine vinegar
2 tablespoons Dijon mustard
1 large clove garlic, minced
big pinch kosher salt
black pepper to taste
⅔ cup extra-virgin olive oil

Toss zucchini and bell pepper with olive oil, salt, and pepper; arrange on large baking sheet with sides. Adjust oven rack to highest position and broil 8 to 10 minutes until spotty brown, turning zucchini slices and pepper halves once. Set aside in large bowl to cool, then cut into bite size pieces.

Cook pasta in salted water according to package directions. Drain thoroughly (do not rinse) and place onto baking sheet. Set aside to cool.

Combine vegetables, pasta, shrimp, tomatoes, olive, feta, red onion, and oregano in large bowl. Add dressing and toss to serve at room temperature. Can be served cold; refrigerate several hours, without dressing, before serving.

Dijon Vinaigrette:
Whisk rice wine vinegar, Dijon mustard, garlic, salt, and pepper together, then slowly whisk in the oil.

Mexican Pasta Salad
6 Servings

1 pound fusilli pasta
1½ tablespoons olive oil
4 large tomatoes, seeded,
  diced (4 cups)
3 cups corn kernels, fresh or
  frozen and thawed
3 large carrots, thinly sliced on
  diagonal, slices cut lengthwise
  into thin strips
½ large red onion, chopped

Dressing:
½ cup mayonnaise
2 tablespoons Dijon mustard
2 tablespoons fresh lime juice
2 jalapeno chilies, seeded, minced
1¼ teaspoons chili powder
1¼ teaspoons ground cumin
½ cup chopped cilantro
salt
pepper

Cook fusilli in large pot of boiling salted water according to package directions until al dente. Drain, rinse pasta with cold water to cool, drain again. Transfer pasta to large bowl. Add olive oil and mix thoroughly to coat. Add diced tomatoes, corn kernels, carrot strips, onion and toss.

Dressing:
Mix mayonnaise, Dijon mustard, and fresh lime juice in small bowl. Mix in minced jalapeno chilies, chili powder, and ground cumin.

Add dressing and chopped fresh cilantro to pasta and mix to blend. Season to taste with salt and pepper.

Bowtie Pasta Salad
12 servings

Pasta Salad:
1 12-ounce package of veggie bowtie pasta (or any tri-colored pasta)
1 12-ounce beef summer sausage cubed into bite-sized pieces
1 3.8-ounce can sliced black olives
¾ of 5¾-ounce jar sliced green olives
1 small white onion, finely diced
1 cup shredded cheddar cheese
1 cup shredded mozzarella cheese

Balsamic Vinaigrette Dressing:
¼ cup balsamic vinegar
¾ cup extra-virgin olive oil
1 teaspoon garlic powder
½ teaspoon salt
½ teaspoon black pepper

Bring 6 to 8 quarts of water to a rolling boil over high heat. Add 12 ounces of pasta and boil uncovered for 11 to 13 minutes or until tender. Drain and rinse with cold water. Pour drained pasta in large bowl. Add the chopped sausage, black olives, green olives, onion, cheddar cheese, and mozzarella cheese to the pasta.

Put balsamic vinegar, olive oil, garlic powder, salt, and pepper in screw-top container and shake well (or whisk in small bowl until thoroughly mixed). Pour half of the dressing onto salad and toss. Add more dressing as needed.

Note: *You most likely will only use half the dressing and can refrigerate the remainder. For best results, make a day ahead of serving and chill in refrigerator. Refrigerate any unused portions.*

Rice & Beans

Arroz Negro
6 to 8 Servings

Chef Grace Dinsmoor *is passionate about Spanish cuisine, and this is one of her favorite recipes. Celebrating 10 years in business,* Modesto *is known for its delicious tapas, attentive service, and fun atmosphere.*

2 teaspoons squid ink (see note)
6 cups vegetable broth
2 lobster tails
½ cup olive oil
1 onion, chopped
2 cloves garlic, minced
½ cup dry white wine
2 cups uncooked Bomba
  rice (see note)

6 shrimp
½ pound squid, cleaned and
  sliced
1 tablespoon sea salt
freshly ground pepper
parsley for garnish
lemon wedges for garnish
lemon aioli (garlic mayonnaise)
  for garnish

In a small pot over medium heat, whisk squid ink into vegetable broth to combine well; heat until warm and set aside. Remove shells from lobster, cut meat into small pieces.

Heat olive oil in a paella pan or large oven-safe skillet. Add onion and garlic; cook, stirring for 2 minutes. Add wine, rice, lobster meat, shrimp, squid, salt, and pepper to taste. Cook for 5 minutes, stirring frequently; gradually stir in stock mixture.

Transfer to the oven and bake at 425°F, uncovered, until broth is absorbed, 20 to 25 minutes. Do not stir; finished paella should have a slightly crusted top. To check for doneness, insert a narrow spatula into mixture and check to make sure liquid has been absorbed. To serve, sprinkle with parsley; garnish with lemon wedges and aioli.

Note: *Bomba or Calasparra Rice from Spain will absorb the broth and remain as separate grains. These may be bought at Williams-Sonoma. Squid ink is available at Asian markets.*

Orange, Spinach, Salmon Risotto
4 Servings

Bernard Pilon, *CEC, was a chef in Montreal and Maryland before arriving in St. Louis in 1995. He has been the Executive Chef at* Norwood Hills Country Club *since 2000, and won the Chef of the Year Award in 2007. His family includes his wife Stephanie, his daughter Olivia, and his son Brian.*

8 ounces of salmon chunks
olive oil
1 small onion, minced
1 tablespoon butter
1 cup arborio rice
2½ cups of fish stock or chicken
stock, warmed

3 cups spinach, clipped and
cleaned
1 teaspoon of orange zest
2 ounces of pine nuts
salt and pepper

Sear salmon lightly in olive oil and reserve.

Cook onion in butter and olive oil. Add rice and cook for 1 minute. Add ½ cup of warmed stock and stir until almost completely absorbed, about 2 minutes. Continue adding the stock, ½ cup at a time, stirring constantly and allowing each addition of stock to absorb before adding the next; approximately 15 to 18 minutes.

Add salmon, spinach, orange zest, and pine nuts. Salt and pepper to taste. Cook 1 minute longer and serve.

Smoked Gouda Risotto with Spinach and Mushrooms
6 Servings

Risotto:
2 cups water
2 16-ounce cans fat-free, less-sodium chicken broth
1 tablespoon butter
⅓ cup chopped shallots
2 cups arborio rice or other short-grain rice
½ cup dry white wine
½ teaspoon salt
1½ cups (6 ounces) shredded smoked Gouda cheese
5 cups (about 5 ounces) chopped spinach

1 tablespoon olive oil
2 cups (about 3½ ounces) sliced shiitake mushroom caps

2 cups (about ½ pound) sliced button mushrooms
2 cups (about ½ pound) sliced cremini mushrooms
2 cups (about 3½ ounces) sliced oyster mushrooms
⅓ cup chopped shallots
¼ cup dry white wine
1½ teaspoons chopped fresh thyme
1½ teaspoons chopped fresh rosemary
1 garlic clove, minced
¼ teaspoon salt
¼ teaspoon black pepper
¼ cup (1 ounce) grated fresh Parmesan cheese
rosemary sprigs (optional)

To prepare risotto, combine water and broth; set aside. Melt butter in a large nonstick saucepan over medium heat. Add ⅓ cup shallots; cover and cook 2 minutes. Add rice; cook 2 minutes, uncovered, stirring constantly. Stir in ½ cup wine and ½ teaspoon salt; cook 30 seconds or until the liquid is nearly absorbed, stirring constantly. Add broth mixture, ½ cup at a time, stirring constantly until each portion of broth mixture is absorbed before adding the next (about 20 minutes total). Stir in Gouda; cook until melted. Stir in spinach; cook until spinach is wilted. Set aside.

To prepare mushrooms, heat olive oil in a large nonstick skillet over medium-high heat. Add mushrooms and sauté 5 minutes or until beginning to brown. Add shallots, wine, chopped thyme, chopped rosemary, and minced garlic, and sauté 1 minute or until wine is absorbed. Sprinkle with salt and pepper.

Divide risotto evenly among 6 bowls; top with mushroom mixture, and sprinkle with Parmesan. Garnish with rosemary sprigs, if desired.

Brown Butter Risotto with Lobster
4 Servings

1 pound (about 2 medium)
frozen lobster tails, thawed
4½ cups reduced-sodium
chicken stock
4 tablespoons butter, at
room temperature
1 cup finely chopped onion

1½ cups arborio rice
½ cup brandy
½ cup grated Parmesan
¼ cup chopped fresh chives
kosher salt
freshly ground black pepper

Bring a medium saucepan of salted water to a boil. Add the lobster tails and continue boiling for 8 to 10 minutes until the shells curl and the lobster meat turns white. Drain, transfer to a cutting board, and cool for 15 minutes. Using kitchen shears or a sharp knife, cut through the top shell lengthwise. Remove the meat and cut into ½-inch pieces. Set aside.

In a medium saucepan, bring the chicken stock to a boil. Keep hot over low heat.

In a large saucepan, melt 3 tablespoons of butter over medium heat. Cook until the butter begins to foam and then turns brown, about 1 to 1½ minutes. Add the onion and cook, about 3 minutes. Add the rice and stir to coat.

Add the brandy and simmer until the liquid has almost evaporated, about 3 minutes. Add ½ cup of stock and stir until almost completely absorbed, about 2 minutes. Continue adding the stock, ½ cup at a time, stirring constantly and allowing each addition of stock to absorb before adding the next. Cook until the rice is tender but still firm to the bite, about 20 minutes. Remove from the heat. Stir in the Parmesan cheese, the remaining 1 tablespoon butter and 2 tablespoons chives. Season with salt and pepper to taste.

Transfer the risotto to a large serving bowl. Arrange the lobster meat on top of the risotto and garnish with the remaining chives.

Gorgonzola Risotto
8 Servings

½ cup chopped walnuts
2 tablespoons margarine or butter
1 medium onion, thinly sliced
1 medium carrot, thinly sliced (about ½ cup)
2 cups uncooked arborio rice or regular long grain rice
3⅓ cups milk
1⅓ cups half and half
⅓ cup crumbled Gorgonzola or blue cheese
1 3-ounce package cream cheese, cut in cubes
¼ teaspoon pepper

Toast walnuts in a small dry skillet over moderate heat until lightly browned; set aside.

Melt margarine in 12-inch skillet or Dutch over medium-high heat. Cook onion and carrot in margarine for 5 to 7 minutes, stirring occasionally, until crisp tender. Reduce heat to medium; stir in rice. Cook, uncovered, stirring frequently, until rice begins to brown.

Mix milk and half-and-half; pour ½ cup milk mixture over rice mixture. Cook uncovered, stirring occasionally, until liquid is absorbed. Continue cooking 15 to 20 minutes, adding milk mixture ½ cup at a time until absorbed and stirring occasionally, until rice is tender and creamy. Stir in cheeses and pepper. Cook about 5 minutes, stirring frequently, until cheeses are melted.

Quick Saffron Risotto with Roasted Asparagus
4 to 6 Servings

12 stalks asparagus, woody ends trimmed
4 tablespoons olive oil
salt and freshly grounded black pepper
4½ to 5 cups chicken stock or water
1 large pinch saffron
1 small Spanish onion, finely chopped
1 clove garlic, finely chopped
1 cup arborio rice
1 cup dry white wine
¼ cup freshly grated Parmesan cheese

Place asparagus stalks on a rimmed baking sheet. Toss with 2 tablespoons olive oil. Season well with salt and pepper. Roast in oven at 425°F until tender, about 6 to 8 minutes. Move asparagus to a cutting board; slice on the bias into ½-inch pieces, set aside.

Bring stock (or water) to a simmer in a medium pan over high heat. Reduce heat so liquid bubbles but doesn't boil. Add saffron.

Heat remaining olive oil in a large, high-sided sauté pan over medium-high heat. Add onion and sauté; stirring until soft about 3 to 5 minutes. Add garlic, cook for 1 minute.

Pour in rice, stir constantly to prevent it from sticking to the pan. After 2 minutes, add wine; stir until wine is completely absorbed. Add 1 cup stock (or water) to pan, stir often. When liquid has been absorbed, add another cup of stock and stir. Repeat steps until risotto is creamy and soft (requiring 4 to 5 cups of stock and about 20 minutes). Stir asparagus and cheese into risotto. Season with salt and pepper to taste.

Serve immediately.

Nutted Wild and Brown Rice
12-plus Servings

½ cup dry sherry	1 cup brown rice
1 cup golden raisins	1 cup slivered almonds
1 cup wild rice	1 cup chopped fresh parsley
4⅔ cups chicken stock	salt
6 tablespoons butter (divided)	pepper

Heat sherry and raisins in a small sauce pan to boiling, reduce heat and simmer 5 minutes, set aside. Bring 4⅔ cups chicken stock to boil. Place wild rice and 2 tablespoons butter into top of double boiler over simmering water. Add 2 cups boiling chicken stock. Cook, covered for one hour. Place brown rice, remaining 2⅔ cups boiling chicken stock and 2 tablespoons butter in a medium-sized saucepan. Heat to boiling; reduce heat to low and cook until all water is absorbed, about 50 minutes. Sauté almonds in the remaining 2 tablespoons butter in a small skillet over low heat until lightly toasted. Combine wild rice, brown rice, raisins, almonds and parsley in a large mixing bowl. Season to taste with salt and pepper. Place in 3-quart dish. Cover and refrigerate until serving.

Note: *Can be prepared the day before; cover and refrigerate.*

Corn and Green Chile Rice
12 Servings

1 cup uncooked regular long grain white rice	1 8-ounce container sour cream
2 cups water	1 4.5-ounce can green chiles, chopped
1 cup cottage cheese	4 ounces shredded Mexican cheese blend
1 11-ounce can Mexicorn	

Cook rice in water according to package directions. Spray a 2-quart casserole with cooking spray. In large bowl combine cooked rice, cottage cheese, Mexicorn, sour cream, and green chiles, mix well. Pour mixture into casserole and then sprinkle with Mexican cheese. Bake at 350°F for 30 to 35 minutes, or until thoroughly heated.

Spring Green Rice
6 to 8 Servings

2 cups uncooked rice
2 eggs, beaten
⅓ cup vegetable oil
2 Vidalia onions, chopped
2 cups grated Parmesan cheese
2 teaspoons salt

1 clove garlic, minced
1 cup finely chopped parsley
1 can cream of mushroom
  soup
1 cup milk (soup can filled with
  milk)

Mix together all ingredients. Place in a 9×13 inch casserole dish. Bake at 375°F for 45 minutes.

Note: *Great for an Easter buffet.*

Spicy Black Beans and Rice
4 Servings

½ cup rice
1 teaspoon olive oil
1¼ cups diced onion
¾ cup finely chopped carrots
1 tablespoon minced garlic
2 tablespoons dry sherry
1 tablespoon balsamic vinegar

1 teaspoon dried thyme
¼ teaspoon salt
½ teaspoon ground black pepper
2 15-ounce cans black beans,
  rinsed and drained
2 bay leaves

Cook rice according to package directions to make 2 cups cooked rice. Set aside.

In a large saucepan, heat oil over medium heat. Add onion, carrots, and garlic; sauté 10 minutes. Add cooked rice, sherry, balsamic vinegar, thyme, salt, black pepper, black beans, and bay leaves. Cover, reduce heat, and simmer 5 minutes or until heated thoroughly. Remove bay leaf before serving.

Note: *Great Lenten meal!*

Red Beans and Rice
8 Servings

1 tablespoon olive oil
2 large cloves garlic, minced
1 large red onion, diced
1 stalk celery, diced
1 green bell pepper, stem and seeds
 removed and diced small
2 16-ounce cans red kidney beans
1 teaspoon onion powder
1 teaspoon salt
¼ teaspoon ground black pepper

1 teaspoon Creole seasoning
1 tablespoon hot sauce (add
 more as needed)
2½ cups chicken stock
1 cup white rice
1 tablespoon butter
1 tablespoon minced fresh
 cilantro leaves

Heat olive oil over medium-high heat in a large saucepan. Sauté garlic, onion, celery, and bell pepper until tender. Stir in kidney beans, onion powder, salt, pepper, Creole seasoning, and hot sauce. Reduce heat to low and let mixture simmer for 20 minutes.

Bring the chicken stock to a boil and stir in rice and butter. Return to a boil, reduce heat to low, cover and cook for 20 minutes without removing the lid. Remove from heat and let stand for 5 minutes.

Fold rice and beans gently together and transfer to a serving dish. Serve garnished with cilantro.

Note: *Can add cooked Chorizo sausage (2 links) for a little more substance.*

Italian-Style Baked Beans
6 Servings

6 ounces thinly sliced pancetta, chopped
2 onions, chopped
4 garlic cloves, minced
1 cup dark beer
1 cup tomato sauce
⅓ cup dark brown sugar
¼ cup balsamic vinegar
3 tablespoons mild-flavored molasses
6 teaspoons Dijon mustard
¾ teaspoon salt
½ teaspoon freshly ground black pepper
4 15-ounce cans cannellini beans, drained

Cook the pancetta in a heavy, large oven-safe pot over medium-heat until crisp, about 8 minutes. Add the onions and garlic, and sauté until the onions are translucent, about 5 minutes. Mix in the beer, tomato sauce, brown sugar, vinegar, molasses, mustard, salt, and pepper. Stir in the cannellini beans. Bring to a simmer.

Transfer pot to the oven and bake at 400°F, uncovered, until the bean mixture bubbles and thickens slightly, stirring occasionally, about 45 minutes.

Meaty BBQ Beans
10 to 12 Servings

1 pound ground beef
½ pound ground pork sausage
10 strips bacon
4 regular cans pork and beans, pick out and discard pork fat
1 cup barbeque sauce
1 cup molasses
4 or 5 dashes Worcestershire sauce
3 or 4 dashes Tabasco
1 teaspoon black pepper
½ cup chopped onion
½ cup chopped green pepper

Cook ground beef and sausage, drain fat. Cook bacon; drain and chop. In a large bowl, mix ground beef, sausage, bacon, beans, barbeque sauce, molasses, Worcestershire sauce, Tabasco, pepper, onion, and green pepper together. Put in a 9×13 casserole dish. Bake at 375°F for 45 minutes.

Black Eyed Pea and Corn Salsa
4 to 6 Servings

8 ounces Italian salad dressing
2 14-ounces black eyed peas, drained
(can substitute with kidney beans)
1 14-ounce can shoe peg corn
2 medium ripe tomatoes, chopped

4 green onions, chopped
¼ cup chopped parsley
1 green pepper, chopped
1 white onion, chopped
2 cloves garlic, minced

Combine Italian salad dressing, black eyed peas, shoe peg corn, chopped tomatoes, onions, parsley, pepper, onion, and minced garlic and refrigerate for 4 hours.

Note: *This very easy side dish is always a hit and is healthy, too. Can substitute own salad dressing.*

Red Lentils with Sesame
8 Servings

2 teaspoons peanut oil
1 teaspoon dark sesame oil
½ cup finely chopped shallots
2 cups dried red lentils
1½ cups water
2 tablespoons low-sodium soy sauce

¼ teaspoon salt
14 ounces chicken broth
1 cup finely sliced
green onions
1 tablespoon toasted
sesame seeds

Heat oils over medium heat. Add shallots; cook 3 minutes or until tender. Add lentils, 1½ cups water, soy sauce, salt, and broth. Bring to a boil. Cover and then simmer for 20 minutes stirring occasionally, until lentils are tender. Stir in green onions. Sprinkle with sesame seeds and serve.

Vegetables & Sides

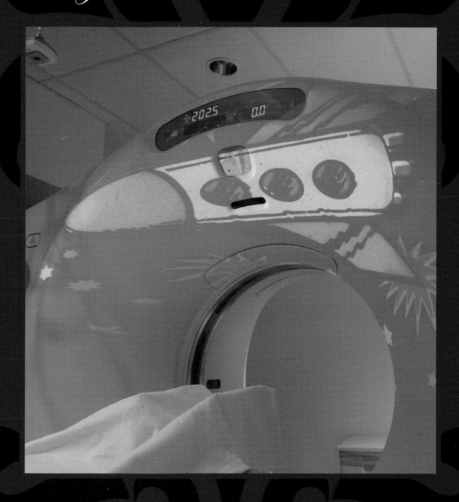

Getting an MRI or CT scan can be a frightening experience. Fun colors on big equipment can make these tests and scans more bearable and help put children at ease. Blast off!

Vegetables

Coliflor al Azfran
(Roasted Cauliflower with Saffron)
4 Servings

Chef David Molina *has been the Executive Chef at* BARcelona Tapas Restaurant *since September of 2002; at BARcelona, he created the Spanish Menu at the first true Spanish Tapas Bar in downtown Clayton. David is currently working on opening Bocci Bar, the newest addition to the BARcelona family, to be completed April 2011.*

Cauliflower:
½ teaspoon turmeric
2 pinches of saffron
1 gallon of water
1 cauliflower head

Sauté:
3 tablespoons olive oil
3 tablespoons pine nuts
3 tablespoons raisins
2 cups white wine
½ cup diced Roma tomatoes
4 cups spinach leaves
salt and pepper to taste

Cauliflower:
Bring turmeric and saffron to a boil in 1 gallon of water. Break cauliflower into bite-size pieces and add to boiling water. Cook for 7 minutes, until cauliflower is tender. Cool using ice bath.

Sauté:
In a hot skillet, add cauliflower, olive oil, pine nuts, and raisins. Sauté until cauliflower is seared on all sides. Add wine, diced tomatoes, spinach, salt, and pepper. Continuously toss in sauté pan until spinach is wilted. Remove from heat and serve.

Oven-Roasted Artichokes with Brie and Mustard Butter Sauce

4 Servings

Like the vibrant neighborhood surrounding it, Scape *is an eclectic blend of classic and contemporary. The inventive American cuisine is set against the backdrop of warmth and sophistication. Chef* Eric Kelly *has a passion for culturally diverse cuisine, and has had continued success in St. Louis.*

kosher salt
4 fresh large artichokes
ice water
12 ounce double-cream Brie cheese
1 teaspoon extra-virgin olive oil
1 tablespoon minced shallots

¼ cup white wine
¼ cup rice wine vinegar
1 tablespoon heavy cream
1 cup (2 sticks) cold butter,
  cut into cubes
ground white pepper
1 tablespoon grainy mustard

Bring a large pot of water to a boil. Stir in 2 teaspoons salt. Meanwhile, cut off artichoke stems and slice ½ inch off the top of each. Add artichokes to boiling water. Place plate on the surface of the water to keep the artichokes submerged. Boil for exactly 25 minutes. Using tongs, carefully remove artichokes. Transfer immediately to a large bowl of ice water. Let cool completely, then remove from ice water and drain upside down for 15 minutes. Use your fingers to open the center of each artichoke. Reach into the middle and pull out the "choke" (the small spiky leaves and thistle-like fuzz). Slice cheese into 8 equal pieces. Stuff the center of each artichoke with a piece of cheese. Using 1 piece of remaining cheese for each artichoke, pull the artichoke "petals" slightly away from the center and smear cheese under the petals. Place artichoke upright in a baking pan; bake at 400°F for 10 to 12 minutes.

While artichokes bake, prepare the sauce. Warm olive oil in a nonstick pan over low heat. Add shallots and sweat, stirring often, 3 to 4 minutes or until translucent, making sure the shallots do not begin to brown. Add wine and vinegar, increase heat to medium, and cook until liquid reduces to a slightly syrupy consistency. Stir in cream; cook until liquid is reduced by half. Using a wire whisk, add butter all at once and whisk constantly until 95% of the butter has melted.

Remove from heat and continue whisking until completely melted. Place a fine sieve over another pan; strain sauce and discard shallots. Stir in a pinch of salt, a pinch of white pepper, and mustard. Keep warm until ready to serve. Carefully remove artichokes from oven with tongs and arrange on serving plates. Drizzle sauce over and around each artichoke.

Green Bean and Mushroom Stir Fry with Black Bean and Oyster Sauces
2 to 4 Servings

When Mai Lee *opened in 1985, it was the first Vietnamese restaurant in St. Louis. Bringing the unique cuisine of Vietnam to their customers, Master Chef Lee Tran and her family have taken Mai Lee from its original, tiny 6-table restaurant to its beautiful new location in Brentwood.*

⅓ pound fresh green beans
⅓ pound mushrooms, halved,
olive or vegetable oil
2 cloves garlic, minced
a few slices of ginger root

Optional:
cilantro
Asian basil

1 teaspoon black bean sauce
½ tablespoon oyster sauce
¾ tablespoon sugar
3 to 4 tablespoons rice
cooking wine
1 pinch cracked black pepper

Blanch green beans and mushrooms in hot water on high heat for 1 to 2 minutes. In separate pan, heat splash of olive or vegetable oil on moderate temperature. Add garlic and ginger to oil and swish around for 15 to 20 seconds. Add vegetables and stir until they adequately absorb garlic and ginger. Add black bean sauce, then oyster sauce and stir 15 to 20 seconds. Add sugar then rice wine; stir 15 to 20 seconds. Season with pepper.

Optional: add cilantro and Asian basil.

Roasted Mushrooms
4 Servings

Liluma *is a New American jewel in the fashionable Central West End. This lively bistro is the place to dine for top-notch French- and Italian-inspired fare that makes inventive use of quality local ingredients.* Chef Brad Watts *does simple but great food with all the local ingredients he can find.*

1 cup port wine reduced to ¼ cup for garnish (optional)
½ cup cleaned and quartered medium (domestic) mushrooms
½ cup cleaned, de-stemmed, and sliced shiitake mushrooms
½ cup cleaned and sliced cremini mushrooms
½ cup oyster mushrooms, cleaned and rough chopped

canola oil for sautéing
garlic, chopped
salt and pepper to taste
4 ounces Brie
extra-virgin olive oil
⅓ cup Italian flat leaf parsley, rinsed and picked from stems

If you decide to use the port wine, start reducing it while you are cleaning and prepping your mushrooms. When all mushrooms are ready, divide into 2 even amounts. Bring 2 sauté pans to medium-high heat. When ready, add enough canola oil to coat the bottom of the pans. Add the mushrooms to each of the pans. The mushrooms will soak up a majority of the oil. If the pans seem to dry, add a little more oil.

Next add ½ teaspoon chopped garlic to each pan. Make sure to give it a quick stir to coat the mushrooms with garlic so it does not burn. Season with salt and pepper. Once mushrooms are cooked, divide among 4 small bowls. Cover each bowl with 1 ounce of the Brie. Place in a 375°F oven for 2 to 3 minutes (just enough to slightly melt the Brie). Drizzle desired amount of extra-virgin olive oil on top of Brie after removing from the oven. When ready, finish with the parsley leafs and the port reduction if desired.

Note: *The reason for using canola oil for the cooking process is because it has a higher smoke point. This means the oil can reach higher temperatures before burning. Refined canola oil is 400°F and extra-virgin olive oil is 375°F.*

Noodleless Vegetable Lasagna

8 Servings

Bethany Budde *is the owner and Executive Chef of* Sqwires Restaurant. *Budde was a pioneer in presenting seasonal menus featuring items that are locally grown and produced. The restaurant name was chosen for its location in the Western Wire Factory building in Lafayette Square.*

1 pound carrots	1 quart fresh tomato sauce
1½ pounds zucchini	½ pound Parmesan cheese
1½ pounds yellow squash	½ pound goat cheese, crumbled
1 pound red onion	1 teaspoon salt
olive oil	1 teaspoon pepper

Slice carrots, zucchini, and squash ⅛ inch thick on hard bias. Slice onion ⅛ inch thick. In mixing bowl, toss carrots with olive oil and salt and pepper. Repeat process for zucchini, squash, and onions. Grill all vegetables separately until cooked through; let cool 15 minutes.

In a 12-inch baking pan, place 1 cup fresh tomato sauce and spread to cover bottom of pan. Layer in this order: zucchini, squash, carrots, onions, sprinkle and spread with ¼ of both cheeses. Repeat 3 times and top with remaining cheese.

Bake at 300°F for 45 minutes. You may need to cover with foil if getting too brown.

Note: *This is not only a great vegetarian option, but also gluten free.*

Tuscan Ratatouille Terrine
12 Servings

Chef Todd Lough *began his culinary career while staying with his grandmother and watching her create amazing food without using a recipe or measuring anything. He spent time in San Francisco and Palm Beach before coming to St Louis, where he was the Executive Chef at Busch's Grove. He is now at* Bixby's at the Missouri History Museum.

3 large beefsteak tomatoes
2 shallots, finely diced
3 tablespoons sherry vinegar
salt and cracked black peppercorns
2 sheets gelatin
¼ cup extra-virgin olive oil
1 zucchini
1 Japanese eggplant
8 scallions
1 tablespoon chopped fresh rosemary
1 tablespoon chopped fresh thyme

1 bunch frisse (curly lettuce)
2 ounces arugula

3 tablespoons extra-virgin olive oil
salt and pepper to taste
1 red bell pepper
1 yellow bell pepper
2 medium red onions
¼ cup balsamic vinegar
1 tablespoon extra-virgin olive oil
2 leeks
2 ounces basil leaves

1 pint diakon sprouts
your favorite flatbread or crostinis

To make tomato coulis, core and cut tomatoes in half; char on grill. Place in food processor with shallots and vinegar and purée. Season with salt and fresh cracked black peppercorns. Strain through fine mesh strainer.

Take half of the tomato coulis and gently warm over double broiler. Soak gelatin sheets in cold water. Remove soft gelatin from water and melt into warm tomato coulis. Whisk olive oil into the other half of the tomato coulis, and set aside. Cut zucchini and eggplant ⅜ thick lengthwise. Season zucchini, eggplant, and scallions with rosemary, thyme, extra-virgin olive oil, salt, and pepper. Lightly grill on charbroiler and chill. Roast, peel, and seed bell peppers and cut into 4-inch wide panels.

Cut red onions into sixths. Place in roasting pan with balsamic vinegar, extra-virgin olive oil, salt, and pepper. Cover tightly with aluminum foil. Bake at 350°F for 15 minutes. Remove foil and cool.

Remove the first 5 layers of each leek, leaving the layers whole. Blanch for 90 seconds in boiling salted water then place in ice water. Brush terrine mold with olive oil. Line terrine mold with leeks. Line mold with alternating layers of vegetables and tomato coulis with gelatin. Fold leeks over the top. Place another identical terrine mold on top. Place in refrigerator and fill the empty terrine mold with water. Allow to set overnight.

Blanch basil leaves in boiling water for 5 seconds; cool in ice water. Squeeze out all water. Place in blender with 4 ounces olive oil and purée. Place in squeeze bottle and use as decorative garnish.

Slice terrine into 12 slices and present with basil purée, greens, sprouts, and flatbread.

Roasted Asparagus with Balsamic Browned Butter
8 Servings

2 pounds asparagus spears, trimmed
cooking spray
¼ teaspoon kosher salt
⅛ teaspoon freshly ground
   black pepper
2 tablespoons butter

2 teaspoons low-sodium soy
   sauce
1 teaspoon balsamic vinegar
cracked black pepper (optional)
grated lemon rind (optional)

Arrange asparagus in a single layer on a baking sheet; coat with cooking spray. Sprinkle with salt and pepper. Bake at 400°F for 12 minutes or until tender.

Melt butter in a small skillet over medium heat; cook 3 minutes or until lightly browned, shaking pan occasionally. Remove from heat. Stir in soy sauce and balsamic vinegar. Drizzle over asparagus, tossing well to coat. Garnish with cracked pepper and lemon rind, if desired.

Baked Artichokes with Gorgonzola and Herbs
4 Servings

4 artichokes
3 lemons
10 ounces mild Gorgonzola cheese,
  crumbled, at room temperature
2 tablespoons cream
2 teaspoons chopped fresh
  thyme leaves
2 teaspoons chopped fresh parsley leaves,
  plus 1 extra tablespoon

1 clove garlic, minced
salt
½ teaspoon freshly ground
  black pepper
3 tablespoons breadcrumbs
1 tablespoon olive oil

Bring a large pot of salted water to a boil over high heat. Trim the artichokes by cutting off the top 1 inch or so. Cut the stem close to the base of the artichoke so the artichoke can sit up straight, and remove some of the bottom leaves. Using kitchen shears, trim the sharp points off of any remaining outer leaves. Add the artichokes to the boiling water. Halve the lemons and squeeze the juice into the boiling water. Toss in the lemons. Cook the artichokes until tender, about 30 minutes. Drain the artichokes and let cool.

Meanwhile, in a small bowl, stir together the Gorgonzola, cream, thyme, 2 teaspoons parsley, garlic, salt, and pepper. In another small bowl stir together the breadcrumbs and remaining 1 tablespoon of parsley.

Remove the center of the artichokes using a small spoon. Stuff the cheese mixture into the center of the artichokes. Place the artichokes into a baking dish. Sprinkle the breadcrumb mixture over the top of the artichokes. Drizzle the tops of the artichokes with olive oil. Bake at 400°F until the artichokes are heated through, the cheese is melted, and the breadcrumbs are crisp and golden, about 25 minutes. Transfer the artichokes to a serving dish.

Asparagus with Cashew Butter
10 Servings

3 pounds fresh asparagus
½ cup butter
6 teaspoons freshly squeezed lemon juice
½ teaspoon dried marjoram
½ cup coarsely chopped salted cashew nuts

Cook asparagus in salted water in large covered skillet until tender, about 18 minutes. Drain and arrange on heated platter. While asparagus cooks, melt butter in small saucepan; add lemon juice, marjoram, and cashew nuts. Simmer over low heat for about 3 minutes. Pour over cooked asparagus.

Cold Asparagus with Grainy Mustard Vinaigrette
4 Servings

1 tablespoon chopped shallot
2 tablespoons balsamic vinegar
2 tablespoons grainy mustard
3 tablespoons olive oil
4 large fresh basil leaves, sliced into thin strips (or ½ teaspoon dried basil)
20 medium asparagus stalks, trimmed and peeled

In small bowl, mix together the chopped shallot, balsamic vinegar, and mustard. Allow to steep for 15 minutes. Pour in the oil slowly, whisking vigorously. Add the basil and set aside.

Steam the asparagus until tender, but still crisp (about 5 minutes). Drain off water, and refresh asparagus under cold running water to arrest cooking and preserve color. Dry on paper towels. May refrigerate until ready to serve or serve at room temperature.Arrange on a serving platter or individual plates. Whisk the vinaigrette again, and pour over the stalks.

Note: *Vinaigrette may be used with other green vegetables.*

Brussels Sprouts Lardons
6 Servings

2 tablespoons good-quality olive oil
6 ounces Italian pancetta or bacon,
 ¼-inch diced
1½ pounds Brussels sprouts,
 trimmed and cut in half

¾ teaspoon kosher salt
¾ teaspoon freshly ground
 pepper
¾ cup golden raisins
1¾ cups homemade chicken
 stock, or canned broth

Heat the olive oil in a large (12-inch) sauté pan, and add the pancetta. Cook over medium heat, stirring often, until the fat is rendered and the pancetta is golden brown and crisp, about 5 to 10 minutes. Remove the pancetta to a plate lined with a paper towel. Add the Brussels sprouts, salt, and pepper to the fat in the pan and sauté over medium heat for about 5 minutes, until lightly browned. Add the raisins and chicken stock. Lower the heat and cook uncovered, stirring occasionally, until the sprouts are tender when pierced with a knife, about 15 minutes. If the skillet becomes too dry, add a little chicken stock or water. Return the pancetta to the pan, heat through, season to taste, and serve.

Brussels Sprouts with Pancetta
4 Servings

2 tablespoons olive oil
3 ounces paper thin slices pancetta,
 coarsely chopped
2 cloves garlic, minced

1 pound fresh Brussels sprouts,
 trimmed and cut in half
¾ cup chicken broth
1 teaspoon Dijon mustard
salt and pepper

In a medium skillet, heat 1 tablespoon olive oil. Add pancetta and sauté 2 to 3 minutes. Add the garlic and sauté another 2 minutes. Remove pancetta and garlic from pan. Add 1 tablespoon olive oil to the pan and cook the Brussels sprouts over medium heat for 10 to 15 minutes until tender and the sprouts begin to brown. Add pancetta and garlic back in to pan. Add the broth and mustard and simmer until broth reduces enough to coat the sprouts. Season with salt and pepper to taste.

Note: *You can substitute bacon for the pancetta and also add shallots.*

German Red Cabbage
6 Servings

1 tablespoon butter
2 large tart apples, peeled and chopped
1 medium sweet onion, sliced thinly
1 medium head red cabbage,
   cored and thinly sliced
1½ cups water or chicken stock
1 cup cider vinegar

½ cup sugar
1 teaspoon salt
6 whole peppercorns
2 whole allspice
2 whole cloves
1 bay leaf
2 teaspoons cornstarch
2 teaspoons cold water

In a Dutch oven, melt butter and sauté apples and onions for 1 to 2 minutes until slightly softened. Add red cabbage, water, vinegar, sugar, and salt. Place the peppercorns, allspice, cloves, and bay leaf on a double thickness of cheesecloth; bring up corners of cloth and tie with kitchen string to form a bag. Add to Dutch oven. Bring to a boil. Reduce heat; cover and simmer for 1¼ hours.

Discard spice bag. In a small bowl, combine cornstarch and cold water until smooth; stir in cabbage mixture. Bring to a boil; cook and stir for 1 to 2 minutes or until thickened.

Note: *This makes an excellent side dish to sausages, beef, and just about any meat dish.*

Thyme Roasted Carrots
6 Servings

2 pounds carrots, peeled, cut on
   diagonal into ½-inch thick slices
1½ tablespoons olive oil

1½ teaspoons fresh thyme
   leaves
1½ tablespoons butter
salt and pepper

Toss carrots, oil, and thyme in large bowl. Sprinkle generously with salt and pepper. Spread carrots in a single layer on large rimmed baking sheet; dot with butter. Roast at 400°F until carrots are tender and brown, stirring occasionally, about 25 to 35 minutes.

Maque Choux
4 Servings

4 slices thick-sliced bacon, diced
¾ cup diced red bell pepper
½ cup diced onion
¼ cup dry sherry
4 cups fresh corn kernels

1 cup heavy cream
1 tablespoon Tabasco sauce
salt and pepper
½ cup thinly sliced scallions

Sauté bacon in a large sauté pan over medium heat until crisp; pour off all but 1 tablespoon drippings. Add bell pepper and onion, and cook until soft, about 5 minutes. Deglaze with sherry until nearly evaporated, scraping bits from bottom of pan. Stir in corn, cream, and Tabasco sauce; simmer until thickened, 3 to 4 minutes. Season with salt and pepper and then stir in scallions.

Creamy Corn Pudding
6 Servings

3 tablespoons butter or margarine
3 tablespoons flour
1 tablespoon sugar
¾ teaspoon salt

¾ cup milk
1 17-ounce can cream-style corn
3 eggs

Melt butter in a heavy saucepan over low heat; add flour, sugar, and salt, stirring until smooth. Cook 1 minute, stirring constantly. Gradually add milk; cook over medium heat, stirring constantly, until thickened and bubbly. Remove mixture from heat and stir in corn. Beat eggs well with a whisk. Gradually stir about a fourth of hot mixture into beaten eggs, then add eggs to remaining hot mixture, stirring constantly. Pour into a buttered 1½-quart casserole. Bake 350°F for 1 hour.

Note: *This recipe is a good side dish at Easter, Thanksgiving, and Christmas!*

Corn Boats
6 Servings

6 ears of corn, in husks
5½ tablespoons unsalted butter, divided
1 tablespoon chopped fresh cilantro
⅛ teaspoon Tabasco sauce
2 tablespoons mayonnaise
2 tablespoons fresh lime juice

10 ounces sharp white cheddar cheese, grated coarsely (about 3 cups)
salt and pepper
½ cup dry breadcrumbs
vegetable oil for brushing husks

Pull a length-wide strip of corn husk (about 1 to 1½ inches wide) from each ear to expose kernels; discard husk strip. Carefully peel back the remaining husks, keeping them attached to the stem ends, and snap the ear from the stem end. Discard the silk from the husks. Tear a thin strip from a tender inner piece of each husk and use it to tie the loose end of each husk together, forming a "boat."

Cut the kernels from the ears of corn and discard the cobs. In a large skillet, sauté the corn in 4 tablespoons of butter, over moderately high heat, stirring until just tender (about 5 minutes). Stir in the chopped cilantro, Tabasco sauce, mayonnaise, lime juice, and 2¾ cups of grated cheese. Stir until cheese is melted. Remove skillet from heat and season mixture with salt and pepper.

In a small skillet sauté the breadcrumbs in the remaining 1½ tablespoons butter over moderately high heat, stirring until golden brown (about 2 minutes).

Preheat the broiler. Brush the insides of the husk boats lightly with oil. Divide corn mixture among the "boats." Top the corn mixture with breadcrumbs and the remaining ¼ cup of cheese. Put the filled boats on a baking sheet and broil about 4 inches from the heat, until the cheese is melted and the tops are browned lightly (about 2 minutes).

Eggplant Soufflé
4 to 6 Servings

1 eggplant, peeled and cubed
¾ cup cracker crumbs
1 small onion, finely chopped
1 10-ounce can cream of mushroom soup

2 eggs, well beaten
¼ cup melted butter

Add cubed eggplant to salted water in a medium saucepan. Boil until eggplant is nearly soft and then drain. Add the eggplant to a bowl with the cracker crumbs, chopped onion, cream of mushroom soup, beaten eggs, and melted butter. Mix well and pour into a greased casserole dish. Bake at 350°F for 40 minutes.

Green Bean Bundles
4 Servings

1 stick butter
½ teaspoon pressed garlic
1 cup brown sugar

1 pound bacon (not cooked)
1 pound package fresh
   trimmed green beans

Melt butter in a saucepan. Stir in garlic and brown sugar.

Cut uncooked bacon strips in halves. Wrap each half bacon strip around 6 to 8 green beans. Place green bean bundles in a 9×13 glass baking pan. Pour butter mixture over green bean bundles. Marinate, covered, in refrigerator overnight.

When ready to serve, bake at 350°F for 30 minutes.

Green Bean Casserole
12 Servings

3 pounds green beans, trimmed
and cut in half
4 large shallots
1 tablespoon olive oil
1½ cups coarse fresh breadcrumbs
1 teaspoon chopped fresh thyme
leaves
½ teaspoon salt, divided

½ teaspoon pepper, divided
½ cup freshly grated
Parmesan cheese
3 cups 1% milk
3 tablespoons margarine
or butter
¼ cup flour
⅛ teaspoon freshly ground
nutmeg

Heat a covered 8-quart saucepan of salted water on high heat. When boiling, add beans and cook, uncovered, for 6 minutes or until bright green and just tender. Drain well and transfer to shallow 3-quart glass or ceramic baking dish.

Meanwhile, finely chop two shallots. Thinly slice remaining shallots; set aside. In 12-inch skillet, heat oil on medium until hot. Add chopped shallots and cook 4 to 7 minutes or until brown and tender, stirring occasionally. Add breadcrumbs and cook 2 minutes or until dry and golden, stirring. Transfer mixture to large bowl. Stir in thyme, ¼ teaspoon salt, ¼ teaspoons freshly ground black pepper, and Parmesan cheese. In microwave-safe measuring cup, microwave milk on high just until milk is warm.

Meanwhile, in same 12-inch skillet, melt margarine on medium. Add sliced shallots and cook 5 minutes or until golden brown and tender, stirring occasionally. Add flour and cook 2 minutes, stirring. Gradually pour milk into flour mixture in slow, steady stream, stirring constantly. Heat to boiling, stirring. Stir 2 minutes longer or until thickened (mixture should have consistency of heavy cream). Stir in nutmeg, ¼ teaspoon salt, and ¼ teaspoon freshly ground black pepper.

Pour sauce over green beans and stir gently until green beans are evenly coated. Spread breadcrumb mixture evenly over green bean mixture in casserole. Bake at 350°F for 30 minutes or until breadcrumbs are golden brown and sauce is bubbling.

Southern Green Beans

6 to 8 Servings

1½ pounds fresh green beans
10 strips bacon
6 tablespoons sugar

6 tablespoons vinegar
¼ cup slivered almonds

Wash the beans; remove ends and strings. Leave whole or cut into 1-inch pieces. In a 2-quart saucepan, cook beans in a small amount of boiling salted water, covered for 20 to 25 minutes or until crisp-tender. Drain and set aside.

In a 10-inch skillet, cook bacon until crisp. Remove bacon and crumble, reserving drippings in skillet. Stir sugar and vinegar into drippings. In a 1½-quart casserole, layer half of the beans, half of the crumbled bacon and half of the almonds. Repeat layering. Pour prepared drippings over all. Bake at 350°F for 45 minutes or until heated through.

Onion Patties

4 to 6 Servings

¾ cup flour
2 teaspoons baking powder
2 tablespoons sugar
½ teaspoon salt
1 tablespoon cornmeal

½ cup powdered milk
cold water
2½ cups chopped onions
cooking oil

Mix together flour, baking powder, sugar, salt, cornmeal, and powdered milk. Stir in enough cold water to form thick batter. Stir in onions and drop by the teaspoon full into hot deep oil in skillet. Flatten patties slightly as you turn them. Fry to a golden brown. Drain on paper towels. Serve hot.

Scalloped Vidalia Onions
6 to 8 Servings

4 pounds Vidalia or other
  sweet onions
1½ teaspoons olive oil
⅔ cup dry sherry
1 tablespoon butter
2 tablespoons flour

1 cup milk
¼ to ½ cup shredded Gruyere
  cheese
¾ teaspoon salt
¼ teaspoon black pepper

Trim and quarter onions and place in 13×9 pan coated with cooking spray. Drizzle with oil, toss to coat. Bake at 400°F for 40 minutes, stirring half way through cooking time. Remove from oven, drizzle sherry over onions, and stir to combine. Bake an additional 40 minutes, stirring once.

With about 10 minutes remaining, melt butter in saucepan over medium heat; add flour, stirring with whisk until smooth. Gradually add milk, whisking until blended; bring to gentle boil. Cook 1 minute, stirring constantly. Remove from heat. Add cheese, salt, and pepper, stirring until smooth.

Pour milk mixture over onions, stirring to combine. Bake for 20 minutes or until mixture is thick and beginning to brown on top. Remove from oven and let stand for 10 minutes before serving.

Note: *Total baking time is 1 hour 40 minutes. Don't overcook. Great with grilled red meat or poultry.*

Stuffed Mushrooms Florentine
12 Servings

12 large mushrooms, 2½- to
   3-inch diameter
2 pounds fresh spinach (or 10-ounce
   package of frozen chopped)
¼ cup butter
1 medium onion, minced

1 egg yolk
½ teaspoon salt
⅛ teaspoon pepper
⅛ teaspoon ground nutmeg
¼ cup grated Parmesan
   cheese

Clean mushrooms and snap out stems. Chop stems finely and set aside. Thoroughly wash and drain spinach. Cook spinach, covered, in just the water that clings to leaves for 4 to 5 minutes. Squeeze all water from spinach and chop finely. If preparing frozen spinach, be sure to drain very well. Melt butter in frying pan over medium heat. Add mushroom caps only to coat with butter then transfer them to an 8×12 baking dish. Add onion and chopped mushroom stems to the pan and cook until onion is translucent. Stir in spinach and remove pan from heat. Combine the egg yolk, salt, pepper, and nutmeg, and 2½ tablespoons of Parmesan cheese. Add to spinach mixture. Mound the mixture in the mushroom caps and sprinkle with the remaining cheese. If made ahead, cover and chill up to 24 hours. Bake at 325°F uncovered for 20 minutes or until heated through and tender.

Snow Peas with Grand Marnier
8 Servings

1 cup water
1 teaspoon sugar
3 10-ounce packages snow peas
   (fresh or frozen)
1 8-ounce can sliced water chestnuts,
   drained

¼ cup Grand Marnier
5 tablespoons butter
1 tablespoon chopped fresh
   mint, or 1½ tablespoons
   dried mint
1 teaspoon salt

In a medium saucepan, bring 1 cup of water to a boil and add the sugar. Drop in the snow peas and cook until barely tender. Drain, and return to pan. Add the water chestnuts, Grand Marnier, butter, mint, and salt and mix well. Cook over medium-low heat until heated through.

Mushroom Compote
10 Servings

3 tablespoons olive oil
2 pounds mushrooms, cleaned,
 trimmed, and caps and stems
 sliced as desired
½ bunch green onions or 1 large
 shallot, chopped
2 cloves garlic, minced
1½ tablespoons fresh thyme leaves
 or 1 teaspoon dried thyme

2 tablespoons chopped fresh
 parsley
black pepper or cayenne as
 desired
1 teaspoon chicken base
½ cup water
½ teaspoon balsamic vinegar

Heat olive oil in a large pan. Add mushrooms, onions or shallots and
sauté until tender. Add minced garlic, thyme, parsley, pepper, chicken
base, water, and vinegar. Cook over low heat until liquid has reduced.
Taste and add more chicken base if a saltier flavor is desired.

Note: *Mushroom Compote is an excellent accompaniment to meats, poultry, and fish. It goes
well with rice, pasta, potatoes, polenta, and omelets or in a grilled cheese sandwich. Toss it into
cooked vegetables or put a spoonful of it on top of a creamy soup. It freezes well.*

Creamed Spinach (Gluten-Free)
4 Servings

16-ounce bag frozen spinach
4 to 8 ounces cream cheese (or Neufchâtel)

Put the spinach in a glass microwaveable dish and steam until just cooked
through. Once the spinach is warmed through, drain in a fine-mesh colander. Squeeze out as much water as possible. Return the spinach to dish.
Add 4 to 8 ounces of cream cheese (depending on desired creaminess)
and stir vigorously until the cream cheese is well mixed in. Reheat the
mixture briefly until warmed through.

Note: *A tasty gluten-free substitute for traditional creamed spinach. Neufchâtel cheese can be
used for low-fat option.*

Spinach Soufflé
4 to 6 Servings

1 bag frozen chopped spinach
(can also use mustard greens or
collard greens)
8 ounces cottage cheese
2 teaspoons dehydrated onion
2 teaspoons seasoned salt

2 teaspoons seasoned pepper
2 teaspoons caraway seeds
pinch of nutmeg
1 cup grated Parmesan cheese
2 teaspoons paprika
6 eggs

Defrost greens in microwave, but do not cook. Drain in colander until all the moisture is removed. Combine greens, cottage cheese, onion, salt, pepper, caraway seeds, nutmeg, Parmesan, and paprika. Beat 6 eggs until light and then fold into other ingredients. Transfer to a 9×13 casserole dish. Bake at 350°F for 45 minutes to 1 hour. This will be quite fluffy but will be more substantial than a traditional soufflé.

Squash and Apple Bake
6 Servings

2 pounds of butternut or buttercup squash
½ cup brown sugar, packed
1 tablespoon flour
1 teaspoon salt
½ teaspoon mace (or nutmeg)
2 baking apples, cored, peeled, and cut into ½-inch slices
2 to 3 tablespoons dried cranberries
2 to 3 tablespoons chopped walnuts
¼ cup butter or margarine, melted

Cut each squash in half. Remove seeds and fibers; peel squash. Cut into ½-inch slices. Arrange in ungreased baking dish. In ziplock bag, combine brown sugar, flour, salt, and mace. Add apples and toss to coat. Arrange over squash. Sprinkle with cranberries and chopped walnuts. Drizzle melted butter over top. Cover tightly with foil. Bake at 350°F for 50 minutes or until squash is tender.

Squash, White Bean, and Kale Ragout
8 to 10 Servings

1 3-pound sugar pumpkin or
  butternut squash
2 tablespoons canola oil or
  unsalted butter
2 tablespoons maple syrup
2½ teaspoons cider vinegar
1 teaspoon kosher salt
1 teaspoon ground black pepper
⅛ teaspoon cayenne pepper
2 tablespoons extra-virgin olive oil
4 large leeks, chopped (white
  and light green parts only)
2 large garlic cloves, minced

2 teaspoons chopped fresh
  rosemary
2 15-ounce cans cannellini,
  beans drained and rinsed
2 cups vegetable broth
¾ pound kale, center ribs
  removed, leaves thinly sliced
  (about 6 cups). Can
  substitute spinach, if desired
2 ounces grated Parmigiano-
  Reggiano cheese (½ cup) or
  more to taste
⅓ cup roughly chopped
  dried cranberries

Peel pumpkin or squash. Trim stem and half lengthwise (easier if you microwave it for a few minutes to soften). Scoop out seeds; cut flesh into 1-inch cubes. Spread cubes on large rimmed baking sheet that has been sprayed with cooking spray.

Combine butter or canola oil, syrup, 1 tablespoon vinegar, salt, ½ teaspoon black pepper, and cayenne in small saucepan. Cook, stirring occasionally, over medium-high heat until butter melts. Pour over squash and toss to coat evenly. Roast at 450°F stirring occasionally until tender and caramelized at edges (about 30 minutes).

Warm olive oil in large skillet over medium heat. Add leeks, garlic, rosemary, and generous pinch of salt. Cook, stirring occasionally, until leeks are very soft but not browned (about 15 minutes). Add beans and broth; simmer about 10 minutes.

Stir in kale or spinach and cheese. Stir until greens are cooked down and tender (about 10 minutes). Stir in pumpkin or squash and chopped cranberries. Season with remaining 1½ teaspoons vinegar and ½ teaspoon black pepper. Serve.

Note: *This can also serve 6 as a main course. Cheese can be increased as desired.*

Creamy Butternut Squash with Parmesan
8 Servings

2½ pounds butternut squash, peeled
  and cut into 1-inch pieces
¾ cup heavy cream
3 fresh sage leaves, finely chopped

½ teaspoon salt
¼ teaspoon pepper
⅔ cup finely grated
  Parmigiano-Reggiano

Toss squash with cream, sage, salt, and pepper in a 2-quart shallow baking dish. Bake, covered, at 350°F for 30 minutes. Stir in half of cheese and sprinkle remainder on top. Roast, uncovered, until squash is tender and beginning to brown, about 20 minutes. Let stand about 5 minutes before serving (cream will thicken).

Note: *Butternut squash can be cut 1 day ahead and chilled in sealable bag (ready-cut butternut squash can be found at Trader Joe's). You can use any herbs that you have on hand.*

Nutty Baked Squash
4 Servings

2 medium acorn squash
⅔ cup cracker crumbs
⅓ cup coarsely chopped pecans
⅓ cup melted butter or margarine

3 tablespoons brown sugar
½ teaspoon salt
¼ teaspoon nutmeg

Cut each squash in half; remove seeds and fibers. Place cut side up in baking dish. Stir together cracker crumbs, pecans, butter, brown sugar, salt, and nutmeg. Spoon equal amounts into each squash half. Pour water into baking dish to ¼ inch depth around squash. Cover tightly with foil. Bake at 400°F for 30 minutes or until tender.

Very Baked Tomatoes
8 Servings

4 tomatoes, the riper the better
¼ cup olive oil
4 cloves garlic, peeled and minced

2 tablespoons chopped fresh
    basil or 1 tablespoon
    chopped fresh rosemary
salt and pepper

Core tomatoes. Slice in half horizontally and place in a baking pan, cut side up. Mix together oil, garlic, basil or rosemary, salt and pepper. Pour over the 8 halves. Bake at 325°F for 2 hours. The tomatoes will exude their juices and collapse, and then begin to caramelize. Remove tomatoes from pan using a slotted spoon and serve.

Roasted Veggies and Potatoes
4 to 6 Servings

1 pound Brussels sprouts, halved
4 to 6 carrots, thickly sliced
½ coarsely chopped medium yellow
    or red onion
1 pound potatoes, cubed (white, Yukon
    gold, sweet or a combination)
2 teaspoons coarse salt

½ teaspoon freshly ground pepper
½ teaspoon finely chopped
    fresh thyme
½ teaspoon finely chopped
    fresh rosemary
1 tablespoon extra-virgin
    olive oil

Combine Brussels sprouts, carrots, onion, and potatoes in large bowl and toss with olive oil. Sprinkle generously with herbs, salt, and pepper. Arrange in a single layer in preheated roasting or jelly roll pan. Roast at 400°F for 25 to 30 minutes until they are golden on the outside and tender when pierced with a sharp knife. Remove from oven and serve hot.

Note: *Be creative and experiment with your favorite vegetables, potatoes, and herbs.*

Root Vegetables with Cream and Fontina Cheese
6 to 8 Servings

1 pound carrots, cut into ½-inch pieces
1 pound new potatoes, quartered
1 pound parsnips, peeled and cut
　into ½-inch pieces
1 pound rutabaga, peeled and diced
2 tablespoons olive oil
1½ teaspoons sea salt
½ teaspoon pepper

1 cup heavy cream
1 cup cubed Fontina cheese
1 tablespoon chopped parsley
1 tablespoon grated Parmesan
　cheese
1 tablespoon breadcrumbs

Place carrots, potatoes, parsnips, and rutabaga in a 13×9 shallow baking dish and toss with olive oil, sea salt, and pepper. Bake at 400°F for 1 hour. For last 10 minutes, stir in cream, Fontina cheese, parsley, and Parmesan cheese. Sprinkle breadcrumbs over top. Remove from oven when bubbly.

Cider Roasted Vegetables
8 Servings

1½ pounds beets, peeled and cut
　into wedges
1½ pounds parsnips, peeled and
　cut into 2-inch chunks
1½ pounds carrots, peeled cut
　into 2-inch chunks or 1½ pounds
　baby carrots, peeled
4 tablespoons brown sugar

4 tablespoons olive oil
2 tablespoons apple cider
　vinegar
1 pound shiitake or cremini
　mushrooms, cleaned, and
　stemmed
salt and pepper

Place vegetables in two small roasting pans. In a medium bowl, whisk together the brown sugar, oil, and vinegar. Pour over the vegetables and toss to coat well. Bake at 450°F until tender, about 1 hour, stirring halfway. Add the mushrooms during the last 10 minutes, toss to coat well, and finish roasting. Season to taste with salt and freshly ground pepper.

Stewed Yams, Apples, and Onions
4 to 5 Servings

1¼ pounds yams
2 medium-sized sweet tart apples
1 medium-sized onion
2 tablespoons olive oil
3 tablespoons water

3 tablespoons packed brown
  sugar
½ teaspoon Creole seasoning
  (Tony Chachere's Original)
½ teaspoon cinnamon
salt

Peel yams and apples. Slice yams into ½-inch slices, then cut in half lengthwise. Cut apple into ½-inch wedges. Cut onion into half, then into ½-inch slices. Heat 1 tablespoon of the oil in a large skillet. When hot, add the yams in a single layer. Cover skillet and cook over medium heat for about 3 minutes or until lightly brown on one side. Flip slices over, add water, cover, and cook another 5 minutes. While that is cooking, put the apples and onions together in a bowl and toss with the remaining 1 tablespoon oil. Add apples and onions to the skillet, and give all ingredients a stir, lifting yams off bottom of pan to mix with other ingredients. Cover and cook for about 5 minutes. Remove from heat and sprinkle with brown sugar, Creole seasoning, and cinnamon. Mix together, cover, and continue cooking until potatoes and apples are fork tender. Taste and adjust for salt.

Baked Sweet Potatoes with Ginger and Honey
12 Servings

9 sweet potatoes, peeled and cubed
½ cup honey
3 tablespoons grated fresh ginger
2 tablespoons walnut oil

1 teaspoon ground cardamom
½ teaspoon ground black
  pepper

In a large bowl, combine the sweet potatoes, honey, ginger, oil, cardamom, and pepper. Transfer to a large cast iron frying pan. Bake at 400°F for 20 minutes. Turn the mixture over to expose the pieces from the bottom of the pan. Bake for another 20 minutes, or until the sweet potatoes are tender and caramelized on the outside.

Note: *Fresh ginger, cardamom, and sweet potatoes will fill your house with a wonderful fall fragrance.*

Golden Parmesan Potatoes
6 to 8 Servings

6 large Idaho potatoes (about 3 pounds)   ⅛ teaspoon pepper
¼ cup flour   ⅓ cup butter or margarine
¼ cup grated Parmesan cheese   chopped parsley
salt to taste

Peel potatoes and cut into quarters lengthwise. Combine flour, cheese, salt, and pepper in plastic bag. Moisten potato slices with water. Shake a few potatoes at a time in a bag to coat the potatoes well with the cheese-flour mixture. Melt butter in a 13×9×2 baking dish. Place potatoes in a single layer in dish. Bake at 375°F for 1 hour turning once half way through baking. When golden brown remove from the oven and sprinkle with parsley. If desired, additional cheese may be added before baking.

Garlic Mashed Potato Bake
6 to 8 Servings

2 pounds red potatoes   8 ounces sour cream
2 tablespoons butter   ¼ teaspoon freshly ground
3 green onions (about ⅓ cup), chopped   black pepper
1 or 2 cloves garlic, minced   salt
4 to 5 tablespoons milk   paprika

Wash potatoes. Do not peel. Cut into similar size chunks, about 2 inches. Cover with cold water and bring to boil. Cover with lid, lower heat and cook until tender. Drain. Put back into pan and cover to keep warm (off heat). In a small saucepan, combine butter, green onions, garlic, and milk. Simmer for about 3 minutes. Stir in sour cream just to warm; do not continue cooking after sour cream has been added. Mash the hot potatoes then add the liquid mixture from saucepan. Mix well and add extra tablespoon of milk if needed for proper consistency. Salt to taste.

You can serve immediately, or if you are making ahead of time, put mixture into an ovenproof casserole dish, sprinkle with the paprika, cover, and refrigerate until ready to bake. Bake covered at 350°F for about 30 minutes or until hot in the center.

Scalloped Potato Gratin
4 to 6 Servings

1½ cups heavy cream
1 sprig fresh thyme
2 garlic cloves, chopped
½ teaspoon ground nutmeg
unsalted butter
2 pounds russet potatoes, peeled
and cut into ⅛-inch thick slices

salt and pepper
½ cup grated Parmesan
cheese, plus more for broiling
½ cup breadcrumbs

In a saucepan, heat the cream with a sprig of thyme, chopped garlic, and nutmeg. Generously butter a casserole dish. Place a layer of potato in an overlapping pattern and season with salt and pepper. Remove cream from heat and pour a small amount over potatoes. Top with grated Parmesan cheese, saving some for topping. Repeat and make 2 more layers. Bake at 375°F uncovered for 45 minutes. Sprinkle with remaining Parmesan cheese and breadcrumbs. Continue baking until brown, about 5 minutes.

Bulgarian Potatoes
10 to 12 Servings

2 cups cottage cheese
1 stick unsalted butter, melted and
cooled slightly
1¼ teaspoons salt

¾ teaspoon pepper
3 pounds russet potatoes
2 large eggs
8 ounces plain yogurt

Purée cottage cheese until smooth. Add butter, 1 teaspoon salt, ½ teaspoon pepper, and blend well. Peel potatoes and cut crosswise into ⅛-inch thick slices. Spread ⅓ potatoes evenly in one layer in greased 2½-quart baking dish and top with scant cup of cottage cheese mixture (will not cover potatoes completely). Repeat layers ending with cottage cheese. Cover tightly with foil and bake on middle shelf at 375°F until potatoes are tender, 1 to 1½ hours. Whisk together eggs, yogurt and remaining salt and pepper. Pour egg mixture evenly over potatoes and bake uncovered until set, about 20 minutes.

Wisconsin Potato Salad
8 to 12 Servings

2 pounds small red potatoes,
washed and unpeeled
1 cup sour cream
½ cup mayonnaise
2 tablespoons chopped fresh dill
or 1 teaspoon dried dill
¼ cup chopped onion

4 ounces shredded Wisconsin
Fontinella cheese
1½ cups peeled, seeded,
chopped cucumber
salt and pepper
cherry tomatoes for garnish

Place potatoes in medium saucepan and cover with cold water. Bring to a boil, cover with lid, lower heat, and simmer until cooked but still fairly firm. Drain and set aside to cool.

In a medium mixing bowl, combine sour cream, mayonnaise, dill, onion, and cheese. Gently stir in the cucumbers. Cut each potato into bite-sized chunks. Season potatoes with salt and pepper and combine with sauce ingredients in mixing bowl. Adjust seasoning. Serve potato salad while still warm or cover and refrigerate until serving time. Garnish with slices of vine-ripened cherry tomatoes.

French-Style Potato Salad
10 to 12 Servings

2½ pounds red potatoes
¾ cup sweet and spicy French dressing
2 cups mayonnaise
2 large cloves garlic, minced
1 tablespoon Dijon-style mustard
1 teaspoon kosher salt

¼ teaspoon coarse pepper
2 hard-boiled eggs, chopped
2 tablespoons capers, rinsed
1 10-ounce package frozen
tiny peas, thawed

In large saucepan, cover potatoes with cold water and bring to a boil. Boil for 10 to 15 minutes or until just tender. Drain, cube, and toss with French dressing. Cool. In medium bowl, combine mayonnaise, garlic, mustard, salt, and pepper. Gently mix in chopped hard-boiled eggs, capers, and peas with potatoes. Serve at room temperature.

Sides

Savory Bread Pudding
4 Servings

Josh Allen *opened* Companion Baking Company *in 1993. His vision was to create wholesome and delicious European breads with simple ingredients. In addition to cafes in Clayton and Ladue, Companion Bread is available in many local restaurants and grocers.*

1 loaf Companion Ciabatta
¼ cup diced pancetta, rendered
    till tender
½ cup golden raisins
¼ cup olive oil
4 teaspoons chopped fresh
    Italian parsley
4 teaspoons chopped fresh thyme
1 large garlic clove, minced

salt and pepper
¾ cup grated Parmigiano-
    Reggiano cheese, divided
2 cups whole milk
6 large eggs
2 teaspoons salt
1 teaspoon freshly ground
    black pepper

Cut bread with crust into small cubes (about 10 cups loosely packed). Lay out on a sheet pan overnight to dry out or toast off in the oven. If toasting off in the oven, spread cubes out on a large rimmed baking sheet. Bake at 375°F until golden and slightly crunchy, stirring occasionally, about 20 minutes.

Put the toasted bread cubes into a very large bowl. Add pancetta, golden raisins, oil, parsley, thyme, and garlic. Toss to coat. Season with salt and pepper to taste, then add ½ cup of Parmesan cheese.

Whisk milk, eggs, salt, and ground pepper in large bowl. Mix custard into bread mixture. Transfer to a buttered 13×9×2-inch baking dish. Sprinkle remaining cheese over top. Bake uncovered at 350°F until set and top is golden, about 1 hour. Let stand 15 minutes.

Note: *Serve with roasted pork chops or pork tenderloin.*

Sicilian Spinach Pie
8 Servings

Adriana's *is a small, family owned lunch café located in the St Louis' Italian section of town, known as 'The Hill.'* Adriana's *opened in 1992 and is run by* Adriana Fazio *and her daughters.*

1 cup chopped onion	1¼ cups plain dry bread
2 tablespoons olive oil	crumbs
6 eggs, lightly beaten	1¼ cups grated Romano
1 teaspoon salt	cheese, plus more for garnish
½ teaspoon ground black pepper	3 10-ounce packages frozen
1 or 2 pinches dried red pepper flakes	chopped spinach, thawed
1 cup tomato-basil pasta sauce or	and squeezed dry
another meatless red sauce, plus	1½ cups ricotta cheese
one more for garnish	

Coat a 9- or 10-inch pie pan with non-stick cooking spray. Sauté onion in olive oil in a skillet over medium heat until translucent. Transfer to a large bowl. Add eggs, salt, black pepper, red pepper flakes, pasta sauce, breadcrumbs, Romano cheese, spinach, and ricotta; stir until well combined and ingredients are well distributed.

Place the mixture in a 9- or 10-inch pie pan that has been sprayed with cooking spray. Smooth the top, mounding gently in the center.

Bake at 350°F (bake at 325°F if using a glass pan) for 60 to 75 minutes, or until firm to the touch. To serve, cut pie into wedges, ladle on additional red sauce, and top with grated cheese.

Panettone Stuffing
8 to 10 Servings

1 (2.2 pound) Panettone (type of sweet bread loaf from Italy)
1 stick sweet butter
2 bunches fresh sage, leaves minced
salt and pepper
½ cup dried apricots, julienned
½ cup dried sour cherries
½ cup golden raisins

1½ cups minced yellow onion
1 cup minced celery or fennel
1 cup minced carrot
up to 2 cups chicken or turkey stock
2 eggs, optional, use if you like a firmer stuffing

Cut the Panettone into ¾-inch squares and place in large bowl. Melt half of the butter in a saucepan over medium heat and continue to cook until light brown, about 5 minutes. Take off the heat and add half the sage. Season with salt and pepper. Pour the sage butter over the bread and toss gently but swiftly. Spread out on 2 cooking sheets and bake at 350°F until light brown, about 15 minutes. Remove from the oven and place back into the bowl. Meanwhile, place the dried apricots, cherries and raisins in a large bowl; add boiling water to cover and then set aside for at least 10 minutes. This will plump and soften the fruit for cooking. Drain fruit once plumped. Raise the oven temperature to 375°F.

Melt the remaining butter and add onion, celery, and carrot. Sauté on medium-low heat until soft. Add dried fruit and remaining sage. Toss into cooled croutons. Gently toss and add chicken broth to moisten; add more broth if you like a softer stuffing. Stir in beaten eggs now, if using. Adjust salt and pepper, to your liking. Turn out into an oven-proof casserole. Bake uncovered until golden brown on top, about 40 minutes.

Note: *Makes a wonderful holiday stuffing to go with your turkey. Mildly sweet and full of flavor.*

Tomato-Basil Bread Pudding
4-6 Servings

Filling:
butter
½ loaf multi-grain bread,
   cut into ¾-inch cubes
3 tablespoons olive oil
1 large or 2 small shallots,
   thinly sliced
2 cloves garlic, minced
12 ounces cherry or grape
   tomatoes, halved
kosher salt and freshly ground black pepper
1 packed cup chopped fresh basil leaves
1½ cups shredded Parmesan cheese

Custard:
6 large eggs, at room temperature
1 cup whole milk
1 teaspoon kosher salt
½ teaspoon freshly ground
   black pepper

Filling:

Butter a 9×13×2 glass baking dish. Add the bread cubes and set aside. In a large skillet, heat the oil over medium-high heat. Add the shallots and garlic. Cook, stirring constantly until fragrant, about 1 minute. Add the tomatoes and season with salt and pepper, to taste. Cook until slightly soft, about 2 minutes. Remove the pan from the heat and stir in the basil. Pour the tomato mixture and Parmesan cheese over the bread cubes and combine well.

Custard:

In a large bowl, beat the eggs, milk, salt, and pepper together until smooth. Pour the custard over the bread mixture and gently toss to coat. Bake in the center of the oven at 375°F until slightly puffed and golden, about 25 to 30 minutes. Remove the pudding from the oven and let cool for 5 minutes. Cut into wedges and serve.

Sweets

As a high-risk baby is prepped for transport to the NICU, mom gets a special transport blankie to keep next to her body. Just before leaving, mom covers baby with the blankie. Her scent and warmth soothes the baby during transport and begin the bonding process.

Desserts

Elegant Stuffed Apples
6 Servings

Stuffed Apples:

⅓ cup firmly packed light brown sugar

2 cups roughly chopped Amaretti cookies

3 tablespoons roughly chopped toasted almonds

3 teaspoons roughly chopped toasted walnuts

¼ teaspoon ground cinnamon

¼ teaspoon nutmeg

4 tablespoons Amaretto liqueur

1 whole egg, beaten

½ cup melted sweet, unsalted butter

½ cup milk

6 large, firm baking apples, such as Cortland apples, cored but not peeled

3 tablespoons butter, cut into 6 pieces

1½ cups apple cider

1½ cups maple syrup

mascarpone cream

Mascarpone Cream:

1 8-ounce container of mascarpone

¼ cup sugar

1 teaspoon vanilla extract

Stuffed Apples:

In a small bowl, mix together brown sugar, Amaretti cookies, almonds, walnuts, cinnamon, nutmeg, Amaretto liqueur, egg, melted butter, and milk. Soak all ingredients in the milk and mix until all ingredients are soft to the touch. Stuff apples with Amaretti cookie and nut mixture. Place apples in a 13×9 glass baking pan. Pour in apple cider and maple syrup. Top each apple with a pat of butter and bake at 400°F for about 30 to 40 minutes, basting every 5 to 7 minutes, until apples are tender. When apples are done, set aside and cover with foil to keep warm. Pour the pan juice into a small saucepan; bring to boil; lower heat; and simmer mixture until it becomes a thick syrup. Pour syrup over each apple, top with mascarpone cream, and serve.

Mascarpone Cream:

Mix 1 container of mascarpone with ¼ cup granulated sugar and 1 teaspoon vanilla extract.

Chocolate-Butterfinger Obsession with Baked Banana Mousse
Makes 4 10-inch Cakes

Casey Shiller, CCE, CEPC, is a St. Louis native and the Coordinator of Baking and Pastry Arts at St. Louis Community College at Forest Park. He was named one of the 'Top 10 Rising Star Pastry Chefs of 2000," and has earned several gold and silver medals for his chocolate sculptures and plated dessert displays.

Crust:
1 pound Oreo cookie crumbs
8 ounces sugar
8 ounces butter, melted

Butterfinger Obsession:
10 ounces milk
12 ounces sugar
12 ounces bittersweet chocolate
14 ounces unsweetened chocolate
1 pound, 2 ounces butter, softened
12 eggs
6 ounces sugar
1 pound Butterfinger Candy
   Sundae Topping Pieces

Baked Bananas:
1 pound light brown sugar
½ ounces ground cinnamon
4 ounces dark rum
4 ounces banana liqueur
2 ounces honey
3 vanilla beans, split
10 ripe bananas

Baked Banana Mousse:
2 quarts heavy cream
1 pound pasteurized egg yolks
1 pound powdered sugar
2 ounces gelatin sheets
10 ounces banana liqueur
Baked Banana Purée (from
   above preparation)

Crust:
Mix cookie crumbs, sugar, and butter together; pat thin layer into bottom of 4 greased 10-inch round cake pans.

Butterfinger Obsession:
Bring milk and 12 ounces of sugar to gentle boil. Remove from heat and add chocolates; stir until melted. Add soft butter and stir until melted.

In a separate bowl, whisk eggs and 6 ounces sugar together until smooth. Stir egg mixture into chocolate mixture. Pour into Oreo-crust-lined cake pans until Obsession is approximately 1 inch thick. Generously cover batter with Butterfinger pieces. Gently swirl Butterfinger into batter. Bake at 300°F with a water bath until fully set—similar to cheesecake. Cool completely.

Baked Bananas:
In a standard hotel or jellyroll pan, pat brown sugar into an even layer. Evenly sprinkle with ground cinnamon, dark rum, banana liqueur, honey, and vanilla beans. Peel the bananas and cut in half lengthwise. Place bananas cut-side-down onto brown sugar. Cover tightly with aluminum foil; bake at 325°F for 15 minutes. Remove foil, flip bananas over and baste with the syrup from the hotel pan. Replace foil; continue baking for 15 additional minutes. Remove foil, stir bananas—they should be very soft at this point. Return to oven, uncovered, and bake 15 additional minutes. Remove from oven, remove vanilla beans, and pour bananas and syrup into food processor. Purée until smooth—mixture will be a thick brown paste.

Baked Banana Mousse:
Whip heavy cream until soft peaks are formed. In mixer, whip egg yolks and powdered sugar until thick ribbons are formed. Bloom (soak) gelatin sheets in cold water until soft. Remove gelatin from water, squeezing gently, and melt with banana liqueur.

Stir baked banana purée into whipped egg yolks. Gently temper some egg yolk mixture into hot gelatin. Pour gelatin into egg yolk mixture. Stir quickly to incorporate. Add soft-whipped cream and quickly stir to incorporate fully.

Pour mousse into cake pans lined with Butterfinger Obsession. Freeze until completely firm. Remove cakes from freezer; using a blowtorch, warm sides and bottom of cake pan. Gently tap upside down to release frozen mousse cake. Invert, thaw, and serve.

Apfelschnitten (Apple Slices)
8 Servings

Crust:
2 cups sifted flour
3 tablespoons sugar
¾ cup butter
3 tablespoons cream
1 egg yolk
grated rind of ½ lemon

Apple Mixture:
1 quart apples, thinly sliced
¾ cup sugar
½ teaspoon cinnamon
½ cup currants (if desired)

Confectioners' Icing:
1 cup confectioners' (powdered) sugar
2 tablespoons butter, melted
½ teaspoon vanilla extract
cream

Crust:
Mix flour and sugar. Cut the butter into the flour and sugar; add the cream, egg yolk, and grated lemon rind. Knead lightly for a few minutes; divide into 2 equal parts and refrigerate for at least 15 minutes. Take each of the divisions of dough and roll out separately on a lightly floured board into rectangles to fit one into the bottom of a 9×13 pan. Cover with apple mixture; place remaining sheet of pastry on top and prick with a fork. Brush with a slightly beaten egg white. Bake at 350°F for about 45 minutes or until apples are tender and pastry is nicely browned. Remove from oven and cool. When cold, spread with Confectioners' Sugar Icing and cut into slices.

Apple Mixture:
Mix 1 quart thinly sliced apples with ¾ cup sugar, ½ teaspoon cinnamon, and currants (if desired).

Confectioners' Sugar Icing:
Mix together 1 cup confectioners' sugar and 2 tablespoons melted butter. Add ½ teaspoon vanilla and enough cream to make a spreading consistency.

Lace Baskets with Marinated Berries
Makes 15 Baskets

Lace Baskets:
½ cup unsalted butter
1 cup plus 2 tablespoons sugar
¼ cup dark corn syrup
2 cups blanched almonds
2 tablespoons flour

Marinated Berries:
1 cup raspberries
1 cup hulled and quartered
  strawberries
1 cup blueberries
1 cup blackberries
¼ cup Grand Marnier
½ cup sugar

Lace Baskets:

In a heavy saucepan, melt butter, sugar, and corn syrup. Grind the almonds with the flour, add to the butter and simmer for 3 minutes. Spoon 4 golf ball-sized balls onto a sheet lined with parchment paper, allowing room for them to spread. Bake about 7 minutes at 350°F until the balls have flattened out and are golden brown. Remove from the oven and cool for 1 minute. While the cookies are still warm, shape over an upside-down custard cup to form a basket. Repeat with remaining dough.

Marinated Berries:

Place raspberries, blueberries, blackberries, Grand Marnier, and sugar into a bowl and toss gently. Allow to macerate for one hour.

Just before serving, fill the baskets with berries. Garnish with ice cream, whipped cream, or chopped pistachios if desired.

Summer Fruit Cobbler
8 to 10 Servings

4 cups fresh fruit, anything in season	¼ teaspoon mace
2 cups sugar	¼ teaspoon salt
1 cup flour	1 cup milk
1 teaspoon baking powder	½ teaspoon vanilla extract
½ teaspoon cinnamon	1 stick melted and cooled butter

Mix together the fruit and 1 cup sugar, let sit for 30 minutes. Sift together the remaining 1 cup of sugar, flour, baking powder, cinnamon, mace and salt. In a separate bowl, combine the milk, vanilla, and butter. Add to dry ingredients and stir just until combined. Pour into a soufflé dish and spoon fruit over top of batter. Bake at 350°F for 30 minutes; increase oven to 400°F and bake an additional 10 to 15 minutes. Let cobbler cool for 20 minutes.

Note: *The batter rises to the top and makes a wonderful summer dessert.*

Raspberries with White Chocolate Mint Sauce
6 Servings

¼ cup milk	2 cups heavy cream
6 sprigs fresh mint	1 quart raspberries
8 ounces white chocolate	

Bring the milk to a gentle boil and steep the mint in it for 5 minutes. Break up the chocolate and melt it in the top of a double boiler over hot water. When the chocolate has melted, pour in the cream, whisking until the mixture is well blended. Pour the milk and mint through a fine sieve and discard the mint. Add the milk to the chocolate, whisking well.

Chill the sauce and serve under or over the raspberries, divided among six plates.

Strawberry Trifle
10 Servings

1 small Sara Lee pound cake
1 18-ounce jar Hershey's hot
    fudge sauce
¼ cup Kahlua (optional)
1 bag Heath Bits of Brickle
2 small instant Jell-O vanilla
    flavored puddings

2 cups cold 2% milk
2 cups heavy whipping cream
1 small package strawberries,
    sliced (can add any favorite
    fruit such as blueberries,
    raspberries, etc.)
1 small container Cool Whip,
    thawed

Cut cake into bite-sized pieces and place on bottom of trifle bowl. Microwave hot fudge sauce as directed on the jar. Add Kahlua to hot fudge and pour mixture over cake. Add bits of brickle, saving ¼ bag. Mix pudding with cold milk and set aside. Whip whipping cream until stiff and fold into pudding. Spread on top of brickle layer.

Arrange strawberries on top of pudding. Spread Cool Whip on top of strawberries. Sprinkle with remaining brickle. Chill until ready to serve.

When serving, use a large spoon to get all the layers in every serving.

Pink Pears with Chocolate
6 Servings

6 medium pears (not too ripe)	1 teaspoon lemon juice
¾ cup sugar	4 whole cloves
1½ cups water	1 3-inch stick cinnamon
1½ cups rosé wine	grated dark chocolate of
½ cup Burgundy or other dry red wine	choice

Peel the pears, removing the core from the bottom end and cutting to, but not through, the stem. Slice ¼ inch from the bottom of each pear to make a flat base. Set pears aside.

Combine sugar, water, Rose wine, Burgundy wine, lemon juice, cloves, and cinnamon stick in a 5-quart Dutch oven. Bring to a boil over medium heat, stirring until sugar dissolves. Place pears in Dutch oven in an upright position and spoon syrup over pears. Cover and simmer for 20 minutes. Transfer pears to a large bowl. Strain syrup and pour over pears, discarding pieces. Submerge pears with syrup and cover tightly refrigerating 2 to 3 hours. Baste occasionally with syrup.

Place each pear on a small plate and drizzle syrup over pear. Sprinkle with grated chocolate.

Note: *Purchasing unripe pears in advance is best. Pears can be ripened in a brown paper bag with a very well ripened apple or banana. Check daily and move pears to refrigerator to control ripening. If pears are too ripe, they will not hold their form during cooking.*

Mixed Berry Strudel
8 to 10 Servings

1 pint blueberries
½ pint raspberries
1 pint strawberries, halved
1 tablespoon flour
2 tablespoons chopped
  crystallized ginger

3 tablespoons light brown
  sugar
2 teaspoons grated orange zest
1 sheet frozen puff pastry,
  thawed
1 egg, slightly beaten

Line a baking sheet with aluminum foil and set aside. In a medium-size mixing bowl, toss together the berries, flour, ginger, sugar, and zest; set aside. If your puff pastry sheets measure 10×12 inches proceed to next step. If not, unfold the puff pastry, and on a lightly floured surface, roll out the puff into a 10×12-inch rectangle. Transfer the dough onto the sheet pan; brush the edges of the pastry dough with some of the beaten egg. Arrange the berry mixture lengthwise down the center. Fold the dough lengthwise toward the center and pinch the ends to seal. Brush the top with the remaining egg. With a sharp knife, cut 3 slits down the length of the pastry. In the center rack of the oven, bake at 400°F for 40 to 45 minutes. The pastry is done when it is a golden brown and feels crispy to the touch. Remove from the oven and allow to cool for 15 minutes before serving.

Bananas Foster
8 Servings

4 medium bananas
¼ cup butter
1 cup packed brown sugar
¼ cup banana liqueur

½ teaspoon ground cinnamon
¼ cup dark rum
2 cups vanilla ice cream

Peel bananas and cut each banana in half lengthwise. Cut each half into 2 pieces. Melt butter in a large nonstick skillet over medium heat. Stir in brown sugar, liqueur, and cinnamon. Bring to a simmer and cook for 2 minutes. Add bananas and cook for 4 minutes until tender. Remove from heat. Add warmed rum to pan and ignite rum with a long match, if desired. Stir bananas gently until flame dies down. Serve over ice cream.

Apple Fritters
8 to 10 Servings

1 cup flour
1 teaspoon baking powder
2 tablespoons sugar
¼ teaspoon salt

1 egg, beaten
¼ cup milk
2 cups chopped apples
oil for frying

Sift flour with baking powder, sugar, and salt. Add egg, milk, and apples and mix together. Drop by teaspoonfuls into hot oil and fry until golden brown. Serve with whipped cream or sprinkle with confectioners' sugar.

Balsamic Berries with Vanilla Ice Cream
6 Servings

1 8.8-ounce package fresh strawberries, hulled and quartered
1 6-ounce package fresh blueberries
1 6-ounce package fresh blackberries
1 quart vanilla ice cream
4 to 6 tablespoons balsamic vinegar

Combine strawberries, blueberries, and blackberries in medium bowl; toss until mixed. Add vinegar and toss again. Put in 8×8 baking dish and bake at 350°F for 20 to 30 minutes. Scoop ice cream in dessert bowls. Top with warm berries.

Note: *You can also put the berries tossed with vinegar in aluminum foil and set on a grill for 20 minutes on low heat.*

Frozen Meyer Lemon Creme with Blackberry Sauce

6 Servings

½ cup plus 2 tablespoons sugar
5 tablespoons plus 1½ teaspoons strained fresh Meyer Lemon juice
3 large egg yolks
1 tablespoon light corn syrup
1 cup chilled heavy cream
1¾ teaspoons finely grated Meyer Lemon peel, divided
1 cup frozen unsweetened blackberries, thawed

Whisk ½ cup sugar, 5 tablespoons lemon juice, egg yolks, and corn syrup in a small metal bowl to blend. Set bowl over saucepan of boiling water; whisk the mixture until it is thick and fluffy and thermometer inserted into mixture registers 180°F, about 3 minutes. Place bowl with yolk mixture over larger bowl filled with ice and water until mixture is cool, stirring occasionally, about 8 minutes.

Meanwhile, using an electric mixer, beat cream, 1½ teaspoons lemon peel, and 1 tablespoon sugar in medium bowl until stiff peaks form. Fold cooled yolk mixture into cream in 3 additions. Cover and freeze until firm, about 4 hours.

Mix berries and any accumulated juices, remaining 1 tablespoon sugar, 1½ teaspoons lemon juice, and ¼ teaspoon lemon peel in small bowl; let stand 10 minutes. Coarsely mash half of the berries in bowl to thicken juices.

Scoop lemon cream into small bowls. Top each with 1 rounded tablespoon berry sauce and serve immediately.

Peach Mousse Espresso
4 to 6 Servings

1 quart coffee ice cream
1 package peach Jell-O

1 cup boiling water
coffee beans for garnish

Bring the ice cream to room temperature; it should be creamy. Dissolve the Jell-O in 1 cup boiling water, combine with ice cream, and stir until thoroughly mixed. Pour into a medium-sized soufflé dish and refrigerate for at least 3 to 4 hours before serving. Top with whipped cream and a few coffee beans.

Note: *You won't believe how easy and impressive this dish is. You can also put the mixture into individual dishes.*

Frozen Chocolate Mousse Cake
6 to 8 Servings

3 8-ounce packages semisweet
   chocolate
¾ cup sugar
1 cup strong brewed coffee

½ cup bourbon
1 cup butter
2 cups whipping cream,
   whipped

Cook chocolate, sugar, coffee, bourbon, and butter in a heavy saucepan over low heat, stirring until smooth. Cool.

Fold chocolate mixture into whipped cream. Spoon mousse into a plastic-wrap-lined 9×5 loaf pan. Freeze 8 hours. Invert on plate and thaw slightly before slicing.

Chocolate Croissant Bread Pudding

6 Individual Servings

2 large croissants cut into 1-inch cubes
5 ounces semisweet chocolate chips
2 cups heavy cream
4 large egg yolks
½ cup sugar
1 tablespoon vanilla extract

Bake cubed croissants at 350°F until golden brown, about 10 minutes. Cool. Reduce heat to 325°F. Divide chocolate among six, ¾-cup greased custard cups. Place toasted croissants on top of chocolate. Set aside.Heat cream in heavy sauce pan until it simmers.

Meanwhile, beat egg yolks in mixing bowl with sugar until well combined. Gradually whisk hot cream into egg yolk mixture and then add vanilla. Pour custard over chocolate and croissants, dividing evenly.

Place cups in large baking pan. Add enough water to baking pan to come halfway up sides of cups to form a water bath. Bake at 325°F for about 40 minutes or until set. Remove from water; cool slightly. Serve warm or at room temperature.

Note: *You can make the custard early in the day and refrigerate it in a covered pitcher until you are ready to bake desserts. They can then be placed in the oven to bake when you sit down to dinner, to serve them warm.*

Gingered Blueberry Shortcake
8 Servings

4 cups blueberries	¾ cup 2% milk
3 tablespoons sugar	1 large egg white
1 tablespoon fresh lime juice	1 tablespoon water
9 ounces flour (about 2 cups)	1 tablespoon turbinado sugar
1 tablespoon baking powder	or granulated sugar
½ teaspoon salt	⅓ cup heavy whipping cream
6 tablespoons chilled butter, cut	2 tablespoons powdered sugar
into small pieces	
3 tablespoons minced crystallized ginger	

Combine blueberries, sugar, and lime juice in a medium saucepan over medium-low heat; cook 3 minutes or until berries begin to pop, stirring frequently. Set aside.

Lightly spoon flour into dry measuring cups; level with a knife. Place flour, baking powder, and salt in a food processor; pulse 3 times to combine. Add butter and ginger to processor; pulse until mixture resembles coarse meal. Place mixture in a large bowl; add milk, stirring just until moist. Turn mixture out onto a lightly floured surface. Press mixture into a 7-inch circle; cut into 8 wedges. Place wedges 1 inch apart on a baking sheet. Combine egg white and 1 tablespoon water in a small bowl. Lightly brush tops of wedges with egg white mixture; sprinkle evenly with turbinado sugar.

Bake at 400°F for 20 minutes or until golden brown. Cool on a wire rack. Place cream in a medium bowl; beat with a mixer at medium speed until soft peaks form. Add powdered sugar, beating until stiff peaks form.

Split shortcakes in half horizontally; spoon ⅓ cup berry mixture over each bottom half. Top each with 1½ tablespoons whipped cream; cover with shortcake tops.

Strawberry Tunnel Cream Cake
8 to 10 Servings

1 10-inch round prepared angel food cake
2 3-ounce packages cream cheese, softened
1 14-ounce can sweetened condensed (not evaporated) milk
⅓ cup lemon juice
1 teaspoon almond extract
2 to 4 drops red food coloring, if desired
1 cup chopped fresh strawberries
1 12-ounce carton frozen whipped topping, thawed
additional whole strawberries, if desired

Place cake on serving plate. Cut 1-inch slice crosswise from top of cake and reserve it to replace. Using sharp knife, cut around cake 1 inch from center hole and 1 inch from outer edge, leaving 1-inch-thick cake walls and 1-inch-thick base on bottom. Remove center cake piece, leaving 1-inch-thick base on bottom of cake. Tear the center cake piece into smaller pieces and reserve the cake pieces.

In large bowl, beat cream cheese until fluffy. Gradually beat in condensed milk until smooth. Stir in lemon juice, almond extract, and food coloring. Stir in reserved torn cake pieces and chopped strawberries. Fold in 1 cup whipped topping.

Fill cavity of cake with strawberry mixture. Replace top slice of cake. Chill 3 hours or until set. Frost cake with remaining whipped topping. Garnish with whole strawberries. Store in refrigerator.

Note: *Very delicious; very pretty.*

Chocolate Mint Decadence
12 Servings

Cake:
nonstick vegetable oil spray
13 ounces bittersweet
   (not unsweetened) or semisweet
   chocolate, chopped
1 cup plus 3 tablespoons
   unsalted butter
1 cup plus 3 tablespoons sugar
⅓ cup water
6 large eggs, room temperature
¼ cup sugar

Ganache:
18 ounces bittersweet (not
   unsweetened) or semisweet
   chocolate, chopped
1½ cups whipping cream
¾ cup raspberries or quartered and
   hulled strawberries

Mousse:
1 pound imported white chocolate
   (such as Lindt), chopped
½ teaspoon unflavored gelatin
7 tablespoons whipping cream
¼ teaspoon peppermint extract
1⅓ cups chilled whipping cream

Garnish:
Fresh mint sprigs
Raspberries or strawberries

Cake:
Spray 9-inch diameter springform pan with 2¾-inch high sides with non-stick vegetable oil spray. Line bottom with parchment. On outside of pan, wrap foil around bottom and up sides of pan. Melt chocolate with butter in heavy large saucepan over very low heat, stirring until smooth. Remove from heat. Cook 1 cup plus 3 tablespoons sugar and ⅓ cup water in heavy small saucepan over low heat, stirring until sugar dissolves. Increase heat and bring to boil. Whisk sugar syrup into chocolate mixture. Cool until just warm, about 15 minutes.

Using electric mixer, beat eggs and ¼ cup sugar in large bowl until mixture is pale yellow and slowly dissolving ribbon forms when beaters are lifted, about 5 minutes. Add warm chocolate mixture to egg mixture and beat until thoroughly incorporated. Pour batter into prepared pan. Place cake pan in large baking pan. Add enough hot water to baking pan to come halfway up sides of cake pan. Bake at 350°F until cake looks dry on top and feels firm near center, about 45 minutes. Remove cake pan from water. Cool completely in pan on rack (cake will fall slightly). Peel off foil.

Ganache:
Melt chocolate with cream in heavy medium saucepan over medium-low heat, stirring until smooth. Let stand until just cool, about 20 minutes. Transfer 1 cup ganache to bowl and reserve to pipe around edge of cake. Pour 1 cup ganache from saucepan over cake in pan. Sprinkle ¾ cup berries over ganache. Refrigerate cake 1 hour. Reserve the ganache remaining in saucepan for web design and cake sides.

Mousse:
Melt white chocolate in top of double boiler over barely simmering water, stirring until smooth. Remove from over water. Sprinkle gelatin over 7 tablespoons cream in heavy small saucepan. Let stand 10 minutes to soften. Cook over low heat until gelatin dissolves, stirring constantly. Whisk cream mixture into melted chocolate. Mix in extract. Transfer to large bowl. Let stand until cool but not set, about 5 minutes. Using electric mixer, beat 1⅓ cups chilled cream in medium bowl to soft peaks. Fold half of cream into white chocolate mixture to lighten. Gently fold in remaining cream. Spoon mousse atop ganache and berries in cake pan. Shake pan gently to settle mousse.

Garnish:
If necessary, whisk remaining ganache in saucepan over low heat until soft enough to pipe. Spoon ¼ cup ganache into parchment cone or icing bag. Cut tip of cone. Starting at center of cake, pipe ganache in a spiral atop mousse, spacing coils ½ inch apart and continuing to edge of pan. Starting at center, draw tip of knife through spiral to edge of pan. Move knife 1½ inches around pan sides, then draw tip of knife through spiral from edge of pan to center. Repeat moving around pan to form web design, spacing evenly and alternating direction of strokes. Chill until mousse sets, 2 hours.

Run small sharp knife around pan sides to loosen cake. Release pan sides from cake. If necessary, stir remaining ganache in saucepan over low heat until just thick enough to spread. Carefully spread ganache in thin coating over sides of cake and mousse, covering completely. Spoon reserved 1 cup ganache in bowl into pastry bag fitted with star tip. Pipe decorative border around edge of cake. (Can be prepared 1 day ahead. Cover and refrigerate.) Arrange mint sprigs around top edge of cake. Garnish platter with raspberries or strawberries.

Eggnog Bread Pudding
8 Servings

4 large eggs
1 quart refrigerated eggnog
10 slices of raisin-cinnamon bread

Coat a 2-quart baking dish with nonstick spray. Whisk eggs in a large bowl and add eggnog. Cut bread into 1-inch cubes and place in prepared pan. Pour eggnog mixture over bread cubes. Let stand 30 minus.

Bake, uncovered at 350°F for 55 minutes or until a knife inserted in the center comes out clean. Serve warm with a dollop of whipped cream, or at room temperature with a sprinkle of powdered sugar.

Note: *This is good with additional raisins and/or nutmeg.*

Pound Cake
12 Servings

1 cup butter
2¾ cups sugar
6 eggs
3 cups sifted flour

¼ teaspoon baking soda
½ teaspoon salt
1 cup sour cream (8 ounces)
1 teaspoon vanilla extract

Cream the butter and sugar together gradually; beat until fluffy. Beat in the eggs, one at a time. In a separate bowl, sift the flour, baking soda, and salt. Mix the sour cream and vanilla together. Alternately add the two to the butter mixture, stirring just until blended. Grease and flour a 9-inch tube pan. Bake at 350°F for 1 hour and 20 minutes.

Lemon Yogurt Cake
8 to 10 Servings

1½ cups flour
2 teaspoons baking powder
½ teaspoon kosher salt
1 cup plain whole-milk yogurt
1 cup sugar
3 large eggs
2 teaspoons grated lemon
  zest—about 2 lemons
1 teaspoon vanilla extract
½ cup canola oil

Lemon Syrup:
⅓ cup freshly squeezed
  lemon juice
⅓ cup sugar

Lemon Glaze:
1 cup powdered sugar
2 tablespoons freshly
  squeezed lemon juice

Grease and flour loaf pan. In one bowl, sift flour, baking powder and salt. In another bowl, whisk together yogurt, sugar, eggs, lemon zest, and vanilla. Slowly whisk dry ingredients into wet ingredients. With rubber spatula, fold in the canola oil. Blend thoroughly and pour batter into prepared pan. Bake at 350°F for 55 minutes.

Lemon Syrup:
Cook lemon juice and sugar over medium heat until sugar is dissolved. Cool cake for about 10 minutes. Remove from pan carefully and place on baking rack. While still warm, spoon lemon-sugar syrup over the cake gently to allow it to soak in. Cool.

Lemon Glaze:
Combine powdered sugar and lemon juice. Drizzle over cooled cake.

Heavenly Chocolate Cake
16 Servings

1¾ cups flour
1 cup sugar
¾ cup unsweetened Dutch-process
  cocoa
1½ teaspoons baking soda
1½ teaspoons baking powder
1 teaspoon salt
1¾ cups buttermilk

1 cup packed light brown
  sugar
2 eggs, lightly beaten (or
  equivalent egg substitute)
¼ cup canola oil
2 teaspoons vanilla extract
1 cup hot strong black coffee
  (can use warm leftover coffee)

Lightly grease 12 cup Bundt pan. Dust with flour, invert, and shake out
excess. In a large mixing bowl, whisk together flour, white sugar, cocoa,
baking soda, baking powder, and salt.* Add buttermilk, brown sugar,
eggs, oil, and vanilla. Beat with electric mixer on medium speed for 2
minutes. Whisk in hot coffee until completely incorporated. The batter
will be quite thin.

Pour batter into prepared Bundt pan and bake at 350°F for 35 to 40 minutes or until a toothpick tests done. Cool the cake in the pan on a rack
for 10 minutes, then remove from pan and cool completely.

Note: *You can do this in a plastic container with a lid then gently shake to combine. You
can also make 2 of these mixes at once and store the second mix in the aforementioned plastic
container; you are then halfway to the next cake!*

Elodie's Chocolate Cake
8 to 10 Servings

10 ounces bittersweet or semisweet
  chocolate, chopped
1 cup unsalted butter, cut into
  small pieces
5 large eggs
1¼ cups sugar

5 tablespoons flour
1½ teaspoons baking powder
powdered sugar
1 pint fresh raspberries
chocolate sauce

Butter and flour a 10-inch spring form pan with 2¾-inch high sides.

Stir chocolate and butter in heavy medium saucepan or double boiler over low heat until chocolate melts and mixture is smooth.

Beat eggs and 1¼ cups sugar in large bowl until well blended and beginning to thicken. Sift flour and baking powder over eggs and fold in. Gradually fold in chocolate mixture. Transfer batter to prepared pan.

Bake cake at 325°F for 20 minutes. Cover pan with foil. Bake until tester inserted into center comes out with moist crumbs still attached, about 30 minutes longer. Uncover cake. Cool in pan on rack (cake will fall as it cools).

Cake can be made one day ahead. Cover and let stand at room temperature. Cut around pan sides to loosen cake. Release pan sides. Sift powdered sugar over cake. Garnish with chocolate sauce and raspberries.

Traditional Vanilla Birthday Cake
12 to 15 Servings or 24 cupcakes

Cake:
1 cup (2 sticks) unsalted butter, softened
2 cups sugar
4 large eggs, room temperature
1½ cups of self-rising flour
1¼ cups flour
1 cup milk
1 teaspoon vanilla extract

Vanilla Butter Cream Frosting:
1 cup (2 sticks) unsalted butter, very soft
8 cups confectioners' sugar
½ cup milk
2 teaspoons vanilla extract
pink food coloring (or your choice of color!)

Cake:
Grease and lightly flour 3 9×2-inch round cake pans then line the bottom with waxed paper. In a large bowl, using the medium speed on an electric mixer, cream the butter until smooth. Add the sugar gradually and beat until fluffy, about 3 minutes. Add the eggs one at a time, beating well after each addition. In a separate bowl, combine the flours and add in four parts, alternating with the milk and the vanilla extract, beating well after each addition. Divide batter among the cake pans. Bake at 350°F for 20 to 25 minutes or until a cake tester inserted into center of cake comes out clean. Let cakes cool in pans for ten minutes. Remove from pans and cool completely on a wire rack.

If you are making cupcakes, line two 12-cup muffin tins with cupcake paper. Spoon batter into the cups about ¾ full. Bake at 350°F until the tops spring back when lightly touched, about 20 to 22 minutes. Remove cupcakes from pans and cool completely on a rack before icing. When cake has cooled, ice between the layers, then ice top and sides of cake. For cupcakes, ice the tops.

Frosting:
Place the butter in a large mixing bowl. Add 4 cups of the sugar and then the milk and the vanilla extract. Beat until smooth and creamy. Gradually add the remaining sugar, 1 cup at a time, until icing is thick enough to be of good spreading consistency (you may not need all of the sugar). If desired, add a few drops of food coloring (light pink is beautiful!) and

mix thoroughly. Use and store icing at room temperature, as icing will set if chilled. Can store in airtight container for up to 3 days.

Note: *Whole eggs in the cake make it moist, and the secret to the butter cream frosting is that you whip it longer than you'd think necessary to get that extra-creamy texture. If ever in New York, visit The Magnolia Bakery!*

Cassata Cake
12 Servings

1 Sara Lee Pound Cake, sliced thin (¼-inch slices)	1 teaspoon vanilla extract
½ gallon whole milk	1 teaspoon cinnamon
2 cups sugar	1½ cups cornstarch
1 orange rind, washed and peeled from orange in one piece if possible	2 ounces shaved chocolate
	½ cup maraschino cherries, quartered

Slice pound cake and line a 9×13 pan with the pound cake slices.

Pour all but 2 cups of the milk into a large saucepan, big enough to hold all remaining ingredients. Add the sugar, orange rind, vanilla, and cinnamon. Stir contents over medium heat until combined and warmed.

Mix the cornstarch into the remaining 2 cups of milk. Stir until the mixture is smooth. Remove the orange rind and add to the warm milk mixture, stirring constantly until the mixture gently boils. Cook for one minute, gently stirring constantly. Remove from heat immediately.

Spoon half the mixture over the pound cake, add another layer of pound cake, and spread remaining mixture on top of second layer of pound cake. Spread evenly and press the cherries into a design on top and sprinkle with shaved chocolate. Refrigerate immediately.

Schwarzwald Torte (Black Forest Cherry Torte)
10 to 12 Servings

Cake:
6 eggs, separated
¾ cup sifted flour
¼ cup sifted cocoa
¼ teaspoon salt
1½ cups sugar
1 teaspoon vanilla extract

Glaze:
1 tablespoon water
¼ cup sugar
¼ cup brandy

Frosting:
2 cups whipping cream
¼ cup powdered sugar
2 tablespoons brandy
shaved chocolate
Maraschino cherries

Cake:
Separate yolks from whites of eggs and allow to come to room temperature. Meanwhile, sift flour once, measure, add cocoa and salt, and sift again. In small bowl of electric mixer, beat egg yolks until thick and lemon colored. Add ¾ cup of the sugar gradually and continue to beat until all has been added and the mixture is thick and light. Transfer to large mixer bowl. Beat egg whites until frothy throughout then add ½ cup sugar gradually, beating constantly. Continue to beat until stiff peaks form. Fold into yellow egg mixture. Sift flour mixture gradually over egg mixture, folding gently but thoroughly. Add vanilla and blend. Turn into two deep 9-inch layer cake pans, the bottoms of which have been lightly greased and floured. Bake at 350°F for about 25 minutes, or until cake tests done. Remove from the oven and cool in the pans 10 minutes.

Glaze:
Combine sugar and water for glaze in a small saucepan. Place over low heat and stir until sugar is dissolved. Remove from the heat and cool slightly, then add brandy. Cut cake layers from sides of pans and remove to wire cake racks. Brush brandy glaze over the top of warm layers and allow to cool.

Frosting:
Combine cream and powdered sugar and chill thoroughly. Beat until thick and light then add brandy. Spread whipped cream on one layer of cake and top with the second layer. Use remainder of cream to frost sides and top. Sprinkle with shaved chocolate and garnish with maraschino cherries. Keep refrigerated.

Note: *To make shaved chocolate, shave thin strips of chocolate from bar, using a swivel-type vegetable peeler.*

Rustic Raspberry Tart with Irish Butter Crust

8 Servings

Crust:
1 cup flour
¼ teaspoon salt
6 tablespoons cold unsalted Kerrygold
   Pure Irish Butter, cut in ½ -inch chunks
1 large egg yolk (reserve white)
3 to 5 teaspoons ice water

Filling:
2 cups raspberries
3 tablespoons sugar
2 teaspoons cornstarch

Crust:

In food processor, combine flour and salt. Add butter to processor, pulsing just until mixture resembles coarse meal. Slowly add egg yolk and water, 1 teaspoon at a time; process just until dough clumps together and begins to form a ball. Set 2 pieces (each about 12×15 inches) plastic wrap on work surface. Lightly dust each with flour. Gather dough and press into a flat disk about 6 inches wide. Set disk in center of 1 piece of wrap. Set remaining plastic wrap, floured-side down on dough. With rolling pin, roll dough evenly into about an 11×12-inch round; occasionally turn round over, lift wrinkled plastic wrap, pull smooth and replace; continue rolling as needed.

To fill the tart, peel off top sheet of wrap and invert onto 15×2 inch baking sheet lined with cooking parchment. Remove remaining plastic wrap. Distribute berries in center of pastry, leaving about a 2-inch border. In small bowl, mix sugar and cornstarch. Sprinkle 3 tablespoons mixture evenly over fruit. Gently fold edges of pastry over berries, pleating edges to fit; leave an opening of 4 to 6 inches wide in center. Brush pastry with reserved egg white from crust. Sprinkle pastry lightly with remaining sugar mixture.

Bake tart on the bottom rack at 425°F until crust is golden on bottom and juices bubble, 25 to 30 minutes. Cool in pan at least 15 minutes. While still warm, use wide spatula loosen tart from pan especially where juices have leaked out. Transfer to serving platter and serve warm or cool. Cut in wedges. Dust with powdered sugar, if desired. Serve with vanilla ice cream or lightly sweetened, softly whipped cream.

Jameson Chocolate-Walnut-Caramel Tart
8 Servings

Crust:
1¼ cups flour
1 teaspoon sugar
¼ teaspoon salt
4 tablespoons cold unsalted Kerrygold
 Irish butter, cut into small pieces
4 tablespoons cold vegetable
 shortening, cut into small pieces
2 to 4 tablespoons ice water

Caramel Sauce:
¼ cup unsalted butter
½ cup sugar
¼ cup heavy whipping cream

Filling:
1 cup chopped walnuts
½ cup bittersweet or semisweet
 chocolate, broken into small pieces
¾ cup light corn syrup
½ cup packed light brown sugar
½ packed dark brown sugar
4 tablespoons unsalted butter,
 cut into pieces
3 large eggs
3 tablespoons Jameson
 Irish Whiskey
1 teaspoon vanilla extract
¼ teaspoon salt

confectioners' sugar for dusting

Crust:
Combine the flour, sugar, and the salt in a food processor fitted with a
metal blade. Add the butter and shortening and pulse 8 to 12 times, or
until the mixture resembles coarse crumbs. Add 2 tablespoons of ice water and process 15 to 20 seconds, or until the dough comes together. Add
the remaining water if necessary and pulse again. Dust a work surface
with flour. Turn out the dough; form it into a ball, then wrap it in plastic
wrap and refrigerate for 1 hour. Remove the dough from refrigerator 10
minutes before rolling.

Butter a 10-inch tart pan with removable bottom. Dust a work surface
with flour. Roll out the dough to a circle 12 inches in diameter. Transfer
to the prepared pan, fold in the excess dough, and press with your fingers
to form thick sides. Freeze for 30 minutes, or until firm. Prick the bottom and sides of the crust with a fork. Line the crust with foil, fill with
pie weights or dry beans, and cover with a pie shield (see note) Bake at
375°F for 18 to 20 minutes. Remove the weights, foil, and shield and bake
for another 12 to 15 minutes, or until crust is browned all over. Remove
from oven and let cool on a wire rack. Maintain oven temperature.

Caramel Sauce:
In a saucepan over medium heat, combine the butter and sugar. Cook, stirring constantly, for 3 to 5 minutes, or until the mixture thickens. Continue cooking until the mixture turns golden brown. Remove from heat and stir in cream. Pour the caramel mixture into the tart crust; spread evenly over the bottom and freeze for 15 minutes, or until set.

Filling:
Sprinkle half the walnuts and all of the chocolate pieces over the caramel mixture. In a large bowl, combine the corn syrup, brown sugars, butter, eggs, whiskey, vanilla, and salt. With an electric mixer, beat until smooth. Pour over the chocolate and walnuts. Sprinkle the remaining half of the walnuts over the top.

Bake the tart at 375°F for about 50 minutes, or until the filling is nearly set in the center. Remove from the oven and cool on a wire rack for 10 minutes. Release the sides of the pan. Dust the tart with confectioners' sugar, slice and serve warm with a dollop of fresh whipped cream.

Note: *A pie shield is a ring of heavy-duty nonstick coated metal that sits on top of the tart or pie. It keeps the edges of the crust from burning before the middle is done. One can make the ring from heavy-duty aluminum foil if needed.*

Caramel-Apple Crumb Pie
10 Servings

Crust:
1 cup flour
⅛ teaspoon salt
2 tablespoons chilled butter or stick
  margarine, cut into small pieces
2 tablespoons vegetable shortening
3 tablespoons plus ½ teaspoon
  ice water
1 teaspoon cider vinegar
butter-flavored cooking spray

Filling:
1 tablespoon butter or margarine
½ cup packed brown sugar
¾ teaspoon ground cinnamon
9 cups sliced peeled Granny Smith
  apples (about 2¾ pounds)
3 tablespoons flour
2 teaspoons lemon juice

Topping:
¼ cup flour
¼ cup packed brown sugar
2 tablespoons chilled butter or
  margarine, cut into small pieces
¼ cup fat-free caramel sundae syrup

Crust:
Lightly spoon 1 cup flour into a dry measuring cup; level with a knife.
Combine 1 cup flour and salt in a bowl; cut in 2 tablespoons butter and
shortening with a pastry blender or 2 knives until mixture resembles
coarse meal. Sprinkle surface with ice water, 1 tablespoon at a time; add
vinegar. Toss with a fork until moist and crumbly (do not form a ball).

Press mixture gently into a 4-inch circle on heavy-duty plastic wrap; cover
with additional plastic wrap. Roll dough, still covered, to a 12-inch circle.
Freeze 10 minutes or until plastic wrap can be easily removed.

Remove 1 sheet of plastic wrap; fit dough into a 9-inch pie plate coated
with cooking spray. Remove top sheet of plastic wrap. Press the crust
into the pie plate and fold the edges under; flute the edges to decorate.
Line the crust with a piece of foil; arrange pie weights (or dried beans)
on foil. Bake at 375°F for 15 minutes or until the edge is lightly browned.
Remove pie weights and foil; cool on a wire rack.

Filling:

Melt 1 tablespoon butter in a large nonstick skillet over medium-high heat. Combine ½ cup brown sugar and cinnamon. Add sugar mixture and apples to skillet; cook 5 minutes, stirring occasionally. Remove from heat; stir in 3 tablespoons flour and lemon juice. Spoon into prepared crust. To prepare topping, lightly spoon ¼ cup flour into a dry measuring cup; level with a knife. Combine flour and ¼ cup brown sugar in a bowl; cut in 2 tablespoons butter with a pastry blender or 2 knives until mixture resembles coarse meal. Drizzle syrup over apple mixture; sprinkle topping over syrup. Bake at 375°F for 30 minutes or until apples are tender. Cool on a wire rack.

Blueberry Sour Cream Pie
8 Servings

1 unbaked 9-inch pie crust

Filling:
1 cup sour cream
2 tablespoons flour
¾ cup sugar
1 teaspoon almond extract
¼ teaspoon salt
1 egg, slightly beaten
1 to 2 pints (about 3 cups) blueberries, cleaned and stemmed

Topping:
4 tablespoons flour
1 tablespoon sugar
⅓ cup chopped pecans
¼ cup (½ stick) unsalted butter, cold

Filling:

Combine sour cream, 2 tablespoons flour, ¾ cup sugar, almond extract, salt, and egg in mixing bowl. Whisk until batter is smooth. Stir in blueberries. Spoon filling into pastry shell, smoothing top with spatula. Bake pie in center of oven at 400°F for 25 minutes. Sprinkle topping over pie and bake for an additional 10 minutes or until lightly browned (you may need to cover edges of crust with aluminum foil to reduce browning).

Topping:

Combine 4 tablespoons flour, 1 tablespoon sugar, pecans, and ¼ cup butter in bowl. Mix well, cutting together with fork or pastry blender. Let pie cool to room temperature. Pie can be made 4 to 5 hours ahead and kept at cool room temperature, or it can be chilled 6 to 8 hours.

Note: *This is the BEST pie, and practically fool proof.*

Cranberry Tart
10 to 12 Servings

1¼ cups plus 2 tablespoons flour
½ cup instant or fine polenta
1¾ cups sugar
1¼ teaspoons salt
freshly grated zest of 1 lemon
4 ounces unsalted butter, diced
1 large egg plus 3 large egg yolks

2 tablespoons extra-virgin olive oil
2 teaspoons vanilla extract
½ cup light corn syrup
3 cups (12-ounce bag) fresh cranberries, rinsed
1 cup heavy cream

Place 1¼ cups flour, polenta, 1 cup sugar, 1 teaspoon salt, and lemon zest in a food processor and process to blend. Add butter and pulse until mixture resembles coarse sand.

In a small bowl, beat whole egg with oil and 1 teaspoon vanilla. Uncover processor, pour in liquid ingredients, and pulse until a ball of dough forms. This may take 20 or more quick pulses. If necessary, sprinkle a little water if mixture does not come together. Form dough into a disk and wrap in plastic. Chill at least 1 hour in refrigerator.

In a 3-quart saucepan, melt remaining sugar over low heat. Stir in corn syrup and bring to a boil. Add cranberries and cook, stirring, about 2 minutes, until they begin to release juice. Remove to a bowl and allow to cool about 20 minutes.

Roll out dough to a 12-inch circle and fit into a 10-inch loose-bottom tart pan. If dough tears, it can easily be pressed together.

In a bowl, whisk together cream and 2 tablespoons flour. Whisk in three egg yolks, remaining vanilla, and a pinch of salt. Pour over cranberries and fold together. Pour into tart shell, place pan on a baking sheet and bake at 350°F for about 40 minutes, until filling bubbles but is not yet firm, and pastry browns. Cool in pan before removing sides.

Strawberry-Rhubarb Pie

6 to 8 Servings

Crust:
2 ⅔ cups flour
1 teaspoon salt
⅔ cup vegetable oil
6 tablespoons cold milk

Filling:
1¼ cups plus 2 teaspoons sugar
⅓ cup all-purpose flour
¼ teaspoon nutmeg
¼ teaspoon cinnamon
3 cups halved strawberries
2 cups thinly sliced rhubarb
2 tablespoon butter, cut up
2 teaspoons milk

To make crust, preheat oven to 400°F. Mix flour and salt. Measure oil and milk together but don't stir. Add to flour and mix lightly. Roll out two crusts on wax paper, one to fit a 9-inch pie plate and one for the top crust. To make the filling, mix sugar, flour, nutmeg and cinnamon. Add fruit, stirring to coat. Can set aside in fridge and then drain later (if adding blueberry or peach, add lemon zest). Pour the filling into the crust. Scatter butter. Add top crust. Pinch edges and ventilate the top. Brush with milk. Sprinkle sugar on top. Bake on cookie sheet for 50 minutes. Can cover edge with tinfoil if cooking too fast.

Jack Daniel's Chocolate Chip Pecan Pie

6 to 8 Servings

3 eggs, lightly beaten
1 cup sugar
2 tablespoons unsalted butter, melted
1 cup dark corn syrup
1 teaspoon vanilla extract

½ cup Jack Daniel's Whiskey
½ cup semisweet chocolate chips
1 cup whole pecans
1 10-inch pie crust, unbaked

Combine eggs, sugar, butter, corn syrup, vanilla, and Jack Daniel's. Mix well. Sprinkle chocolate chips over bottom of unbaked pie crust. Cover with pecans. Pour filling over chips and pecans. Bake at 375°F for 35 to 40 minutes, or until knife inserted halfway between center and edge comes out clean. Set aside 30 minutes before cutting.

̣nut Cream Pie
̣rvings

1 cup sugar	1 teaspoon vanilla extract
1 cup milk	1 cup flaked coconut
1 cup heavy cream	¼ teaspoon salt
3 egg yolks, beaten	9-inch pie shell, baked
3 tablespoons cornstarch	1 cup heavy cream
¼ cup butter	additional coconut for garnish

Heat sugar, milk, and cream in a 1-quart saucepan over medium heat. Blend egg yolks and cornstarch. Add small amount of hot milk to yolk mixture to temper. Mix well and return to the hot milk. Boil until thick, about 3 minutes. Remove from heat. Add butter, vanilla, coconut, and salt. Stir until butter melts. Cool. Pour mixture into pre baked pie shell. Whip and sweeten cream; spread over pie. Garnish with grated coconut. Serve chilled.

Note: *An exceptional version of a classic.*

Mystery Pecan Pie
6 to 8 Servings

8 ounce package cream cheese, softened	1¼ cups chopped pecans
4 eggs	1 cup light corn syrup
⅓ cup sugar	¼ cup sugar
1 teaspoon vanilla extract	¼ teaspoon salt
	9-inch unbaked pie shell

Cream together cream cheese, 1 egg, ⅓ cup sugar, and 1 teaspoon vanilla. Beat until fluffy. Spread mixture on bottom of pie shell. Sprinkle pecans over cheese mixture. Beat 3 eggs until well mixed but not foamy. Do not over-beat. Add corn syrup, ¼ cup sugar, 1 teaspoon vanilla, and salt. Mix well. Pour over pecans. Bake at 350°F for 40 minutes or until nuts are lightly browned. Top will rise and fall as it cools.

Cookies

Kifli Cookies
Makes 56 Cookies

1 cup butter
½ pound cream cheese
¼ teaspoon salt
2 cups flour

Filling:
1 cup chopped walnuts
½ cup sugar
1 teaspoon cinnamon

Mix together butter, cream cheese, salt, and flour. Refrigerate overnight. Shape into 14 balls. In a separate bowl, mix together chopped walnuts, sugar, and cinnamon. Roll refrigerated dough into 6-inch flat rounds and cut into quarters. Fill each quarter with filling. Take 2 ends and roll into a cone. Bake at 350°F for 12 minutes.

Carrot Drop Cookies
Makes 48 Cookies

4 to 6 carrots, peeled
1½ sticks of butter, softened
¾ cup sugar
1 egg
2 cups flour
2 teaspoons baking powder
½ teaspoon salt

Icing:
½ stick butter, softened
1½ cups sifted powdered
  sugar
1 tablespoon orange rind and
  enough juice to make a
  smooth icing
variety of sprinkles

Boil carrots in water until soft. Mash with potato masher. Mix butter, sugar, and egg in mixer. Add 1 cup mashed carrots, flour, baking powder, and salt into mixer until combined. Drop by rounded teaspoon on cookie sheet and bake at 350°F for 8 to 10 minutes. When cool, ice each cookie and dip in favorite sprinkles. To make the icing, blend butter and powdered sugar. Add the orange rind and the orange juice, a teaspoon at a time until smooth.

Note: *Don't be fooled by the name! These treats are soft and delicious. At Christmas, dip the cookies in red and green sugar crystals, chocolate jimmies, and colorful nonpareils. At Easter, use spring colored sprinkles. Soft and delicious!*

Amaretti Cookies
Makes 40 Cookies

8 ounces canned almond paste
1 cup superfine or castor white sugar
2 large egg whites
extra white sugar or Swedish Pearl Sugar for dusting cookies

Line two baking sheets with parchment paper. Have ready a pastry bag fitted with a ½-inch plain tip.

Using a food processor or electric mixer, break the almond paste into small pieces and place in bowl of food processor or mixer, with the sugar. Pulse or mix on low speed, until the mixture is very fine. Add the egg whites in three additions, processing or mixing well after each addition. Continue processing or mixing the dough until very smooth (about one minute for the processor and about 3 or 4 minutes for the mixer).

Fill the pastry bag with the almond mixture. Pipe 1½-inch mounds onto the parchment paper, spacing about 1 inch apart. After filling the baking sheet with cookie mounds, take a damp paper towel and lightly press the top of each cookie to smooth out the surface (to flatten out the tip of dough at the top of each cookie caused from piping). Lightly sprinkle a little sugar on top of each cookie.

Bake at 375°F for 15 minutes, or until the cookies have risen, are a deep golden color, and have tiny cracks. Remove from the oven and place baking pan on a rack to cool. When cool, gently peel cookies from parchment. If they stick to parchment, turn the paper over, take a damp paper towel and gently wipe the bottom of the parchment paper to loosen the cookie.

Note: *Make your own superfine sugar by processing regular granulated white sugar in your food processor for about 30 seconds or until sugar is ground very fine.*

Mexican Wedding Cakes
Makes 36 Cookies

⅔ cup toasted nuts (pecans,
walnuts, hazelnuts)
2 cups flour, divided
1 cup unsalted butter, room temperature

¼ cup confectioners'
(powdered or icing) sugar
1 teaspoon vanilla extract
¼ teaspoon salt

1 cup powdered sugar, sifted

Toast Nuts:
Place nuts on a baking sheet and bake at 350°F on middle rack for about 8 minutes, or until lightly brown and fragrant. Cool. Once the nuts have cooled completely place them, along with 2 tablespoons of the flour from the recipe, into your food processor, and process until they are finely ground (but not a paste). In the bowl of your electric mixer (or with a hand mixer), beat the butter and sugar until light and fluffy (about 2 minutes). Beat in the vanilla extract. Add the remaining flour and salt and beat until combined. Stir in the nuts. Cover and refrigerate the dough for about one hour or until firm.

Line 2 baking sheets with parchment paper. Form the chilled dough into 1-inch balls and place them 2 inches apart on the prepared baking sheets. Bake at 350°F for about 12 to 15 minutes, or until the edges of the cookies start to brown. Remove from oven and place on a wire rack to cool for about 5 minutes.

Meanwhile, line another baking pan or tray with parchment or wax paper. Sprinkle about ½ cup of the confectioners' sugar on the bottom of the pan and then place the slightly cooled cookies on top of the sugar. Place the remaining ½ cup of sugar in a fine strainer or sieve and then sprinkle the tops of the cookies (or you can just roll the cookies in the sugar). Store in an airtight container.

Note: *The secret to great tasting Mexican Wedding Cakes is to use a high quality butter and pure vanilla extract. Butter is graded according to flavor, color, texture, aroma, and body and one easy way to tell the quality of the butter is by the letter code or numerical number listed on the butter's package. The highest grade is AA (93 score), then A (92 score), followed by B (90 score). Buy a vanilla extract that is labeled "pure."*

Peanut Butter Milk Dud Cookies
Makes 36 Cookies

½ cup margarine
½ cup smooth peanut butter
½ cup sugar
½ cup brown sugar
1 egg

1¼ cups flour
½ teaspoon baking powder
¼ cup baking soda
¼ teaspoon salt
1 large box Milk Dud candy
½ cup sugar

Beat together margarine, peanut butter, sugar, and brown sugar. Add egg to mixture and beat until smooth. Stir together flour, baking powder, baking soda, and salt. Stir flour mixture into margarine/peanut butter mixture. Chill in refrigerator 30 minutes.

Form ball of dough around a Milk Dud. Roll ball in sugar. Bake at 375°F on ungreased cookie sheet for 10 minutes. Remove from cookie sheet and cool on wire rack.

Butter Balls
Makes 24 Cookies

¼ pound butter
4 heaping tablespoons sugar
1½ cups chopped nuts

4 teaspoons vanilla extract
2 cups flour, unsifted
½ cup powdered sugar

Cream together butter and sugar. Add nuts, vanilla, and flour; mix well. Roll mixture into balls and place on cookie sheet. Bake at 325°F for 30 minutes. Roll balls in powdered sugar while still warm. Let cool on wax paper and then store in air-tight container.

Ranger Cookies
Makes 48 to 72 Cookies

1 cup margarine or butter-flavored Crisco	2 cups flour
	½ teaspoon baking powder
1 cup sugar	½ teaspoon baking soda
1 cup brown sugar	½ teaspoon salt
2 eggs	2 cups Rice Crispies cereal
1 tablespoon vanilla extract	1 cup coconut flakes

Cream margarine, sugar, brown sugar, eggs, and vanilla together. Add flour, baking powder, baking soda, and salt. Stir in Rice Crispies and coconut flakes. Drop in small spoonfuls on ungreased cookie sheet with sufficient space for cookies to spread. Bake at 350°F for 10 minutes. Cookies will not look brown when done (if brown, they will be overdone).

Note: *These cookies are chewy and crunchy! Other ingredients can be added for a different look and taste including butter brickle, chocolate chips, mint chips, or butterscotch chips. For variety, place one of following in center of dropped cookie before baking: Gum Drop, Chocolate Kiss, or M&M.*

No Bake Butterscotch Cornflake Cookies
Makes 36 to 40 Cookies

6 cups cornflakes (measure before crushing)
1 12-ounce package butterscotch chips
1⅓ cups chunky peanut butter

Crush cornflakes. Melt butterscotch chips and peanut butter in a double boiler over hot water. Stir in cornflakes, mixing well. Drop by spoonfuls on wax paper. Cool until set. Place in covered container.

S'More Cup Cookies
Makes 24 Cups

1½-ounce pouch chocolate
chip cookie mix
½ cup butter or margarine, softened
1 egg
24 round caramels in milk chocolate
candies, unwrapped (Rolos)

72 mini marshmallows,
(about ¾ cup)
⅓ cup semisweet chocolate
chips

Spray mini muffin cups with cooking spray. Make cookie dough according to package using butter and egg. Shape into 1½-inch balls and place one into each muffin cup. Bake at 350°F for 13 minutes or until edges begin to brown. Remove from oven. Press one candy into each cookie until even with cookie top. Top with 3 marshmallows. Bake a few minutes longer until marshmallows are puffy. Cool 10 minutes, loosen edges of each cookie and remove to cooking rack. Put chocolate chips in small resealable plastic bag and microwave on high 1 minute or until softened. Squeeze bag until chocolate is smooth. Cut off small corner of bag and squeeze to drizzle over marshmallows.

Note: *Any chocolate cookie dough recipe or refrigerated cookie dough can be substituted in this recipe.*

Chocolate Turtle Cookies
Makes 20 Cookies

1 ⅔ cups shelled pecans (about 100)
1 16½-ounce package refrigerated
chocolate chip cookie dough

20 caramels, unwrapped
2 tablespoons milk

Soak pecans in water for 5 minutes. Arrange 5 pecans on ungreased baking sheets (1 for head, 4 for legs), leaving about a 1-inch circle in center. Shape slightly rounded tablespoons of cookie dough into balls. Place over circle onto pecans. Repeat with remaining pecans and dough, placing turtles two inches apart on baking sheets. Bake at 375°F for 9 to 11 minutes, or until edges are crisp. Cool on baking sheets on wire racks for 1 minute and then move to wire racks to cool completely. Microwave caramels and milk in medium, microwave-safe bowl on high power for 1½ minutes. Stir. Microwave at additional 10 to 15 second intervals, stirring until smooth. Drizzle over turtles.

Note: *Dough from one batch Original Nestle Semisweet Chocolate Chip Cookies (from recipe on Semisweet Chocolate Morsels package) may be used as well.*

Deep Dark Chocolate Biscotti
Makes 30 Cookies

9½ ounces whole-wheat flour
  (about 2 cups)
2 tablespoons flaxseed
½ teaspoon baking soda
¼ teaspoon salt
⅓ cup sugar
⅓ cup packed dark brown sugar

2 large egg whites
1 large egg
1½ teaspoons vanilla extract
⅔ cup dark chocolate chips
  (such as Hershey's)
¾ cup unsalted almonds

Weigh or lightly spoon flour into dry measuring cups; level with a knife. Combine flour, flaxseed, baking soda, and salt in a bowl, stirring with a whisk. Combine sugars, egg whites, and egg in a separate bowl; beat with a mixer at high speed for 2 minutes. Add vanilla; mix well. Add flour mixture to egg mixture; stir until combined. Fold in chocolate and almonds.

Divide dough into 3 equal portions. Roll each portion into a 6-inch-long roll. Arrange rolls 3 inches apart on a baking sheet lined with parchment paper. Pat to a 1 inch thickness. Bake 350°F for 28 minutes, or until firm. Remove rolls from baking sheet and cool 10 minutes on a wire rack.

Cut rolls diagonally into 30 (½-inch) slices. Place, cut sides down, on baking sheet. Reduce oven temperature to 325°F; bake 7 minutes. Turn cookies over; bake 7 minutes (cookies will be slightly soft in center but will harden as they cool). Remove from baking sheet and cool on wire rack.

Chocolate Hazelnut Biscotti
Makes 12 Biscotti

1 cup chopped lightly roasted hazelnuts	3 ounces chopped semisweet chocolate
2 cups flour	
⅔ cup sugar	2 eggs
1¼ teaspoons baking powder	1 tablespoon vanilla extract
¼ teaspoon salt	8 ounces bittersweet chocolate
8 tablespoons butter, cubed	

Roast hazelnuts at 350°F for 5 minutes. Combine flour, sugar, baking powder, and salt in a food processor. Add the butter and blend until coarse. Pour mixture into a large bowl and add chopped hazelnuts and chopped semisweet chocolate.

In separate mixing bowl, beat eggs. Set 2 tablespoons of beat eggs aside. Add vanilla to larger egg quantity and then add to dry mixture. Dough will be somewhat dry. Set dough on floured surface and divide into 4 to 6 logs, ¾ inch in height. Place on cookie sheets and brush with egg wash.

Bake at 350°F for 25 to 35 minutes. Take out and cool for 20 minutes. Reduce oven temperature to 325°F. Slice the logs into ½-inch slices. Place again, cut side down, on baking sheet. Bake for 10 minutes and then turn them over and bake them on the other side for 10 minutes.

Meanwhile, melt bittersweet chocolate in a small microwave-safe, glass bowl in the microwave. Once the biscotti have cooled, dip one end into the melted chocolate and place onto a cooking sheet lined with wax paper. Place in refrigerator for faster set up of chocolate.

Bars & Squares

Lemon Bars

24 Servings

Cravings Restaurant *is an intimate bistro in Webster Groves, serving European inspired dishes with an Asian twist. Cravings focuses on local ingredients and emphasize 'made from scratch' and high quality products.* Tim Brennan *is the chef/ owner of* Cravings, *and has twice received the Midwest Regional James Beard Award for Desserts.*

Crust:
3 cups unbleached flour
½ teaspoon salt
¾ cup sugar
12 ounces unsalted butter
grated zest of one lemon

Lemon Bar Filling:
8 large eggs
3 cups sugar
½ cup unbleached flour
1 teaspoon baking powder
1 cup fresh squeezed lemon juice
2 cups fresh blueberries

powdered sugar for dusting

Crust:
Place all the crust ingredients in the bowl of a food processor. Process until the dough comes together in a ball. Line a 12×18 cookie sheet (with sides) with foil. Brush with melted butter. Press dough evenly into the foil-lined cookie sheet. Bake at 350°F for 25 to 30 minutes or until golden brown.

Lemon Bar Filling:
Mix together the eggs and sugar until well blended. Sift together the flour and baking powder, then add to the egg and sugar mixture. Gently stir in the lemon juice.

Sprinkle the blueberries over the baked crust. Pour the lemon custard on top. Bake at 350°F for 30 to 40 minutes until set in the center. Cool at room temperature for 25 minutes. Refrigerate or freeze until completely firm. Invert on a cutting board of the same size. Peel off the foil and invert again. Dust the top with powdered sugar.

Note: *It is best to cut the bars while frozen or completely cooled.*

Linzer Squares
Makes 16 Squares

1½ cups flour
1 tablespoon unsweetened
　cocoa powder
½ teaspoon ground cinnamon
⅛ teaspoon ground cloves
¼ teaspoon freshly ground nutmeg
¼ teaspoon salt
¾ cup unsalted butter, room
　temperature

½ cup sugar
1 large egg
1 cup ground almonds or
　hazelnuts
1 cup raspberry preserves
　or jam
confectioners' (powdered)
　sugar for dusting

In a separate bowl, whisk together the flour, cocoa powder, cinnamon, cloves, nutmeg, and salt. In the bowl of your electric mixer, or with a hand mixer, cream the butter and sugar until smooth and creamy. Add the egg and beat until fluffy. Stir in the ground nuts and the flour mixture. Cover with plastic wrap and place the dough in the refrigerator for about 1 hour.

Lightly butter, or spray with a non-stick vegetable spray, a 9×9 baking pan. Take the dough from the refrigerator, remove ⅔ of the dough and place the remaining dough back in the refrigerator. Place the ⅔ portion of the dough between two sheets of plastic wrap or parchment paper and roll the dough into a 10-inch square. Remove the top sheet of plastic wrap and place the square of dough into square baking pan, plastic wrap side up. Pull off the second sheet of plastic wrap and, with your fingers, press the dough onto the bottom and ½ inch up the sides of the pan. Spread the raspberry preserves evenly over the dough.

Remove the remaining dough from the refrigerator and place between two sheets of plastic wrap or parchment paper. Roll the dough into slightly larger than a 9 inch square. With a pastry cutter or pizza wheel, cut the square into ½-inch strips. Lay half the strips over the jam, spacing evenly over the squares. Lay the remaining strips crosswise over the first layer of strips and press the ends into the edges of the bottom crust. (If you find the strips of dough too soft, place the strips on a baking sheet and freeze for about 10 minutes.) Do not worry if the pastry tears; just press the pieces back together.

Bake at 350°F on middle rack for about 30 to 40 minutes or until the pastry starts to brown and the raspberry preserves are starting to bubble. Place on a wire rack to cool completely. Cut into 2-inch squares. It is best to store these squares a day or two before serving so the flavors have time to mellow and mingle. Just before serving, the squares can be dusted with confectioners' (powdered or icing) sugar. These squares can also be frozen.

Note: *With beautiful lattice pastry on top and fruity preserves in the middle, this torte-like dessert will please the eye and the palate!*

Viennese Raspberry Squares
Makes 36 Squares

2 eggs separated	⅔ cup sifted powdered sugar
⅓ cup butter	1 cup finely chopped toasted
1 cup flour	almonds or walnuts
⅓ cup sugar	⅓ cup red raspberry preserves
¼ teaspoon cream of tartar	

In a medium mixing bowl, bring egg whites to room temperature. Set aside. For crust, in another medium mixing bowl, beat butter with an electric mixer on medium speed for about 30 seconds or until softened. Add about half the flour. Then add the sugar and egg yolks. Beat on medium to high speed until thoroughly combined, scraping sides of bowl occasionally. Stir in the remaining flour. Press crust mixture into an un-greased 9×9×2 inch baking pan. Bake at 350°F for 15 minutes.

Meanwhile, thoroughly wash and dry the beaters. For meringue topping, add cream of tartar to the egg whites. Beat on medium until soft peaks form (tips curl). Gradually add the powdered sugar, beating until stiff peaks form (tips stand straight). Gently fold in chopped nuts. Set meringue topping aside.

Spread preserves over top of the HOT baked crust. Then carefully spread meringue topping over the preserve layer. Bake at 350°F for about 20 minutes more or until top is golden brown.

Note: *Store in refrigerator.*

Rugelach Bars
Makes 36 Bars

Cream Cheese Dough:
12 tablespoons (1½ sticks) cold
   unsalted butter, cut in ½-inch pieces
1 8-ounce package cream
   cheese, softened
2 cups flour
½ teaspoon salt

Chocolate Filling:
1 cup walnuts or pecans
6 ounces semisweet chocolate, cut into pieces
½ cup granulated white sugar
1½ teaspoons ground cinnamon
¾ cup finely chopped dried apricots
grated zest of one orange
3 tablespoons light corn syrup
3 tablespoons unsalted butter, melted

Glaze:
1 large egg yolk
1 tablespoon water

Garnish:
3 tablespoons granulated
   white sugar or sanding sugar

Cream Cheese Dough:
Place the cold butter and cream cheese in the bowl of your electric mixer. Mix on low speed until the cream cheese is broken down but the butter is still chunky. Add the flour and salt and, on low speed, beat until crumbly and just beginning to hold together. (There should still be some small pieces of butter visible in the dough.) Divide the dough into 2 equal pieces. Flatten each piece of dough into a rectangle and wrap in plastic. Chill in the refrigerator several hours or overnight.

On the next day make the Chocolate Filling:
Place the walnuts or pecans on a baking sheet and bake at 350°F for about 8 to 10 minutes or until lightly browned and fragrant. Remove from oven, cool, and then finely chop. Set aside. In the bowl of your food processor, pulse the cut chocolate until very finely chopped. Transfer to a large bowl and stir in the chopped nuts, sugar, ground cinnamon, dried apricots, orange zest, corn syrup, and melted butter. Set aside.

Have ready a 9×13×2-inch baking pan that has been lined with parchment paper. Remove 1 rectangle of the dough from the refrigerator and, between two 9×13-inch pieces of waxed paper or parchment paper, roll the dough into a rectangle that is the size of your baking pan. Line your pan with the rolled out dough, trimming as needed. Spread the chocolate filling over the dough. Remove the second dough from the refrigerator and roll it out the same as the first. Place the rolled-out dough on top of the chocolate filling, trimming the edges as needed.

Glaze:
Mix the egg yolk and water together in a small bowl, and brush the top of the bars with the glaze. Sprinkle with sugar.

Bake at 350°F for about 35 minutes or until golden brown. Remove from oven and place on a wire rack to cool. Cut into 1×3-inch long bars.

Lemon Squares
Makes 24 Squares

1 cup flour
½ cup butter or margarine
½ cup powdered sugar
2 eggs

¼ teaspoon salt
1 cup sugar
2 tablespoons lemon juice

Cream together flour, butter, and powdered sugar. Pour mixture in ungreased 9×12-inch pan and bake at 350°F for 20 minutes. In another bowl, beat eggs, salt, sugar, and lemon juice. Pour liquid on top of the baked crust and bake for another 25 minutes. Cool and cut into squares.

Carrot-Walnut Bars
Makes 24 Bars

1½ cups flour
1 cup packed brown sugar
1 teaspoon baking powder
1 teaspoon ground cinnamon
½ teaspoon baking soda
2 eggs, beaten
⅔ cup cooking oil
1 teaspoon vanilla extract
1½ cups finely shredded carrots
¾ cup chopped walnuts
½ cup coconut

Cream Cheese Frosting:
1 3-ounce package cream cheese
¼ cup butter, softened
1 teaspoon vanilla
2¼ to 2½ cups sifted powdered sugar

In a large mixing bowl, stir together flour, brown sugar, baking powder, cinnamon, and baking soda. Stir in eggs, oil, and vanilla until thoroughly combined, then stir in carrots, walnuts, and coconut. Spread batter into a greased 13×9×2 baking pan.

Bake at 350°F for 20 to 25 minutes or until a wooden toothpick inserted near the center comes out clean. Cool completely in pan on a rack. Frost with cream cheese frosting. Cut into bars.

Cream Cheese Frosting:
In a large mixing bowl, beat cream cheese, butter, and vanilla with an electric mixer on medium to high speed until light and fluffy. Gradually add 1 cup of the sifted powdered sugar, beating well. Gradually beat in enough of the remaining powdered sugar to make frosting of spreading consistency.

Note: *Store frosted cake, covered, in refrigerator.*

Cheesecake Bars
16 Servings

⅓ cup packed brown sugar
½ cup chopped walnuts
1 cup flour
⅓ cup melted butter
¼ cup sugar

1 8-ounce package cream
  cheese
1 egg
1 tablespoon lemon juice
2 tablespoons milk
1 teaspoon vanilla extract

Mix the brown sugar, walnuts, and flour together. Stir in the butter; work by hand until it resembles coarse crumbs. Set aside 1 cup of mixture for topping; press the rest firmly into the bottom of an 8×8 pan. Bake at 350°F for 12 to 15 minutes. Leave the oven on. While crust is baking, cream sugar and cream cheese together. Add the egg, lemon juice, milk, and vanilla; beat thoroughly and pour over the baked crust. Sprinkle the remaining crumb mixture over the top and bake for an additional 25 minutes. Cool completely before cutting into 2-inch squares.

Note: *Doubles easily to fit into a 9x13-inch pan.*

Key Lime Squares
Makes 12 Squares

5 tablespoons butter, melted
1 cup crushed Walkers Shortbread
  Cookies
¼ cup sugar
½ cup finely chopped macadamia
  nuts, plus some coarsely chopped
4 egg yolks

1 14-ounce can Borden Eagle
  brand sweetened condensed
  milk
1 3-ounce package cream
  cheese
½ cup key lime juice
1 cup heavy cream, whipped

Combine butter, cookies, sugar, and ½ cup macadamia nuts; press into 9×9 ungreased pan. Place in freezer while preparing filling. Using a food processor, combine egg yolks and milk; add cream cheese. Slowly add key lime juice. Pour into chilled crust and refrigerate overnight. Top with whipped cream and 8 to 10 coarsely chopped macadamia nuts.

Turtle Brownies
Makes 24 Bars

1 bag Milk Maid caramels	2 cups pecan halves
⅔ cup evaporated milk (one small can)	4 cups chocolate chips (may
¾ cup softened butter	use part semisweet and part
1 German chocolate cake mix	milk chocolate or all semi
	sweet)

Melt caramels and half of the evaporated milk in microwave. Set aside. Mix the other half the evaporated milk with the butter and cake mix with wooden spoon or electric mixer. Press half this mixture into bottom of 13×9 pan sprayed with cooking spray. Bake at 350°F for 6 minutes. Remove from oven and sprinkle pecans and chocolate chips. Pour caramel sauce over the entire top. Crumble remaining cake mix on top. Bake for about 16 to 17 minutes until golden. Cool completely on a rack and then chill in refrigerator. This is very important before cutting into desired size bars.

Note: *This is a very good but rich dessert. Cutting takes a bit of patience. You will receive many "encore" requests for these brownies!*

To Die For Brownies
Makes 16 Brownies

4 squares unsweetened chocolate	1 cup sifted flour
1 cup butter	1½ cups chopped walnuts
2 cups sugar	(optional)
3 eggs	½ cup semisweet chocolate
1 teaspoon vanilla extract	chips

Melt chocolate and butter in microwave on 30-second intervals. Mix after each interval to ensure that you do not overcook. Blend in sugar, then eggs. Stir in vanilla and flour. Add 1 cup of walnuts, if using. Spread in greased 13×9-inch pan. Sprinkle chocolate chips and remaining walnuts on top. Bake at 350°F for 30 to 35 minutes.

Note: *You will make these over and over again!*

Peanut Butter Squares
Makes 24 Squares

2 sticks butter or margarine
1½ cups crushed graham crackers
1 cup peanut butter

1 box powdered sugar
12 ounces chocolate chips

Melt butter and mix with graham cracker crumbs, peanut butter, and powdered sugar. Pat mixture into a 9×13 pan. Melt chocolate chips in microwave and then pour over top of mixture and smooth evenly. Cut into squares and refrigerate.

Oreo Truffles
Makes 42 Truffles

1 package of Oreo cookies
1 8-ounce package cream cheese
2 8-ounce packages Baker's Semisweet Baking Chocolate/
Chocolate Chips

Crush 9 of the cookies to fine crumbs in food processor; reserve for later use. In lieu of a food processor, a ziplock bag and rolling pin can be used to crush cookies. Crush the remaining cookies and place in a medium-sized bowl. Add the cream cheese into crushed cookies and mix until well blended. Roll cookie mixture into a 1-inch sized ball.

Melt the chocolate in a saucepan on low heat. Line two baking sheets with wax paper. Dip the cookie balls into the melted chocolate. Roll the ball around to cover completely. Place on baking sheet lined with wax paper. Sprinkle the balls with fine crumbs (from initial 9 cookies). Refrigerate until firm, about 1 hour, then store in refrigerator in a covered dish.

Candy

Buckeyes
Makes 36 Pieces

2 cups smooth peanut butter
1 stick margarine or butter, melted
½ cup brown sugar
1 teaspoon vanilla extract

2½ cups powdered sugar
almond bark or Baker's
  dipping chocolate (found in
  grocery baking section)

Mix peanut butter with melted butter. Add brown sugar and vanilla. Mix thoroughly. Add powdered sugar and mix until blended. Roll into 1-inch balls and cool in refrigerator for 30 minutes.

Melt dipping chocolate in microwave according to package directions. Dip cooled peanut butter balls in chocolate and cover most of the ball (leave a bit of peanut butter showing). Place on parchment paper lined cookie sheet and cool until hardened in refrigerator.

Note: *These are great gifts for the holidays! Place 10 to 15 balls in a plastic bag and tie with your favorite ribbon. The kids will love to both make AND eat these!*

Peanut Butter Cups
Makes 70 Cups

1 package chocolate bark
peanut butter
1 package of Ritz Crackers

Melt chocolate bark in the microwave. Spread a small amount of peanut butter onto half of the crackers. Top with the remaining crackers to make a sandwich. Dip each sandwich in melted chocolate until completely covered. Place sandwich on waxed paper until chocolate is firm.

Chocolate Covered Strawberries
Makes 24 Strawberries

1 pound fresh strawberries with leaves
16 ounces milk chocolate chips
2 tablespoons shortening

Insert toothpicks into the tops of the strawberries. In a double boiler, melt the chocolate and shortening, stirring occasionally until smooth. Using toothpicks, dip the strawberries into the chocolate mixture. Turn the strawberries upside down and insert the toothpick into Styrofoam for the chocolate to cool. Refrigerate.

Toffee Bars
Makes 40 Pieces

1 sleeve saltine crackers
2 sticks butter
1 cup brown sugar

1 12-ounce package chocolate chips
½ cup chopped pecans

Line cookie sheet with foil. Crush crackers in package and pour onto foil. Melt butter and add brown sugar. Cook on low heat for 3 minutes. Pour over crackers and bake at 350°F for 5 minutes. Sprinkle all chocolate chips over hot cookie sheet. Put back in oven until chips melt. Remove and spread chocolate evenly with spatula. Pour chopped pecans on top, refrigerate, and break into pieces to serve.

Festive Fudge
Makes 30 Pieces

2 cups sugar
⅔ cup evaporated skim milk
12 regular marshmallows
½ cup butter
pinch of salt

1 cup semisweet chocolate
  pieces
1 cup chopped nuts
1 teaspoon vanilla extract

In a 2-quart heavy saucepan, mix the sugar, evaporated milk, marshmallows, butter, and salt. Cook, stirring constantly, over medium heat. Bring to a gentle boil (mixture will be bubbling all over top). Boil and stir 5 minutes more. Remove from heat. Stir in chocolate pieces until completely melted, then add nuts and vanilla. Spread into a buttered 8-inch square pan. Cool completely before cutting.

Holiday Almond Bark
Makes 24 to 30 Pieces

6 ounces semisweet chocolate chips
2 cups whole unsalted almonds, divided
2 3-ounce bars white chocolate

Melt chocolate chips in microwave-safe bowl on high for 1 minute or 1½ minutes, until nearly smooth. Stir until smooth then stir in 1 cup of almonds. Melt the white chocolate in separate microwave-safe bowl until shiny (1 minute or less). Stir until smooth then stir in the second cup of almonds. Line a cookie sheet with waxed paper that is firmly tucked under ends. Alternately spoon dollops of each mixture, side-by-side, onto waxed paper, forming a thick layer of chocolate. With a knife, cut and swirl to create a marbled effect. Put in cool place until firm. Break into pieces when cooled.

Seasonings, Sauces, & Marinades

The St. Louis Fetal Care Institute of Cardinal Glennon, St. Mary's, and SLU School of Medicine evaluates and intervenes during troubled pregnancies. They operate on babies while still in the womb, so they may grow, be born, and have a chance at life.

Chocolate-Ginger Sauce
Makes 1 Cup

Chris Desens *is currently the program director for the* Culinary Institute at Hickey College. *He has thirty years of varied industry experience including national and international culinary competitions. He is a certified culinary judge through the American Culinary Federation, a Certified Executive Chef, and a member of the American Academy of Chefs.*

½ cup heavy cream
1 tablespoon chopped
   fresh ginger

2 ounces Bolivian chocolate,
   pistoles (discs)
Grand Marnier, as needed

Bring cream and ginger to boil. Remove from heat, cover and steep for 30 minutes. Return to boil; strain ginger-cream mixture into chocolate and stir until melted. Add Grand Marnier to desired consistency. Hold for service.

Sauce au Chocolate Supreme
6 Servings

1 cup cocoa powder
2 cups sugar
2 cups Karo light corn syrup
1 cup heavy cream

6 tablespoons unsalted butter
pinch of salt
vanilla extract
liqueur

Place cocoa powder, sugar, corn syrup, heavy cream, butter, and salt into heavy saucepan and heat together over medium-high flame. Boil gently, while stirring constantly for about 3 minutes or until smooth. Season with vanilla extract and/or liqueur compatible with chocolate (Grand Marnier, bourbon, etc). Use while hot or cool and refrigerate in a tightly sealed container.

Note: *Will keep refrigerated for months.*

Fish Marinade
Makes ²/₃ Cup Marinade

2 cloves garlic, minced
⅓ cup vegetable oil
⅓ cup low salt soy sauce
1 tablespoon sugar

3 green onions, chopped
¼ teaspoon black pepper
1 tablespoon sesame seeds

Blend ingredients together and pour over fish. Marinate for 3 hours. Bake or grill according to the type and thickness of the fish.

Note: *Marinate with 2 pounds of the fish of your choice, tilapia, grouper, tuna etc.*

Pretty Chicken Marinade
4 Servings

⅔ cup olive oil
⅔ cup reduced sodium soy sauce
¼ cup fresh lemon juice
2 tablespoons liquid smoke

2 tablespoons spicy brown or
Dijon mustard
2 teaspoons ground black pepper
2 teaspoons garlic powder

4 boneless, skinless, chicken breasts

Combine the marinade ingredients in a large ziplock bag. Add the chicken and marinate in the refrigerator for 1 to 6 hours, turning every few hours. Grill or broil chicken, discarding leftover marinade.

Note: *You will get much more juice from citrus fruits if they are room temperature or warmer. Roll the fruit on the kitchen counter, poke a few holes in the skin, and microwave at 10 second intervals (up to 30 seconds). The fruit will yield much more juice. A hand held juicer works well and your recipe will taste much better than if you substitute bottled juice.*

Luau Barbeque Sauce for Pork
4 Servings

2 4½-ounce jars baby food peaches
½ cup firmly packed brown sugar
⅓ cup ketchup
⅓ cup vinegar

2 tablespoons soy sauce
2 cloves garlic, minced
1 teaspoon salt
1 teaspoon pepper

Combine all ingredients. Brush some sauce on pork while it is cooking, reserving some to serve on the side. It can be used for ribs, pork chops or any kind of meat. This is especially good on grilled pork.

Marinade for Pork Tenderloin
4 to 6 Servings

¼ cup soy sauce
¼ cup brown sugar
4 garlic cloves, minced

Place soy sauce, brown sugar, and garlic in a large ziplock bag. Mix thoroughly. Add pork tenderloins to the bag and marinate for 3 to 24 hours in refrigerator. Grill and enjoy!

Note: *Enough marinade for 2 1-pound pork tenderloins. You can substitute flank steak for the pork tenderloin.*

Marinade for Pork Tenderloin
10 Servings

½ cup red wine
½ cup soy sauce
½ cup honey
2 tablespoons brown sugar

1 teaspoon minced garlic
½ teaspoon ginger
1 teaspoon onion powder

Combine all marinade ingredients. Marinate pork for at least 6 hours, preferably overnight. Grill on your barbecue as your grill directs, or roast at 325°F for 1 to 1½ hours until meat thermometer reaches 160°F.

Note: *Enough marinade for 4 pork tenderloins.*

Rosemary Marinade for Flank Steak
6 to 8 Servings

½ cup soy sauce
½ cup olive oil
4½ tablespoons honey
6 large garlic cloves, minced

3 tablespoons fresh rosemary
or 1 tablespoon dried
1½ tablespoons coarsely
ground black pepper
1½ teaspoons salt

Mix all ingredients in 13×9-inch glass baking dish. Add steak and turn to coat. Cover and refrigerate several hours, turning occasionally. The longer you can marinade the steak, the more tender it will be. Overnight works best. Remove meat from marinade; discard marinade. Grill or broil steak to desired doneness, about 4 minutes per side for medium rare. Transfer steak to work surface. Let stand 5 to 10 minutes. Cut across grain into thin strips. Arrange on platter and serve.

Note: *Enough marinade for a 2¼-pound flank steak.*

Easy Marinade
4 Servings

1 16-ounce bottle balsamic vinaigrette (Paul Newman's Own preferred)

A bottle of good quality balsamic vinaigrette is a great marinade for steak, chicken or pork. It tenderizes the meat and adds a wonderful flavor. Also great on grilled vegetables.

Marinade for Vegetables
8 Servings

1 cup of olive oil
¾ cup white wine vinegar
1 tablespoon sugar
1 tablespoon Accent
1 tablespoon dill weed
1 teaspoon salt
1 teaspoon pepper
1 teaspoon garlic salt

1 head cauliflower washed and cut into
   bite-sized pieces
1 bunch broccoli cut into bite sized pieces
1 pound of cherry tomatoes halved
1 pound of black olives
1 pound mushrooms cut into
   bite-sized pieces
1 can or jar artichoke hearts marinated
   and quartered

Combine the oil, vinegar, sugar, Accent, dill weed, salt, pepper, and garlic salt in a glass bowl and whisk until combined. Place cauliflower, broccoli, tomatoes, mushrooms, and artichoke hearts into a large ziplock bag. Pour the oil and vinegar mixture over the vegetables in the bag and refrigerate overnight, turning the bag over as your time permits. Serve the next day.

Note: *Great make-ahead, colorful vegetable dish. Can use toothpicks for serving or slotted spoon.*

Gus' Salt
Makes 15 Cups

6 pounds kosher salt
1 cup Lawry's seasoning

1 cup garlic powder
1 cup medium-coarse black pepper

Mix all ingredients together. Store in airtight container.

Note: *This makes a great seasoned salt. Perfect for everyday table use, marinating meats and vegetables, and in cooking. Keep a shaker jar right on the counter.*

Cinnamon Butter Spread
Makes 1 Cup

1 cup soft margarine
1 cup sugar
4 tablespoons cinnamon

Mix together well. Keep any leftover cinnamon butter in refrigerator. Spread on bread and broil in toaster oven or regular oven until bubbly. You can also toast the bread lightly first and then spread the butter mixture on top and broil.

Note: *A kids' favorite! A good way to make a lot of cinnamon toast at one time.*

Kids' Favorites

The Footprints program at Cardinal Glennon Children's Medical Center, in partnership with Saint Louis University, provides resources and support so all children with life-threatening or terminal illnesses and their families can live full lives along their journey. Footprints is committed to improving quality of life by providing the highest quality of care for children and their families.

Buckwheat Pancakes
Makes 2 Cups Mix

Chef D'Aun Carrell *is Central Chair for the* American Culinary Federations' Chef and Child Foundation, *bringing better nutritional education to children. Chef D'Aun conducts childhood nutritional science curriculums for educators, parents and health directors.*

½ cup buckwheat flour
¼ cup flour
¼ cup cornmeal
3 tablespoons sugar
1 tablespoon baking powder
2 teaspoons salt

¼ teaspoon nutmeg
1 egg
3 tablespoons olive oil
1¾ cups soy milk
1 teaspoon vanilla extract

In a large bowl, whisk the flours, cornmeal, sugar, baking powder, salt, and nutmeg to distribute evenly. In a medium bowl, whisk the egg, olive oil, soy milk, and vanilla to blend. Add wet mix to dry. Fold with spatula until all dry disappears. Pour into squeeze bottle using a funnel. Let stand 5 minutes to thicken. Heat and lightly oil griddle. Make a tester pancake with just a 1-inch squeeze of bottle onto hot griddle. When bubbles appear all over the surface, turn over and cook until pancake slides. Keep cooked cakes warm in oven. Try shapes and letters with batter. Top with fresh fruit, maple syrup, or fresh fruit jam.

Cheesy English Muffins
6 Servings

3 English muffins split in half and buttered
6 slices bacon, cut in half

6 thick slices tomato
6 slices of American cheese or Velveeta

Split and butter the English muffins and toast under the broiler on one side until lightly browned. Remove from the oven and set aside. Broil bacon on a cookie sheet until crisp. Top each muffin half with thick tomato slice, 2 broiled bacon strips, and slice of American cheese or Velveeta. Return to broiler and broil 5 inches from heat until cheese melts.

Snapping Chicken Fingers
10 Servings

Chef D'Aun Carrell *is Central Chair for the* American Culinary Federations' Chef and Child Foundation *bringing better nutritional education to children. Chef D'Aun conducts childhood nutritional science curriculums for educators, parents and health directors.*

2 pounds frozen or fresh chicken breast fillets	8 ounces canola oil
1 16-ounce jar French dressing	20 bamboo skewers

Place bamboo skewers in water to soak. Rinse chicken fillets and dry on paper towels. Whisk French dressing and canola oil together. Place chicken fillets in flat glass or stainless steel tray and pour dressing and oil mixture on top. Turn each fillet over to completely coat all sides. Cover with plastic wrap and chill for 1 hour. Using plastic gloves, push a skewer through each fillet lengthwise, trying to go the full length without breaking through. Place kebabs on grill or hot griddle. Wait 2 minutes. The chicken should easily separate from the hot surface if it is done. Do not force it. Turn the kebabs over and cook 2 more minutes. Sides should be golden brown with no burn spots. Keep warm in foil-covered pan until ready to serve. Enjoy!

Caramel Corn Puffs
4 to 6 Servings

2 cups brown sugar	1 tablespoon vanilla extract
1 cup butter	1 8-ounce bag Corn Puffs by O-ke-Doke
½ cup light corn syrup	1 16-ounce can mixed nuts
½ teaspoon baking soda	

Boil sugar, butter, corn syrup, and baking soda for 5 minutes over medium-high heat. Add vanilla and stir. Put puffs and mixed nuts in a large bowl. Pour the liquid mixture over puffs and nuts, taking care as the sugar mixture will be hot. Mix well. Spread puffs and nuts evenly on two greased 15×10×1 baking sheets. Bake at 250°F for 45 minutes, stirring every 15 minutes. Spread on waxed paper to cool. Store in an airtight container.

Baked Apples
4 Servings

4 large apples
¼ cup wheat germ
¼ cup raisins
2 tablespoons sunflower seeds
2 tablespoons chopped walnuts
juice from ½ lemon

¼ teaspoon cinnamon
1 tablespoon brown sugar
⅛ teaspoon salt
1 tablespoon flour
¾ cup apple juice

Core the apples and place them in a greased baking dish that has a cover. Try to keep the apples close together in the pan. Mix the wheat germ, raisins, seeds, nuts, lemon juice, cinnamon, brown sugar, and salt in a medium-sized mixing bowl. Stuff the hollow of each apple with the mixture, using a spoon or a rubber spatula. Mix the flour and apple juice in a small bowl, and pour some over each apple. Bake the apples at 350°F for about 40 minutes, covered. Let them cool a little before serving.

Cherry-Pineapple Dump Cake
8 to 10 Servings

1 20-ounce can crushed pineapple
1 21-ounce can cherry pie filling
1 18.25-ounce package
   yellow cake mix

¾ cup butter or margarine,
   melted
½ cup chopped pecans,
   toasted
ice cream or whipped topping

Spread can of crushed pineapples with juice on bottom of a lightly greased 13×9 pan. Top pineapple with cherry pie filling and sprinkle cake mix evenly over fruit. Drizzle with melted butter and sprinkle with chopped pecans. Bake at 350°F for 50 to 60 minutes or until golden and bubbly. Serve with ice cream and/or whipped topping.

Chocolate Delights
Makes 12 Delights

1 6-ounce package butterscotch chips
1 6-ounce package semi-sweet chocolate chips
1 5-ounce can chow mein noodles
½ cup chopped pecans, optional

In top of double boiler, melt together butterscotch and chocolate chips. Remove from heat. Add chow mein noodles and pecans. Mix well. Drop by teaspoons on wax paper. Let stand for 1 hour.

Note: *For variations, you can add coconut flakes, miniature marshmallows, M&M's, or substitute any kind of nut for the pecans. Peanut butter chips can be substituted for the butterscotch chips.*

Cookies on a Stick
4 Servings

½ cup sugar
¼ cup butter
2 tablespoons shortening
1 egg
1 teaspoon vanilla extract

1¼ cups flour
½ teaspoon baking powder
½ teaspoon salt
1 cup chocolate chips
wooden ice cream sticks

Beat sugar, butter, shortening, egg, and vanilla. Stir together flour, baking powder, and salt and combine with butter mixture. Drop by teaspoonfuls onto a cookie sheet and flatten slightly. Place 1 wooden ice cream stick and some chocolate chips on top. Top with another teaspoonful of dough. Press together with fingers. Bake at 400°F for 8 minutes.

Easy Monkey Bread
6 Servings

1 tube refrigerated quick biscuits (6 count)
¼ cup cinnamon sugar
cooking spray
Bundt pan (ring-shaped pan that has a tube in the center)

Coat the Bundt pan thoroughly with cooking spray. Cut each biscuit into 4 pieces. Roll each piece of biscuit into a ball. Roll in cinnamon sugar mixture until covered. Drop pieces around the sprayed Bundt pan and bake at 400°F for about 10 minutes, or until the biscuits are done and brown on top. Flip the bread out of the pan and pull apart to serve.

Gingerbread Men
Makes 12 to 14 Gingerbread Men

1 18.25-ounce package spice cake mix
½ cup flour
2 eggs
⅓ cup oil

⅓ cup dark molasses
2 teaspoons ground ginger
gingerbread man cookie cutter
assorted candies for
  decorating

Combine cake mix, flour, eggs, oil, molasses, and ginger (the mixture will be soft). Refrigerate 2 hours. Roll dough to ¼-inch thickness on a lightly floured surface. Cut with gingerbread man cookie cutter. Place cookies on an ungreased baking sheet, 3 inches apart. Decorate. Bake at 375°F for 8 to 10 minutes or until the edges start to brown. Remove immediately to a cooling rack.

Homemade Pretzels
Makes 12 Pretzels

1 packet yeast	4 cups flour
1½ cups warm water (about 105°F)	1 egg
1 tablespoon sugar	coarse salt
1 tablespoon salt	

Mix yeast, warm water, sugar, and salt together with a fork in large mixing bowl. Add flour and stir until well blended. Remove dough from bowl; knead on a floured surface until smooth. Break off pieces and roll into "snakes." Shape the snakes into initials, traditional pretzel shapes, or whatever shapes you like. Don't make them too thick or they will be doughy; too thin and they will break. Put them on cookie sheet sprayed with cooking spray. Beat the egg and brush it on the pretzels with a pastry brush or back of a spoon. Sprinkle with salt if desired. Bake at 425°F for 12 to 15 minutes or until golden brown. Cool on baking sheets. Transfer pretzels to rack to cool further unless you prefer to eat them warm.

Note: *These are best made the day they are to be eaten.*

Kid's Chow
4 to 6 Servings

1 stick margarine	1 12-ounce box Rice Chex cereal
1 cup creamy peanut butter	1 pound powdered sugar
1 12-ounce bag semi-sweet chocolate chips	1 large, unused paper grocery bag

In medium saucepan, melt butter, peanut butter, and semi-sweet chocolate chips until completely melted. Do not boil. Put box of cereal in large bowl. Pour melted mixture over cereal. Stir gently until covered. Sprinkle enough powdered sugar to cover the bottom of a clean paper grocery bag. Add some cereal mixture to bag, then some powdered sugar and alternate until finished with the cereal mixture and powdered sugar. Seal and shake until a clump is no longer felt. Store snack mix in an airtight container.

Layered Cookie Cake
10 to 12 Servings

1 1-pound package Oreos
2 6-ounce boxes chocolate pudding
milk for making pudding

⅓ cup sugar
1 10-ounce carton Cool Whip
1 8-ounce package cream
  cheese, softened

Crush Oreos and set aside. Make pudding according to package directions and set aside. Mix together softened cream cheese, sugar, and Cool Whip. Layer in 13×9×2 pan starting with crushed Oreos (reserving some for the top), then the pudding, then the cream cheese mixture. Put remainder of crushed Oreos on top. Refrigerate until ready to serve.

Lazy-Day Lasagna
8 Servings

1 15-ounce container ricotta cheese
2 tablespoons grated Parmesan
  cheese
1 teaspoon Italian seasoning
1 26-ounce jar spaghetti sauce

8 lasagna noodles, uncooked
1 8-ounce bag shredded
  mozzarella cheese

Put the ricotta cheese, Parmesan cheese, and Italian seasoning in a medium bowl. Stir with spoon until mixed. Spoon 1 cup of the spaghetti sauce evenly over bottom of a greased 9×13 baking dish. Top with 4 of the uncooked lasagna noodles. Spread 1 cup of the ricotta cheese mixture over noodles, using the back of the spoon. Sprinkle with 1 cup of the mozzarella cheese. Spread 1 cup of the spaghetti sauce over mozzarella cheese. Make another layer with 4 lasagna noodles, the rest of the ricotta cheese mixture, and 1 cup spaghetti sauce. Be sure the spaghetti sauce completely covers the noodles. Sprinkle with the rest of the mozzarella cheese.

Bake at 350°F for 40 to 45 minutes or until the lasagna is hot in center and cheese is melted. Use pot holders to take pan out of oven as it will be very hot and heavy. Let lasagna cool for 15 minutes.

Magic Wands
Makes 10 Wands

3 ounces chopped white chocolate
10 long pretzel logs
decorative candies or colored sugars

Place chopped chocolate in a microwave-safe bowl. Microwave on high at 30-second intervals, stirring each time, until the mixture is smooth.

Hold a pretzel over the melted mixture. Carefully spoon melted mixture over the end of the pretzel log. Place the wand on a sheet of waxed paper. Sprinkle the chocolate end of the pretzel with decorative candies or sugars before it hardens. Repeat with remaining logs and melted mixture. Let stand at room temperature until the melted mixture becomes firm, about 1 hour.

Note: *Can be made with milk chocolate or dark chocolate.*

Meatballs
Makes 18 Meatballs

2 pounds ground beef
½ cup Parmesan cheese
2 soft bread slices, cubed
   (approximately 1 cup)
¼ cup parsley

2 eggs
1½ tablespoons salt
½ teaspoon garlic salt
½ teaspoon black pepper

Mix the ground beef, Parmesan cheese, bread, parsley, eggs, salt, garlic, salt, and pepper together. Form into 18 balls and bake at 350°F for about 30 minutes until cooked through, or fry them in a sauté pan until browned and cooked through. Simmer in pasta sauce for 30 minutes and serve with your favorite pasta.

Note: *The meatballs are also delicious served as a sandwich on an Italian Roll with provolone or mozzarella cheese.*

Nitey-Nite Cookies
Makes 48 Cookies

2 egg whites	1 cup chopped nuts
⅔ cup sugar	1 cup chocolate chips

Preheat oven to 350°F. Beat egg whites until stiff, adding sugar gradually. Stir in nuts and chocolate chips. Drop by teaspoonfuls on foil lined cookie sheets. Put it in the oven and turn it off. Do not open until the morning!

No-Bake Blueberry Pie
8 Servings

1 quart blueberries	2 tablespoons flour
1 cup sugar	9-inch baked pie shell
¾ cup water, must be cold water	

Put 1 cup berries into saucepan with sugar. Dissolve flour in ½ cup water; add the rest of the water. Pour the water and flour mixture into the pan with the berries. Cook 10 minutes over medium heat. Remove from heat. Add remaining berries and put mixture into baked pie shell. Chill and serve with whipped cream.

Peanut Butter Balls
Makes 30 Balls

¼ cup softened margarine	2 cups quick rolled oats
½ cup peanut butter	¼ cup mini semi-sweet
½ cup light brown sugar	chocolate chips

In a medium bowl, mix all of the ingredients together. Form into 30 balls. Refrigerate. Ready to serve in 15 minutes. Store in refrigerator.

Spaghetti Pie
6 Servings

6 ounces spaghetti
2 eggs
⅓ cup Parmesan cheese
2 tablespoons margarine

1 cup cottage cheese
½ cup ground beef, cooked,
    drained, and crumbled
1 8-ounce jar spaghetti sauce
1½ ounces shredded mozzarella

Cook and drain spaghetti noodles. Lightly beat eggs. Add Parmesan to eggs. Pour egg and cheese mixture over noodles. Stir to mix. Grease a 9-inch pie plate with margarine. Pour spaghetti mixture into pie plate and press into base and sides to form a crust. Pour cottage cheese over crust. Mix ground beef and spaghetti sauce and pour over cottage cheese layer. Bake at 350°F for 20 minutes. Add mozzarella and bake another 5 to 10 minutes. Let pie sit for 5 minutes before slicing to serve.

Strawberry Pizza
8 Servings

¼ cup plus 4 tablespoons sugar,
    divided
½ cup margarine
1 cup flour
8-ounce package of ⅓-less-fat
    cream cheese, softened

½ teaspoon vanilla extract
1½ pounds or 1½ quarts
    strawberries
1 tablespoon cornstarch

In medium bowl, combine 2 tablespoons sugar, margarine, and flour until crumbly. Press into a 12-inch pizza pan that has been sprayed with non-stick cooking spray. Bake at 350°F for 10 to 15 minutes or until light brown around the edges. Cool. In small mixing bowl, combine cream cheese, vanilla, and ¼ cup sugar; beat until creamy. Spread over cooled pizza crust. To make the glaze: Mash enough of the strawberries to measure 1 cup. In small saucepan, over medium heat, combine 2 tablespoons sugar and the cornstarch; add mashed berries and heat to boiling. Boil and stir 1 minute. Cool. Spread over cream cheese mixture. Cut remaining berries into thin uniform slices. Arrange over top of glaze in circles, beginning at the outside edge, overlapping slices slightly. Refrigerate 2 hours before serving.

Note: *You can use store-bought strawberry glaze instead of making your own.*

Nutty Granola Bars
16 Servings

¾ cup honey
2 tablespoons unsalted butter, plus
  more for baking dish
3 cups old-fashioned rolled oats
1⅓ cups slivered almonds (6 ounces)
coarse salt

1 cup raisins or other dried
  fruit
⅓ cup creamy almond
  butter or other nut butter
¼ cup light brown sugar

In a small saucepan, heat ¼ cup honey and butter over low heat. Cook, stirring, until butter melts, 2 minutes. In a large bowl, combine oats, almonds, and pinch of salt. Drizzle honey mixture over oat mixture and stir until combined. Wipe saucepan clean. Spread mixture evenly onto a large, rimmed baking sheet. Bake at 325°F until golden brown, about 20 minutes, stirring occasionally. Let cool completely on sheet for 10 minutes. Return to large bowl and add dried fruit; stir to combine.

Lightly butter an 8-inch square baking dish. In saucepan, combine ½ cup honey, almond butter, and brown sugar over medium heat. Cook, stirring occasionally, until mixture comes to a boil and sugar dissolves, about 10 minutes. Drizzle over oat mixture and stir until combined; transfer to baking dish. With a spatula, firmly press granola into dish. Refrigerate until firm, about 1 hour. Cut into 16 bars or squares. Store in an airtight container at room temperature, up to 5 days.

Note: *These granola bars are a healthy, power-packed treat, and have no added preservatives. Experiment with different combinations of dried fruit and nuts.*

Watermelon Galore Juice
2 Servings

¼ small watermelon
1 cup apple juice
1 tablespoon honey

Cut the watermelon into small chunks, and remove the seeds and the rind. Purée the chunks, apple juice, and honey in a blender or food processor until smooth.

Tasty Grape Dessert
12 Servings

1 pound red grapes, halved
1 pound green grapes, halved
1 8-ounce container sour cream
1 8-ounce package cream cheese
(softened)
1 teaspoon vanilla extract

Topping:
½ cup brown sugar
½ cup chopped pecans
3 or 4 Butterfinger candy bars,
crushed

Wash and dry grapes and cut them in half. In large bowl mix sour cream, cream cheese, and vanilla. Fold in grapes. In medium bowl, combine the brown sugar, pecans and crushed Butterfinger pieces. Mix half of topping mix with grape mixture and spread in a 9×13 pan. Sprinkle with the rest of the topping. Refrigerate until ready to eat.

Berry Banana Shake-Up
2 Servings

4 scoops low-fat vanilla frozen yogurt
10 fresh strawberries, cleaned

½ banana

Combine all ingredients in a blender and blend until smooth. Pour into a cup and enjoy!

Berry Cranberry Smoothie
2 Servings

1½ cups cranberry juice
½ cup frozen bananas

1½ cups mixed frozen berries
(strawberries, blueberries,
and blackberries)

Put the cranberry juice into a blender. Add the bananas and mixed fruit. Blend until smooth and enjoy.

Note: *This is a great way to use those brown, overripe bananas!*

Cocoa Berry Smoothie
2 Servings

¾ cup apple juice
1 cup vanilla yogurt
2 cups mixed berries (strawberries, raspberries, and blueberries)
2 to 3 tablespoons sweetened powdered cocoa

Put the apple juice and yogurt into a blender. Add the berries and the cocoa powder; blend until smooth.

Magic Brew
12 servings

1 8-ounce carton vanilla yogurt
1 cup orange juice
4 cups orange soda

Put the vanilla yogurt, orange juice, and 2 cups of orange soda in the blender. Cover and blend on high until combined. Pour the mixture into 2 ice cube trays. Cover with plastic wrap. Freeze for 6 hours. Just before serving, remove the frozen cubes from 1 of the ice cube trays. Put the cubes in the blender and add 1 cup of orange soda. Cover and blend on high until slushy. Pour into 6 glasses. Repeat with remaining cubes and orange soda.

Orange Razz Frosty
2 Servings

1 cup orange juice
1 cup frozen raspberries
1 cup vanilla frozen yogurt

Put the orange juice into a blender. Add the raspberries and frozen yogurt and blend until smooth.

Non-Edible Fun

Children's Bubbles

1 cup water
⅓ cup Joy dishwashing liquid

2 tablespoons light corn syrup

Mix solution well and allow it to set for 1 hour before using. Cover and label any leftover solution and store it in the refrigerator.

Finger Paint

3 tablespoons sugar
½ cup cornstarch   food coloring

2 cups cold water
dash of liquid detergent

Mix the sugar and cornstarch and then add the water. Cook over low heat, stirring constantly, until well blended. Divide the mixture into 4 or 5 portions and add a different food coloring to each, plus a pinch of detergent (facilitates cleanup).

Oobleck

½ cup cornstarch   ¼ cup water   food coloring

Combine ingredients in a bowl. Pour onto a tray or cookie sheet. Watch what happens. Add more cornstarch and water to the mixture. Observe changes. Put small objects in the Oobleck, such as beads or pennies for your child to find. Watch it "dance" to loud music. Explore with hands, Popsicle sticks, or cookie cutters. Mixture may be stored in an airtight container and reused.

Scented Play Dough

2½ cups flour
1 tablespoon cream of tartar
2 packages Kool-Aid (dry powder)

½ cup salt
3 tablespoons vegetable oil
2 cups boiling water

Mix flour, cream of tartar, Kool-Aid, and salt. Stir in oil and boiling water. Dough will be hot; allow to cool. Knead dough. Add additional flour if dough is too sticky. Dough may be stored in an airtight container.

Index of Recipes

Kids' Favorites

Lamb Entrees

Pasta

Pasta Salads

Pork Entrees

Poultry Entrees

Rice & Beans

Vegetarian Entrees

Warm Appetizers